MAD ABOUT
THE MEKONG

Into India
When Men and Mountains Meet
The Gilgit Game
Eccentric Travellers
Explorers Extraordinary
Highland Drove
The Royal Geographical Society's
History of World Exploration (general editor)
India Discovered:
The Recovery of a Lost Civilization
The Honourable Company:
A History of the English East India Company
The Collins Encyclopaedia of Scotland
(co-editor with Julia Keay)
Indonesia: From Sabang to Merauke
Last Post: The End of Empire in the Far East
India: A History
The Great Arc: The Dramatic Tale of how
India was Mapped and Everest was Named
Sowing the Wind: The Mismanagement of
the Middle East 1900–1960

JOHN KEAY

MAD ABOUT
THE MEKONG

Exploration and Empire
in South-East Asia

HarperCollins*Publishers*

HarperCollins*Publishers*
77–85 Fulham Palace Road,
Hammersmith, London w6 8jb
www.harpercollins.co.uk

Published by HarperCollins*Publishers* 2005

2   4   6   8   9   7   5   3   1

A catalogue record for this book
is available from the British Library

ISBN 0 00 711113 4

Maps by John Gilkes

Set in PostScript Linotype Adobe Caslon and
Monotype Modern Extended by
Rowland Phototypesetting Limited, Bury St Edmunds, Suffolk

Printed and bound in Great Britain by
Clays Limited, St Ives plc

FOR ALEXANDER

CONTENTS

PLATES

(Unless otherwise stated, photographs are by Julia Keay. The engravings based on Louis Delaporte's drawings appeared in Francis Garnier's Voyage d'exploration en Indo-Chine, *published in 1873.)*

TEXT ILLUSTRATIONS

(Apart from the two group portraits of the members of the expedition, the engravings are based on Louis Delaporte's drawings, and appeared in Francis Garnier's Voyage d'exploration en Indo-Chine, *published in 1873)*

MAPS

ACKNOWLEDGEMENTS

This book, while describing one journey up the river, is the result of another. The second, like the first, involved some twenty-five different boats and rather more boatmen and boatwomen. I am ashamed to say that I never knew or have forgotten most of their names, but without their intimate knowledge of the river, their skills with paddle, oar and engine, and their unfailing concern for a timid traveller, the trip would have been unthinkable.

I first saw the Mekong in 1984 while making a series of radio documentaries. At a time of considerable difficulty for Westerners in south-east Asia, David Perry overcame the red tape, produced the programmes and minded the presenter with rare delicacy. In Phnom Penh, Cham Borey provided guidance plus a harrowing account of life and death under the Khmer Rouge, and in Chiang Mai the Lintners, Bertil and Hseng Noung, explained the complexities of insurgency and drugs in the Golden Triangle. More recently they helped unravel the mystery of '9:11'.

In 2002 encouragement and some invaluable information came from Darren Campbell and Peter Degen in Phnom Penh. Their acquaintance I owe to Dr Jaroslav Poncar whose panoramic photography now extends from Ladakh through Tibet and India to Angkor.

Laos supplied its own brand of gentle inspiration in the persons of two exceptionally kind and discerning mentors, both now deceased – Dr Oudom Souvannavong and Alan Davidson. In the midst of celebrating the 2003 award of the Erasmus Prize, Alan shared his reminiscences of Laos in the 1970s and of the *pa beuk*.

I treasure that evening as I do the elegance of his prose in countless books. Dr Oudom accompanied a 1999 trip via Luang Prabang to Ban Houei Xai and was to have been awaiting us at Pakse in 2002. The news of his death in a traffic accident, received via the public phone on Khong Island, was the most distressing moment of the entire trip.

In Paris, Jean-Philippe Arrou-Vignod fielded some tricky translation queries and facilitated entry into the formidable new Bibliothèque Nationale. Besides the customary acknowledgement of this and other libraries, I would like to record my debt to a publisher. For some years the White Lotus Press in Bangkok has been reprinting nineteenth-century and early-twentieth-century accounts of south-east Asia (including those of Garnier and de Carné), as well as more recent works on the area. I can't believe that it is a very profitable exercise, but perhaps a word of appreciation from one avid reader will encourage others. All the works in the bibliography whose place of publication is shown as Bangkok have come from the presses of White Lotus.

Finally and rather self-consciously, my thanks to various loved ones. Catriona Stewart insists, rightly, that the idea of a sail up the Mekong was hers; she could not come but made sure we went. Susanah Mackay-James and Dorothy Jackson did come, from Chiang Khong to Dali. They shared the expense and enlivened the drama, making a difficult section of the river more fun and less fraught. Alexander, to whom this book is dedicated, also came for part of the trip. As an aquaculturist he took to the river like a thirsty fish and fell in love with it, just like his parents; they found him the best company in the world. Julia came the whole way. We went as one. The courage was hers, and the book is ours.

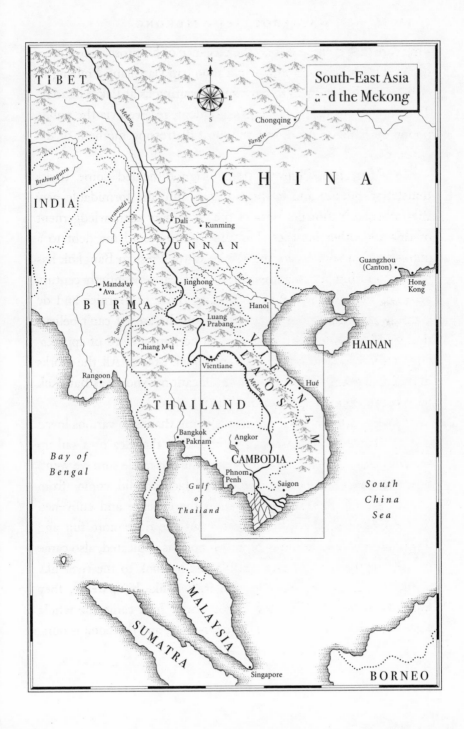

South-East Asia and the Mekong

FOREWORD

In the great age of exploration, while momentous expeditions in Africa were grabbing the English-language headlines, a French initiative through the heart of south-east Asia was arguably more ambitious than any of them. The Mekong Exploration Commission of 1866–68 outmarched David Livingstone and outmapped H.M. Stanley. It also outshone them in that display of sociological categorising, economic sleuthing and political effrontery that was expected of nineteenth-century explorers. In darkest Africa the British were feeling their way, but the French in tropical Asia unashamedly advertised their patriotic intentions, planted their flag and promoted their rule wherever they could. Empire-building was their business. An 'empire of the Indies', otherwise French Indo-China, would duly emerge as a direct outcome of the expedition.

The human cost of travel in the south-east Asian subcontinent was as high as in Africa, and the disappointments just as acute. Danger overtook the Mekong expedition within a week of its official departure; tragedy struck within a week of its effective conclusion. In between, as they clocked up the months and the kilometres in a marathon of survival, the explorers fought their way through the equatorial forests of Cambodia and Laos to climb from the badlands of remotest Burma onto blizzard-swept tundra along the China–Tibet border. Rarely was at least one of the six officers – and sometimes all of them – not delirious or incapacitated. Tigers barred their path, village maidens diverted their attentions, forbidden cities yielded up their secrets. The boats got smaller and the river more impetuous. They took to the jungle, riding on elephants, bullock carts and horses; mostly they just sloshed through the monsoons knee-deep in mud and festooned with leeches. If only as an epic of endurance, the story of the Mekong Exploration Commission dwarfs nearly all contemporary endeavours.

Yet − and hence this book − it is to most people unknown. Doudart de Lagrée, Francis Garnier and their companions are not household names. Any geographical features once called after them have long since been erased from the maps; and histories and anthologies of exploration habitually ignore them (my own included). One might suppose this to be an anglophone conceit. Had the Commission been British, London would now be graced with statues of the Mekong pioneers, streets would be named after them, and symposia convened for them. Their mistake, as Garnier himself wryly put it just before his premature death, lay in being born French.

Posthumous amends had, I presumed, been made in Paris, but it was during an encounter with the French ambassador in London that I first found a chance to confirm this. By way of something to say, I enquired how the Commission was commemorated in France. The ambassador looked blank. A charming and erudite diplomat, he evidently didn't understand the question. I plied him with names, dates and places. He shook his head.

'Never heard of them, I'm afraid.'

'But that's like a British ambassador saying he's never heard of Dr Livingstone, or Scott of the Antarctic.'

'Ah, but you don't understand. In France we have a different attitude to the colonial past.'

A visit to Paris eventually bore this out. Except in the Bibliothèque Nationale and among the treasures poached from Angkor in the Musée Guimet, mention of the Commission brought nothing but Gallic shrugs. A friend whom I counted as an ardent supporter eventually confessed that even he only knew of the expedition because of my incessant prattling about it. Rue Garnier turned out to be named not for Francis Garnier; likewise the tomb in the Père Lachaise cemetery that is commonly awarded to him. Both pertain to some other Garnier. The short entry under 'Garnier, Francis' in the popular Larousse dictionary of biography contains only a sentence on the expedition; there is no entry at all for its leader, Doudart de Lagrée.

If one excludes the writings of its own personnel, scarcely any more accounts of the expedition exist in French than in English. The most recent and well researched (J.-P. Gomane, 1994) appears never to have got beyond the limited circulation accorded to a typewritten thesis so scrunched into its binding as to be almost unopenable. The most ambitious and accessible reconstruction (Osborne, 1975) is by an Australian.

Celebrating dead exponents of a somewhat discredited profession seems to be an anglophonic obsession. The French ambassador, though far too diplomatic to say so, appeared to imply that while the British were today mired in nostalgia for their imperial past, the French were above such things and in healthy denial of their own colonial aberrations. Without going into the reasons for this – which may derive as much from present confidence as from past trauma – I felt encouraged. Here was a story that could usefully be retold.

The history led to the geography. Intrigued by the expedition, I became enthralled by the river. For reasons that will emerge, the Mekong is quite unlike any of the world's other great waterways. Far from inviting navigation it emphatically challenges it with an unrivalled repertoire of spectacular water features. As if not in themselves sufficiently discouraging, the expedition found these appalling physical difficulties compounded by political uncertainties. Colonial rule would fail to remove either, and for the past half-century ideological, bureaucratic and piratical obstructions have barred the river's course more effectively than ever.

But there has recently been a change. In the late 1990s border restrictions were eased, new rivercraft were introduced in Cambodia, and some controversial channel-clearance was begun on the Sino– and Lao–Burmese borders. For the first time in living memory retracing the route of the Mekong Exploration Commission became feasible, if not easy. A golden age in Mekong navigation looked to be dawning.

Sadly it could prove to be short-lived. Water conservation tops the agenda of all the riverine states, while hydro-electricity provides some of them with their main export-earner. In Chinese Yunnan the river is already dammed. So are many of its downstream tributaries; the chainsaw and the mechanical digger are everywhere gouging roads round unsuspected contours; and extant plans threaten to transform the entire hydrography. Natural forest, traditional livelihoods, and the occasionally alarming interplay of menace and innocence in this great green basin may all be swept away within the next few decades.

The rehabilitation of the river could prove its undoing. On the other hand, rehabilitating the story of its exploration may be instructive. Scarcely anywhere has been more traumatised by recent history than mainland south-east Asia. Retracing the expedition's trail means revisiting the aftermath of more twentieth-century wars – international, civil, 'secret' and ethnic – than even the Balkans can boast. (The Vietnam war was the third but by no means the last.) It means circumventing the best natural forest because of the unexploded ordnance, tripping through smiling landscapes memorable for unparalleled savagery, and paddling up tranquil reaches still infamous for narco-insurgency. The experience takes the edge off unalloyed enjoyment and, for a Westerner, invites self-recrimination.

But stay the whip; for the Eden into which the Mekong Exploration Commission first blundered also fell far short of the idyllic. Slavery, banditry and the prevalence of almost every known tropical disease so appalled the Frenchmen that they seemed to justify colonial intervention. The explorers did not, though, berate the prevailing rulers, and mostly they thought well of the Buddhist establishment. They just diagnosed and prescribed. Blaming the acknowledged ills of one society, or one century, on the presumptions of another demeans them both.

It is simply the sequential nature of events, and in this case of intervention – its logic and its consequences – that may be instructive. As with the river at the heart of this story, natural obstructions and human interference contain merit as well as menace. Flooded forest provides the ideal spawning ground for fish; hillside erosion upriver guarantees alluvial abundance in the Delta; and the colonial cake-cutting urged by the expedition probably forestalled more cataclysmic strife than it created. Like fully-fledged trees being tumbled perilously through the rapids, events take their course, not easily deflected yet foreseeable as to season and direction by those who trouble to study the current and read the weather.

AN INDO-CHINA CHRONOLOGY

THE ADVENT OF THE FRENCH

1859   French naval force seizes Saigon.

1862   Three Mekong Delta provinces round Saigon ceded to the French.

1864   Franco–Cambodian Treaty makes truncated Cambodia a protectorate.

1865   French naval ministry champions exploration of Mekong.

1866–68 Mekong Exploration Commission.

1867   French seize remaining Delta provinces.

1869   Survivors of Mekong expedition return to France.

1870   Paris besieged in Franco–Prussian War.

1872   Dupuis takes arms shipment to Yunnan up the Red River.

1873   First French intervention in Tonkin (North Vietnam); death of Garnier.

THE FRENCH ADVANCE

1883   New French offensive in Tonkin brings protectorate over the Annam emperor.

1885–86 British invasion and annexation of Upper Burma.

1886–91 Pavie contests Siamese (Thai) sovereignty in Laos.

1891–93 French attempt to navigate Falls of Khon; Stung Treng seized.

1893   Paknam Incident and French blockade of Bangkok. Franco–Siamese Treaty ends Siamese sovereignty in Laos.

1894–95 Pavie/Scott clash over Franco–British buffer (Muong Sing).

1896 Anglo–French Declaration secures neutrality of truncated Siam. British Burma's claims to Muong Sing withdrawn.

1904 Franco–Siamese Convention adjusts Siam–Cambodia frontier, accords Laos west bank enclaves at Bassac and Luang Prabang.

1907 Franco–Siamese Treaty brings return to Cambodia of 'lost provinces' (including Angkor).

FRENCH WITHDRAWAL AND US INTERVENTION

1930 Nguyen Ai Quoc ('Ho Chi Minh') founds Indo-Chinese Communist Party.

1942–45 Japanese overrun south-east Asia.

1945–54 First (French) Indo-China War.

1949–50 Triumph of Mao's Communists in China. Some Chinese Nationalists (KMT) relocate in Shan states.

1954 Geneva Accords and defeat at Dien Bien Phu end French rule.

1962 Military (General Ne Win) seize power in Burma.

1963–73 CIA's 'Secret War' in Laos.

1965–66 First US ground troops arrive in south Vietnam.

1967 'Second Opium War' as Shan, KMT and Lao drugs barons clash.

1968 500,000 US troops in Vietnam. US bombing of Cambodia begins.

1973 Paris Agreements herald withdrawal of US troops from Vietnam.

1975 Saigon falls to North Vietnamese, Phnom Penh to Khmer Rouge, and Pathet Lao triumph in Laos.

1975–79 Cambodia under Khmer Rouge.

1979 Vietnamese invade Cambodia, install puppet (Heng Samrin) regime.

1988 Burma's military rulers suppress democratic victory (Aung San Suu Kyi).

1989 Vietnamese withdraw from Cambodia. Burma's insurgent Communist leaders come to terms with Rangoon.

1991–93 Paris Peace Accord leads to UN deployment in Cambodia and elections.

1997 Hun Sen overthrows elected Cambodian government, engineers own mandate (1998, 2003).

MAD ABOUT
THE MEKONG

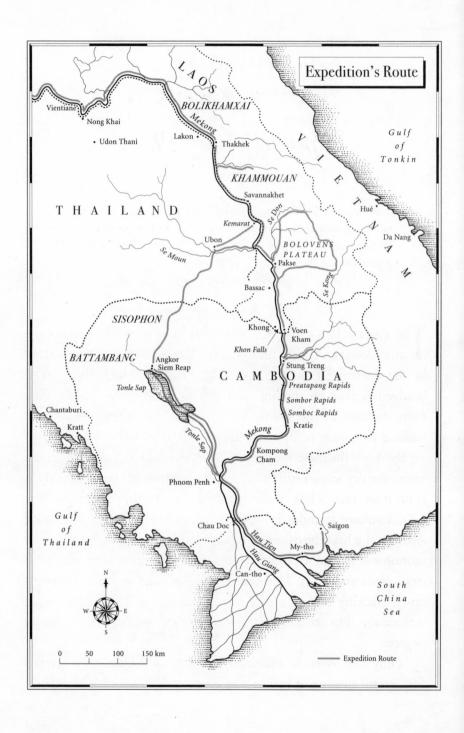

Expedition's Route

LAOS
BOLIKHAMXAI
Vientiane
Nong Khai
Udon Thani
Lakon
Mekong
Thakhek
Gulf of Tonkin
KHAMMOUAN
Savannakhet
Hué
THAILAND
Kemarat
Se Don
Ubon
Se Moun
BOLOVENS PLATEAU
Pakse
Da Nang
Bassac
Se Kong
VIETNAM
SISOPHON
Khong
Voen Kham
Khon Falls
BATTAMBANG
Angkor
Siem Reap
Stung Treng
CAMBODIA
Preatapang Rapids
Tonle Sap
Sombor Rapids
Sombor Rapids
Chantaburi
Kratie
Kratt
Tonle Sap
Mekong
Kompong Cham
Phnom Penh
Gulf of Thailand
Chau Doc
Saigon
My-tho
Hau Tien
Hau Giang
Can-tho
South China Sea
N
W E
S
0   50   100   150 km
Expedition Route

ONE

Apocalypse Then

'Each bend of the Mekong as added to my map seemed an important geographical discovery. Nothing could distract me from this abiding concern. It came to possess me like a monomania. I was mad about the Mekong...'

FRANCIS GARNIER

I N   E A R LY   J U N E   the Mekong in its remote middle reaches is at its lowest. At that time of year, sixteen hundred kilometres to the north-west on the uplands of eastern Tibet, the river's headwaters may be rippling with the first snow-melt, while the same distance to the south, the monsoon may already be pummelling the paddy fields of the Delta. But at its hill-pinched waist on the Lao–Burmese border the river has scarcely begun to rise. Here, the dry season still holds its fiery breath and the odd shower is no more than a lick of the tongue on parched lips. Behind the hills desultory thunder brings no relief. Beetles and cicadas fall silent in the heat; birds seem reluctant to fly. A smoke haze hangs motionless in the treetops, clogging the nostrils with the ash from slash-and-burn. Drained of all glow, the sun sets ingloriously, tracking behind a pall of parched fog to a mid-afternoon extinction. The thermometer stays stuck at thirty-something degrees.

Only the river is refreshingly animated. Darting through fifty-metre narrows, it bellies into pools a kilometre wide and then squirms, like a sleek and well-fed snake, down a barren trough isolated from the tousled shade of its banks by humped sandbars and a wilderness of spectacular upthrusts of black bedrock. Where the rock ventures into its path, the river hisses a caution and recoils in a tangle of eddies, welling up, flicking at the sunlight and glancing aside to nose out other options before slithering prodigiously over the obstruction in a cascade of watery colours.

Midway between Thailand and Chinese Yunnan, a succession of such encounters comprises the Tang-ho rapids. They extend, with intermissions, for perhaps 150 kilometres and confront the navigator with an awesome prospect of boiling whirlpools and spuming cataracts. In June 1867 they were the final straw for the Mekong Exploration Commission. After a year of canoeing up Asia's most capricious river, the six Frenchmen who had undertaken its exploration conceded defeat. From here on they would take to the steep banks, then to the hills and the forests, plotting the river where possible but increasingly deflected from its course by obstructive princelings and their own debilitated condition.

Their proximity to China alone kept them going. Deep in the forest gloom they would stumble on a paved trail and then a humpbacked bridge built of cut stone and once inset with ceramic tiles. Evidently the civilising light of the Celestial Empire had once penetrated these dark recesses. A mandarin's robes and the staccato sound of spoken Chinese sent the Frenchmen into raptures. In China their credentials would be acknowledged and their credit was good. After months of floundering amid malarial jungle, terrorised by tigers, devoured by leeches, often feverish and increasingly destitute, their salvation seemed nigh. They dreamed of wearing shoes again and sleeping in sheets, of tableware and postal facilities and the privacy of stone walls and stout doors. They were not to know that forsaking the river was the prelude to catastrophe, or that the controversies, no less than the crises, were yet to come.

Sensing only that the Mekong was about to elude them,

Francis Garnier, the expedition's restless surveyor, set off alone from the Tang-ho rapids on a last day's excursion upriver. With a compass in his hand and a cold chicken in his haversack, he picked his way past the rapids, and as the sun slanted over the trees on the hilltops, became overwhelmed by an acute sense of wonder. The great river and the boundless forest were utterly deserted. He felt like a trespasser in paradise. He shouted to reassure himself but quickly resented the sound. His shadow, marching across the sandbanks beside him, was no less intrusive: it seemed, as Garnier put it, 'to violate the virginity of a natural world that until now had escaped the profanity of man'.

Behind an outcrop of rock he surprised a young stag drinking from the river. Though only ten paces away, it stood its ground, and when he stopped to reach instinctively for his rifle, the stag actually moved towards him. 'It came to me like a memory of Eden,' he would write. Both thrilled and intimidated, he had no regrets about being unarmed, yet still could not resist making a grab for its antlers. The stag bolted and Garnier cursed his own impatience. It should have been like a fairy story, he thought, or one of La Fontaine's fables. If only, instead of grabbing at it, he had engaged it in polite conversation.

After a hard scramble through the tangled forest to circumvent a portal of rock, he rejoined the river and, now sweating profusely, went for a swim. He was barely out of his depth when two elephants broke cover. One turned back; the other, a big dark tusker, waded into the water beside him. Garnier backed into midstream and prepared to take flight by launching himself into the main current. 'The proboscidean' fixed an eye on him and occasionally waved its trunk in his direction. But it did not approach. It seemed content just to wallow and shower itself with river-water. Naked and defenceless, Garnier cautiously floated into the bank and, grabbing his clothes, fled across the sands and into the forest. The elephant paid no attention. Later, on glancing back, Garnier could still see the spray from the fountain of its trunk raining down in a prism of sunlight.

Lunch was taken in the shade, then it was time to turn back. In the heat of the day the silence was more absolute than ever. Garnier longed to erase his own tracks in the sand; they too seemed to sully surroundings of such heart-rending beauty. Yet that night, back in camp when he told of his adventures, a colleague's suggestion that they revisit this huntsman's 'Eldorado' with shotguns and rifles met with no objection. For repaying nature's 'pacific and almost friendly' reception with bullets Garnier felt a mild pang of remorse but said nothing. Bloodlust prevailed. Evidently virgin lands meant fair game – and that included the river itself.

This long, lyrical and perhaps fanciful passage stands out in the records of the Mekong Exploration Commission because it is so untypical. Disappointment and hardship had more often been the expedition's lot; destitution and death would as surely follow. A day in paradise, for Garnier at least, was a moment of tranquillity set amid buffeting cascades of menace and misfortune. Here Heaven met Hades round every bend in the river. 'This solitary Mekong scene,' he concluded, 'one of the last that it was given to me to see, would remain deeply etched in my memory.'

The passage is immediately preceded, and partly explained, by another admission. He had succumbed, he says, to a '*monomanie de Mékong*'. It was he who had insisted on pursuing the river long after it had become an irrelevance to the expedition's political and commercial concerns. It was he who had deflected their course from the most direct route to China into the dangerous no-man's land of the Shan states on the Lao–Burmese border. The river for Garnier had come to eclipse all else, including the expedition's safety. What mattered was to map its every twist, chart its every rapid, explore its every secret. He had become, he says, obsessed by it, possessed by it, mad about it.

Mountaineers commonly get obsessed by particular peaks,

exaggerating their mystique and slavering over their icy profile. A river obsession is more of a rarity. It takes an especially determined explorer and a peculiarly wayward river. Joseph Conrad set his *Heart of Darkness* in Africa and positioned the terrible Kurtz on the upper reaches of the Congo. In the film *Apocalypse Now* Francis Ford Coppola, while appropriating the Conrad story and retaining Kurtz, transposed the river. Recognising a renegade American holed up in the jungles of south-east Asia as a latter-day Kurtz, he simply swapped the Congo for the Mekong. There was little to choose between them; they were rivers 'of a kind'. Up both lurked twilight forces of good and evil, forbidding yet enticing, virgin yet corrupting. And just as for Conrad the Congo was the obvious setting for an exploration of that 'heart of darkness' at the core of early twentieth-century civilisation, so for Coppola the Mekong was the obvious setting for a visionary parable of damnation in the late twentieth century.

A more historically-minded Coppola could have taken as his model the Mekong Exploration Commission. The same sense of dread would dog the Commission, the same pockets of renegade authority would confront them, and the same questioning of their own credentials would result. Even today, above the Tang-ho rapids, obscure ethnic groups jealously maintain an insurgent status which goes back to colonial times, while disputed enclaves harbour a variety of illicit activities, all narcotics-related. The Golden Triangle, though now wishfully billed as an 'Economic Quadrangle', retains a reputation for pristine lawlessness which makes borders almost irrelevant. Thailand, Laos, Burma and China here abut one another in as mouthwatering a set of co-ordinates as one could wish for. But the maps are always misleading, and the bulldozing of unauthorised dirt roads or the declaration of phantom states renders them instantly out of date.

Garnier, like Kurtz, would have little difficulty in recognising the region today. Even spouting 'proboscideans' have returned to the river. Their legs are the retractable steel pilings of Chinese drilling rigs, the waterspout comes from detonating charges laboriously sunk into the bedrock, and the proboscis belongs to a mechanical excavator poised on the rig's foredeck to scoop out the debris. China takes the Economic Quadrangle seriously. The benefits of investment depend on making the river navigable; and that means taming the Tang-ho rapids. But when the work is finished, navigation will be possible for a maximum of six months a year. For the rest of the time, when the river is low, the rapids will remain as fearsome and insuperable as they appeared to the members of the Mekong Exploration Commission nearly 150 years ago.

As expeditions go, that which first ventured into the Mekong's 'heart of darkness' deserves classic status. It ought to rank with, say, the African travels of Dr Livingstone. In 1871 Livingstone was the recipient of an honorary award at the first meeting of the International Geographical Congress; the only other such award at that prestigious gathering went to Francis Garnier.

Some twenty strong, the Commission disappeared into the unknown for over two years, and when it re-emerged – those who did – it would sweep the board at every geographical equivalent of the Oscars. Anticipating H.M. Stanley's Congo expedition of twenty years later, it would also change the geography and ultimately the whole political complexion of the region. Thanks to the Mekong Exploration Commission a French empire would be hacked from what the expedition insisted on calling 'Indo-China'; and under this dispensation Cambodia would be rescued from extinction, Laos ingeniously contrived, and in defiance of the French, a unitary Vietnam would be painfully projected.

Yet the French were ambivalent about exploration as such and were wont to disparage it as an Anglo-Saxon conceit deficient in scientific rigour. Worse still for the expedition's survivors, word of their achievements would coincide with momentous events at home as France was repeatedly worsted, and Paris itself besieged, during the Franco–Prussian war. It would thus fall to others, especially the British, to heap honours on the Mekong Exploration Commission and to be the first to hail it as 'one of the most remarkable and successful exploring expeditions of the nineteenth century'.

It was also one of the best-documented expeditions of the period. Besides an official record in four hefty volumes, we have a lavishly illustrated account which appeared in serialised instalments in a leading French journal, plus two lengthy personal accounts. Remarkably for the 1860s, there are even 'before and after' group portraits of the six principal participants.

The 'before' picture, an engraving based on a photograph, has something odd about it. Just as the expedition itself tackled the river backwards, starting where it ended and going doggedly against the flow ever after, so the picture appears to have been reversed. Presumably this had something to do with the technical problems of transferring a negative to an engraved plate. It would account for later confusion in the captioning of the picture and would explain why, for instance, Lagrée and Garnier have their hair partings on the wrong side; or why Delaporte – or is it de Carné? – appears to be looking away from the camera. All is adjusted by simply inspecting the picture in a mirror.

The original photo was taken just days before the expedition headed off into the unknown. Some of the men may never before have faced the camera. The picture would serve as an official memorial and, in the not unlikely event of their failing to return, as a cherished memento for family and friends. To a suspicious mind it is also telling evidence of a dangerously self-conscious formality that would dog the whole expedition.

The Saigon photographer, a Monsieur Gsell, would not be

accompanying them. His apparatus was far too cumbersome and his glass plates far too fragile. But at government expense he and his equipment had been shipped up through the Mekong Delta and into Cambodia. There, in June 1866, the expedition officially assembled – then promptly split up. While awaiting the necessary documentation, and by way of getting acquainted, the Commission's six French officials betook themselves to Siem Reap at the far end of Cambodia's Tonle Sap, or 'Great Lake'. A week of tramping and archaeologising amongst the Cyclopean ruins of Angkor would follow.

They were not the first Europeans to visit the ancient Khmer capital, but they were the first to attempt a systematic record of it. They tested their survey instruments by observing for latitude and longitude, by measuring the kilometres of wall and waterway, and by mapping much of the vast complex. Late into the night they sat amongst the statuary conjecturing about the beliefs and resources of Angkor's builders, then they slept within its bat-infested cloisters.

For the photo a suitable site was chosen on the steps leading up to one of the temple terraces. Hats – a sun helmet, a bowler, a Vietnamese straw cone – were discarded yet left 'in shot'. With the same exaggeratedly casual air, the members of the expedition draped themselves over the warm stonework and stared imperiously at the camera, six bearded bachelors on the threshold of a great adventure.

Just so, explorers of the Nile like Burton, Speke and Baker, all of whose exploits had climaxed in the previous five years, might have posed in front of the pyramids before trudging off into the Dark Continent – except that they did no such thing. British sensibilities were offended by such rank displays of professionalism. Her Majesty's Government involved itself in exploration only to the extent of conceding what Lord Salisbury would call 'an Englishman's right to have his throat cut when and where he

Members of the Mekong Exploration Commission at Angkor Wat, June 1866.
Left to right: Garnier, Delaporte, Joubert, Thorel, de Carné, Lagrée.

chose'. Notching up discoveries was reckoned by the British a sporting activity, reserved principally for gentlemen, conducted with a minimum of fuss, and administered by an august scientific body – the Royal Geographical Society.

That such amateurism had nevertheless produced handsome political dividends was undeniable. To Gallic minds, it was also deeply irritating. Amongst the men on the steps at Angkor a sneaking admiration for their British counterparts was overlaid by professional jealousy and intense suspicion. For far too long, they grumbled, France had allowed her rival a free hand in the world's *terra incognita*. It was time to tear a leaf out of Albion's album. Just as the Nile had given Britain its entrée into Africa, the Mekong would give France its entrée into Asia.

Scrutinising the photo, one is impressed more by its poignancy than its bravado. Far from sustaining the intended air of relaxed informality, it is as if the postures adopted by the explorers had been carefully rehearsed and their relative positions measured out with a ruler. On the extreme right (or left, if one uses the mirror), *le Commandant* Ernest Marc Louis de Gonzagues Doudart de Lagrée sits slightly apart from his colleagues, and not actually on the steps but on a ledge beside them. His legs are crossed, his shoes have buckles, and a well-placed sleeve displays the gold braid of his rank. Positioned not so as to make space for his name but so as to emphasise the scope of his authority, Lagrée (for short) affects a certain dignity. An aristocrat by birth and a product of the prestigious École Polytechnique in Paris, he was indisputably the leader. At forty-three and with a hint of grey, he was by far the oldest as well as being the most senior in rank and the only member of the expedition with an already notable record of service in south-east Asia.

Three years previously, in 1863, Lagrée had been deputed to pioneer France's first push up from the Mekong Delta into Cambodia. His orders had been to explore the river's course in that country and to persuade the Cambodian king to sign an exclusive defence treaty with France. On both counts he had succeeded. Siam's (Thailand's) prior claims to suzerainty over Cambodia's King Norodom had been dismissed with a well-timed display of firepower, a treaty had been signed, and Lagrée had stayed on at Norodom's court as France's representative. That Cambodia had just become, in effect, a French protectorate was in no small measure thanks to *le Commandant* Doudart de Lagrée.

Encouraged by the thought that where he went, the tricolour had a way of following, it was Lagrée's idea that the new Mekong expedition first sail across the Great Lake to Siem Reap and Angkor. Neither place was then part of Cambodia. In a protracted decline and fall to rival that of Rome, the Khmer empire had been disintegrating ever since Jayavarman VII completed the stalagmite of Janus-like statuary which is Angkor's Bayon in the thirteenth century. Southern Vietnam, as it now is, including the Mekong

Delta, had been lost by the Khmers over the next three hundred years; so had most of the middle Mekong and the Menam basin in Thailand; and in the late eighteenth century, as Vietnamese and Thais squeezed the Cambodian heartland ever harder, the eastern end of the Great Lake, including Angkor, had been annexed by Bangkok.

The French, as Cambodia's new keepers, now disputed this cession of what they chose to call the 'lost' or 'alienated' Cambodian provinces. It helped that Angkorian scholarship provided cover for occasional visits and that Angkorian preservation provided a ready pretext for administrative interference. Lagrée had himself been in Angkor for several weeks in 1865 and again in early 1866. He had begun the mapping of the site and had commissioned translations of inscriptions which demonstrated that it was indisputably of Cambodian provenance. But Bangkok was unmoved; and in the course of these labours the climate had taken its toll of the indefatigable Lagrée. Suffering from a recurrent and acute form of laryngitis, he had formally requested home leave. Admiral de Lagrandière, the colonial governor in Saigon, suggested he defer the request, then asked him 'out of the blue', as he put it, to accept the leadership of the Mekong Exploration Commission. 'Why not?' replied Lagrée, and 'I began to laugh.' So, apparently, did the Admiral.

The joke, unexplained at the time, would soon turn decidedly sour. Laughter of any sort would not be much heard once the expedition got underway. To his companions Lagrée would remain an enigmatic supremo, neither overbearing nor unsympathetic but aloof, sometimes hesitant, often hard to hear (the laryngitis obliged him to whisper), and so weighed down by his responsibilities as to seem indifferent to the derring-do possibilities of the enterprise. Alternatively he was a pillar of strength and decency and 'possessed of every psychological and moral quality needed for the success of the expedition', as Garnier would put it. By implication, any fault lay not in his lofty character but in his state of health and in the more erratic calibre of his companions.

To reach the expedition's Cambodian assembly point, Lagrée and his companions had already sailed from Saigon up through the Mekong Delta, crossing in the course of this three-hundred-kilometre voyage from French territory to Vietnamese territory to Cambodian. Then, as now, the political geography of the river was horribly confusing. As a rule major rivers – like the Yangtse, Mississippi, Amazon, Nile, Congo, Ganges – flow through just one or two countries. This is because a river basin tends to spawn the homogeneous and mutually dependent society which makes an excellent nucleus for a unitary state. Big rivers naturally make for big states, and so the Amazon integrates much of Brazil, the Yangtse much of China, and the Ganges much of India. Rivers, in essence, unite. They do not make good borders, however invitingly delineated on the map, nor do they lend themselves to being bisected by borders. On the contrary, 'natural frontiers' properly follow the outermost rim of a river's watershed, however problematic the business of definition in such remote tracts.

To this rule the Mekong has long been a conspicuous exception. Historically it has spawned only one notable civilisation, that of Cambodia's Khmers. But although Angkor, the Khmer capital, did indeed profit prodigiously from the freakish behaviour of the Mekong, it remained geographically tangential and politically indifferent to it. Likewise French Indo-China, while it would be postulated on the Mekong basin, would serve only to emphasise the incoherence of the lands which comprised that basin. For much of the river's course the French would elevate it into an internationally recognised border which, in the second half of the twentieth century, would become that least permeable of all frontiers, an ideological divide. As the only substantial section of the Iron Curtain (or here sometimes the 'Bamboo Curtain') to be suspended along a riverbed, it cut most of south-east Asia in two, opposing the beneficiaries of a freer world on one bank to the ideologues of a fairer world on the other, and so turning every boat trip into an escape epic.

Today no fewer than six countries nestle along the river (China, Burma, Laos, Thailand, Cambodia, Vietnam); and for about a third of its length it still serves as an international frontier. Uniquely it has not, then, united the peoples strung along its course, nor encouraged much traffic and transit between them. As the Mekong Exploration Commission would quickly discover, there are good, indeed unassailable, reasons for this aberration.

But they are not apparent in the Delta. In fact, in its lowest reaches between Phnom Penh (at the apex of the Delta) and the South China Sea (as its eastward base), the Mekong bustles about its business most responsibly, smiling beneath colossal skies as if to deny a lifetime of upstream excesses. Brimming through low-lying farmland and slopping into innumerable channels and waterways, it here supports a vast population, fronts a galaxy of jaunty riverside towns, provides a carriageway for all manner of river craft, and generally exhibits the benevolent features associated with deltaic abundance. It is, in short, highly deceptive; and the Mekong Exploration Commission could be forgiven for being deceived.

Saigon itself, which in 1866 was just an enclave of French rule in an as yet uncolonialised Vietnam, is not actually on the Mekong Delta. It has its own river, the Donnai, to which it stands much as London to the Thames, the port of Saigon being the furthest point upriver to which ocean-going ships can conveniently sail. To reach the neighbouring Delta, you must today board a hydrofoil on the Saigon riverfront, skim down the Donnai's leaden reaches past oilrigs and freighters to its estuary, and then turn right at the South China Sea.

Alternatively you can take a shortcut by making an earlier right turn into the Arroyo de Poste. An *arroyo* is a creek, a minor watercourse. This one, a linkage of wiggling tributaries and narrow canals, connects the sullen mangrove-fringed Donnai to a lusher landscape along the Tien Giang, the most northerly branch of the Mekong. It was the route taken in June 1866 by *Canonnières 32* and *27*, the pocket-gunboats by which the French explorers sailed up to Cambodia; and according to Lieutenant Garnier, it was too well known to merit description.

In that photo taken at Angkor, Lieutenant Marie Joseph Francis Garnier is the man lolling at the opposite end of the group to *le Commandant* Doudart de Lagrée. A gaunt little figure with deep-set eyes, he sprawls on the steps like the others and is not obviously set apart from them. One leg, though, is drawn up so that the foot can rest on the equivalent ledge to that on which Lagrée is enthroned at the other end. The foot is making a point. Garnier, as one of the instigators of the expedition, its surveyor and hydrologist, and the most senior in rank after *le Commandant*, was officially Lagrée's deputy and so, by implication, second-in-command. Indeed the Mekong Exploration Commission is commonly referred to as the 'De Lagrée-Garnier Expedition' and sometimes, more controversially, as just the 'Garnier Expedition'. Garnier would write both the official account of it and the best-known of the personal accounts. He would also collect all the medals and the plaudits. When Lagrée's supporters objected, Garnier would respond with double-edged testimonials to his superior. 'He was for us less a *commandant* than a father,' he would write.

This at least rang true. A wiry twenty-six, Francis Garnier was much the smallest of the party and quite young enough to be Lagrée's son. At Naval School the young François (he later changed the spelling to 'Francis') was nicknamed 'Mademoiselle Buonaparte', an unflattering reflection on the contrast between his trim diminutive build and his loud extravagant ambitions. For grand vision as for outstanding stamina and courage, no one must be able to fault Francis Garnier. Single-minded, impulsive and intrepid, he was out both to prove himself and to prove that he was right. He had, in short (so to speak), all the attributes of the indomitable explorer, including an acute sense of his own self-importance. This ruled out anything recognisable as humour. Like the distant Lagrée, the driven Garnier would not be easy company. Happily the remaining four on the steps at Angkor would betray more appealing traits.

By way of the Arroyo de Poste the expedition reached the Tien Giang branch of the Mekong at the town of My-tho, then headed upstream. The river is said to have nine mouths, nine being a fair approximation to the geographical reality as well as an exceptionally auspicious number throughout Buddhist south-east Asia. In mythology and art the river is usually represented as a nine-headed serpent or dragon (*Cuu Long*). But the nine open-mouthed heads on their nine sinuous necks grow from just two scaly torsos, the Tien Giang or Upper River and the Hau Giang, Bassac, or Lower River. Each about a kilometre wide, the Tien Giang and the Hau Giang comprise the main navigational channels up through the Delta, braiding together the seven other effluents until they themselves converge to form the parent stream at Phnom Penh.

On either side of these twin conduits the Delta fans out to both the South China Sea and the Gulf of Siam (or Thailand). The map shows the Delta as eighty thousand square kilometres of very green land criss-crossed by a capillary of waterways. In reality, for at least half the year it is eighty thousand square kilometres of very glassy water criss-crossed by a web of causeways. The Mekong falls only six metres in its last eight hundred kilometres, but so low-lying is the Delta that the river in flood appears, and often is, the highest thing around. The land is so flat that from an upper deck you must allow for the curvature of the earth's surface in counting the tiers of a distant pagoda; the lower ones may have ducked below the horizon. In fact the river feels as if it were itself cambered, with the boat driving along its crown, and lateral channels plunging to left and right or spilling under bridges to explore the orchards and inundate the cabbages.

After forcing its way for thousands of kilometres through mountain gorge and deepest forest, it is as if the river can scarcely believe its good fortune. Like a sluice released, it wells across the plain, exploring the *arroyos*, tugging at pontoons, basking in backwaters and generally making the most of its first and last unimpeded kilometres. Here nothing is quite what it seems. The man hoeing his field knee-deep in verdure turns out to be punting across it, his hoe a pole and his footing a boat. Behind him, along a tree-lined avenue, a rice barge churns into sight pushing a menacing bow wave. The Delta is said to produce more rice than any area of comparable size in the world. Beneath the glinting panes of water lie meadow and mud at no great depth. But rice-growing being a form of hydroponics, for the last six months of the year the fields are lakes and the landscape is a waterscape.

All that is not water in this aqueous world is ordained to wallow. Rusting car ferries shuttle across the main rivers with their decks awash. Upstream glides a mountain of pineapples propelled by a spluttering screw; downstream comes a haystack pirouetting on the current with a rudder and stern sticking out behind. Any craft boasting more draught than the thickness of a banana looks distinctly piratical, an impression heightened by the large painted eyes which adorn every prow and scan the flood ahead, lashless, boss-eyed and bloodshot, for any aquatic impertinence. By these eyes alone can one distinguish the houseboat from the house. Both are otherwise precarious constructions of water-blackened timbers festooned with clothing and potted geraniums.

Sampans, the river's equivalent of bicycles, are the exception; they have no eyes because their bows, like the rest of the boat, lurk below the wash. Standing in midstream, the boatgirl plies her oars with the dexterous click of chopsticks, leaning into them and flicking through the stroke with the toss of a glossy ponytail. Porcelain forearms are encased in long-sleeved gloves, and trousered legs aflutter with the tails of a white *ao dai* (the long-skirted and daringly slit dress beloved of the Vietnamese). She dips in time with the stroke like a decorous metronome. This is how angels would row. Villages perched on nests of drunken stilts loom from the haze like preening storks. Children and ducks upend in the water; lawns of water hyacinth undulate along the bank.

Even the weather is of a mind to wallow. Above the eastern horizon billowing pillars of cloud mount to the stratosphere as the gathering gloom below is ignited with a *son et lumière* spectacle. Steel-grey and flecked with ochreous rust, another storm is lumbering up from the South China Sea. Hastily tarpaulins are hauled over open holds. A high-sterned country boat, junk-like but for the absence of a sail, guns its engine and heads for shelter. In the gathering gloom a string of tanker-barges carrying diesel for Cambodia is overhauled by the deluge.

Floods in the Mekong Delta rival cyclones in the Bay of Bengal as one of Asia's meteorological clichés. Seldom does the rainy season (June–October) pass without an inundation, and in towns like My-tho on the Tien Giang and Can-tho on the Hau Giang the provident householder owns a liferaft. Here sampans may be seen jostling with bicycles at the traffic lights. In adjacent homes families cuddle up on top of the furniture to watch TV across a room afloat with toys. Property and crops suffer; but the Delta is used to these things, and fewer lives are lost than in the flash floods which occasionally affect the hilly areas of Vietnam. Nor is the river wholly to blame. The storms and tides surging in from the sea bear an equal responsibility.

A curious feature of these monsoon inundations in the Delta is that, while exacerbated by incoming tides, they appear to occur only in the evening. In the morning there are no floods and no visible tide. Inescapably therefore, the Mekong Delta seems to receive only one tide a day; and two tides every twenty-four hours being the rule throughout the rest of our planet, this phenomenon looks to be unique.

Such a freak of nature should surely have engaged the attention of Francis Garnier as the Mekong Exploration Commission's hydrologist. But in his haste to whisk the expedition up to Angkor as quickly as possible, Garnier wastes not a word on the matter. Nor, to be fair, do most other writers on the Delta. In fact this tidal oddity is so little remarked and so clearly unnatural that one might suppose it imagined.

Confirmation can be found, though, in the appendices to volume two of a little-read but delightful work by H. Warington Smyth entitled *Five Years in Siam*. During his five years in the employ of the Siamese (Thai) government as a minerals prospector Warington Smyth also noticed the occurrence of what he calls 'diurnal tides' (once-daily, as opposed to the universal 'semi-diurnal', or once-half-daily, tides). Writing in the 1890s and with reference to Thailand's Menam river (or Chao Phraya) below Bangkok, he too had been puzzled and felt the matter worth investigating. This he had done with thoroughness, making his own observations throughout his five years, looking up such tide records as existed, and consulting all manner of seafarers.

'The tides in the Gulf of Siam', he begins, 'present peculiarities which are at first very confusing to the observer.' These peculiarities 'originate in the China Sea' and are detectable, in varying degrees, all down the coast from Hong Kong to Saigon and on round into the Gulf of Thailand and Bangkok. At certain times of the year, just after a full or new moon, and most noticeably in the estuarine approaches of rivers which are in flood, alternate tides vary markedly in size and duration. Thus it happens, continues this paragon of memorialists, that the flow of the lesser tide, usually that in the morning, may be overwhelmed, indeed completely obliterated, by the ebb of the greater, usually that in the evening.

Warington Smyth follows this with complicated notes on how the lesser tide, over a twenty-eight-day period, gradually swells as it gets later in the day until eventually it usurps both the dimensions and the hour of the last great tide. Sadly he ventures no opinion as to why this phenomenon occurs. Even today the workings of the attractive mechanism by which the moon and sun control the action of the tides are not widely understood. But he does note that 'the highest tides are much influenced by the wind' and that a brisk easterly can 'add another half a foot' even in the Gulf of Thailand, which is a more sheltered shore than that of south Vietnam.

This diurnal mother-of-a-tide ought, of course, to spell disaster to the Delta. A salty inundation, albeit only once a day, would soon sour the world's most productive ricebowl and turn the green dazzle of paddy into maudlin thickets of mangrove like those along the Donnai below Saigon. What prevents such a disaster is the power of the mighty Mekong. The inrushing tide meets the outrushing river, and in the best traditions of ecological equilibrium they compromise. The river rises, its progress barred by the tide. The backing-up of the river by a big 'diurnal' is measurable as far upstream as Phnom Penh and beyond. But there and throughout the three to four hundred kilometres down to the sea, salination is barely detectable. The floodwaters surging through My-tho and Can-tho leave no salty sensation and are, in a manner of speaking, fresh. The river thus defends the Delta from its deadliest foe since the rising waters are overwhelming its own, not the China Sea's.

So too is the silt. For their major export crop the Vietnamese have to provide only seed and labour. The rest is down to the river. The farmers of the Delta plunge their rice seedlings into

Mekong water and then anchor them in Mekong mud. In general, facts about the river are disputed. Is it the world's fourteenth longest or its twelfth? Is its discharge the fifth largest or the sixth? No two books agree; even the river-mad Garnier never hazards a guess on such matters. But that it reigns supreme as the world's most industrious earthmover seems highly likely. The Mekong in spate discharges not muddy water but runny mud. A cup of Turkish coffee, heavily sugared, has less sediment per cubic centimetre. In its suspended grit, modern propeller screws get so quickly blunted that riverside repair shops offer a regrinding and replacement service.

To offload this sediment – a sludge of mica and minerals from Tibet, Yunnanese phosphates, nitrogenous Burmese clays and leafy loams from Laos – the river waits until the plains of Cambodia and the Delta. There, as those capricious 'diurnals' halt its flow, and as its level drops after the monsoon floods, it deposits its burden in a silk-glistening tilth of prime growing potential.

Admittedly, when the Mekong Exploration Commission headed upriver in 1866, the diurnal tides may not have been very evident. From Saigon the expedition took three days to reach Cambodia. At night they moored by the banks of the Hau Giang and slept in the boats. Otherwise they stopped only at My-tho to load coal for the *canonnières'* boilers. It was early June, and according to both Garnier and Louis de Carné (who also wrote a personal narrative of the expedition), the monsoon rains were then just beginning. The river would have been rising but not yet in flood; and if the moon was also unfavourable, the effect of the tides might have been negligible.

But if June is a bad month for observing tidal variation, it is the best of times for observing a still stranger phenomenon. Possibly unique to the Mekong and certainly germane to would-be empire-builders, this second fluvial aberration is as much the *sine qua non* of Cambodia as the 'diurnal' tides are of the Delta. Yet it too would elude the *savants* of the Commission. Perhaps they felt that until they ventured into what French maps called *territoires peu connus* they were off-duty so far as science was concerned. Measuring Angkor's great wat was by way of an exercise. Likewise, their speculation on how such a jungle kingdom could have produced the world's most monumental city was something of a formality and still rates high on the conversational bill-of-fare of every tourist. It never seems to have occurred to Lagrée and Garnier that between the mysterious river they were engaged to explore and the inexplicable splendours amid which they first congregated there lay a simple, if bizarre, cause-and-effect connection.

TWO

❖

Shuttle to Angkor

'The Mekon [in Cambodia] is a vast melancholy-looking river,
three miles broad, covered with islands, and flowing with the
rapidity of a torrent.'

LORD ASHBURTON,
President of the Royal Geographical Society, 1862

L IKE THE IMPETUOUS GARNIER, his young colleague
Louis de Carné, the author of what would be the first account
of the expedition to be published, allows just a paragraph for
transporting the Commission's personnel from Saigon to Angkor.
The farewells had been fond, says de Carné. Some shook his hand
'as if we were doomed', more predicted 'a speedy return after an
abortive attempt'. Otherwise there was little to report. Six enervat-
ing months into his first Eastern posting, de Carné insists that he
personally felt nothing, no excitement, no trepidation, just 'a
worldly indifference'. More a superior *ennui*, it would permeate
his narrative and stay with him for the rest of his pathetically brief
life. The climate showed him no favours; but in the light of later
disagreements this early reserve smacks of pique. Like an unwanted
playfellow scuffing a stone with studied indifference, Louis de
Carné nursed the heavy heart of a misfit.

In the group photo de Carné is the one at the back dressed
in black and with the thickest of spade-like beards; sunk in reverie,
he looks to be slightly out of it already. At twenty-two he was the

youngest of the party, and as a junior official in the French Ministry of External Affairs he was the only civilian, all the others being naval officers. Additionally he seems to have taken instant exception to the bullish and undiplomatic Francis Garnier. In the pecking order he rated 'Mademoiselle Buonaparte' as just another naval scientist, one among several and with no greater claim to the direction of the expedition than the rest. Only *le Commandant* could command; and it was thus to the more soft-spoken and dignified Lagrée that de Carné attached himself.

Like Lagrée, de Carné had aristocratic connections. His father was a *comte* and a member of the Académie Française, and his uncle was the self-same Admiral de Lagrandière who was governor of the colony. Young Louis de Carné owed his appointment entirely to this connection, a fact of which Garnier would miss no opportunity to remind him. As the expedition's political officer reporting directly to the Quai d'Orsay, de Carné's position was potentially influential; yet it was prejudiced by his inexperience and fraught with ambivalence. Unaccustomed to naval discipline, he was expected to submit to it. Untutored in any relevant science, he was liable to be treated as a dogsbody by his more qualified companions. And as one unknown to the colony's naval establishment, he was widely suspected of being an informer for the civil authorities and the government of the day in Paris.

The government in Paris was that of the high-handed Louis Napoleon, otherwise Napoleon III. A nephew of Napoleon Bonaparte, Louis Napoleon had been chosen as French president in 1848 and had successfully installed himself as emperor in 1852. The next two decades were therefore those of the 'Second Empire', a period of ambitious national reconstruction well exemplified by Baron Haussmann's proud grey boulevards in Paris and by a succession of sometimes quixotic enterprises overseas. An attempt to foist the francophile emperor Maximilian on the Mexicans would prove disastrous; so nearly were similar schemes in the Levant.

On the other hand gains were made in west Africa and the Pacific. And after a long absence, the tricolour had been seen again in the Far East.

Other nations, notably the British and the Dutch, liked to think that they had come by their colonies either accidentally or as a result of patient trade and an earnest desire on the part of the locals for the security afforded by heavy cannon and accessible law courts. The French had no such illusions. They sought exotic dominions because, without them, France looked like a second-rate power. Nor could they be too particular as to how they acquired them. National prestige was at stake, and casual enterprise had failed. In the eighteenth century France had lost an empire in India to the British; in the nineteenth she had been consistently outbid in China, again mainly by the British. The British were also established in Lower Burma, Ceylon (Sri Lanka), Malaya and Borneo; and they were menacingly well-placed in Siam (Thailand), where the Thai determination to hang on to Cambodia's 'lost provinces' around Angkor owed much to a stiffening British presence.

By the 1850s, then, not much unattached Asiatic shoreline was left. If the Second Empire were to make any impression in the East, it had to move fast and ask questions later. The questions so deferred would include such details as what the place was for, how it would pay for itself, and what other nations, especially the British, would make of it. But the place itself was not in question. Between India and China the only remaining option had been the long thin strand which is now Vietnam.

Then called Annam, Vietnam was under an Annamite emperor based in Hué (roughly halfway up the Vietnamese coast) who claimed sovereignty over both Tonkin in the north (where Hanoi is) and 'Cochin China' in the south (where Saigon and the Delta are). Rarely, though, did Hué's sovereignty go uncontested; and the consequent spectacle of repeated rebellions, disputed successions and arbitrary attacks on Vietnam's mission-run native Christian communities had duly emboldened the government of Louis Napoleon to stake its claim. The plight of the missions meant that the clergy in France, on whose support Louis Napoleon relied, welcomed the idea; so did French commercial interests anxious for ready access to Oriental produce like cotton, silk and hardwoods.

The international situation also obliged. In 1858 Britain's watchful eye was turned to India as all available troops were diverted for the suppression of what the sahibs of the Raj called the 'Indian Mutiny'. Simultaneously there had occurred a lull in a joint Anglo–French assault on the Chinese empire. The French fleet, with time to spare, had been ordered south. Assisted by troops from the Philippines, whose Spanish rulers also supported missionary activity in Annam, it effected a landing at Tourane (now Da Nang), the nearest seaport to Hué. Tourane was slated to become a French trading station equivalent to British Singapore; and the emperor in Hué, presented with this *fait accompli*, was confidently expected to grant France commercial privileges elsewhere in Vietnam and protectoral status over the whole country.

Not surprisingly the Annamite emperor had other ideas. His troops gave a good account of themselves on the landward route to Hué, while the French ships found it impossible to force the city by way of its Perfume River. Stalemate ensued; and for the French, delay meant defeat – from the climate if not from the Annamites. After some fateful debate over the respective merits of Tonkin and Cochin China, the fleet sailed away, heading south again. In the judgement of its commander, the location of Saigon midway between Hong Kong and Singapore, plus the rice surplus of the Delta and the inland access afforded by the Mekong, were a persuasive combination.

Saigon had been duly surprised and taken in early 1859. Annamite forces responded by laying siege to the now French town; for over a year the garrison barely held its own. A second French expedition in 1861, on which the then twenty-one-year-old Francis Garnier served with typically rash distinction, saved the day. The Annamites were repulsed, and their emperor was obliged to cede to France the three small provinces adjacent to Saigon that comprised about half of the Delta.

A bridgehead had thus been established, though it was not quite what was intended. Instead of a protectorate over the whole of Annam – a cut-price arrangement with enormous potential – the Second Empire had been lumbered with a minuscule colony that was expensive to administer and not in the least bit prestigious. Saigon could never rival Singapore because it was sixty kilometres up the dreary Donnai with nothing to trade but rice. Moreover it afforded no obvious protection to Annam's Christian communities, all of them a thousand kilometres away in Tonkin.

With the addition of Lagrée's protectorate over a truncated Cambodia, such was the very limited extent of the French presence in south-east Asia when the Mekong Exploration Commission set off in 1866. Two years earlier even Louis Napoleon had been prey to second thoughts. The foreign affairs ministry in the Quai d'Orsay, Louis de Carné's employer, was under pressure from the British, who upheld Bangkok's claim to sovereignty over Cambodia. Moreover the French exchequer was facing a financial shortfall exacerbated by sustained resistance in the Delta that necessitated military expenditure of about twenty million francs a year against tax receipts of two million. The colony would never pay for itself; it was time to pull out, argued the government.

The Cambodian protectorate put a slightly rosier complexion on things, but it was the verdict of the naval establishment that carried the most weight. In Paris the Ministère de Marine (that is the navy ministry, or admiralty) had responsibility for all colonial operations. The Annamite initiative had been conducted by the Navy, the colony was run by the Navy, nearly all its officials were naval officers, and in Saigon as in Paris the Navy now adamantly opposed the retrocession of any territory.

In this debate – essentially a spat between the ministries of external affairs and marine affairs but with undertones of the running battle (it would run for forty years) between an ever cautious metropolis and an over-adventurous colony – Francis Garnier figured conspicuously. To rescue a shipmate washed overboard he had once leapt into the South China Sea; the man was fished out, and Garnier famously promoted. With the same hopeful bravado he now launched himself to the rescue of the colony. *Soirées* were held in Saigon and a pressure group of like-minded friends was formed; to whet commercial appetites an exhibition of colonial artefacts and produce was organised; and to better inform the home authorities a number of publications appeared, all proclaiming the future potential of 'Indo-China' in the most extravagant terms. Petitions bore the signature of Francis Garnier, but pamphlets carried the byline of 'G. Francis' – an alias of such crystal transparency that one wonders why he bothered.

In identical language, all urged the exploration of the Mekong as the certain saving of the colony. The river's navigational potential was crying out to be realised; the rich mineral deposits (especially gold and silver) of its tributaries and the resins and timbers of its forests could only be exploited by French expertise and enterprise; likewise inland China, the country from which the river was believed to flow, waited only on French initiative for its fabled produce to come gushing downstream, so making the Mekong the rival of the Yangtse, and Saigon a second Shanghai.

The enthusiasm of Garnier and his companions could not be faulted; nor could their arguments be easily rebuffed in the then state of ignorance about the river. The powerful Navy Minister had gratefully taken up the cry, threatening resignation if not heeded. The struggling colony had been reprieved. And in 1865 the Mekong Exploration Commission had been authorised.

It would be an exaggeration to say that the colony's future depended entirely on the success of the expedition; other factors would be just as influential. But the weight of colonial expectation was considerable and it bore heavily on all the expedition's personnel, none more so than Garnier. Whether or not the Mekong itself lived up to his billing as a highway to inland China, he for one was resolved that the expedition must somehow proclaim the political, strategic and economic advantages of extending French rule in the region. In effect, he must make the case for what he called 'a new empire of the East Indies rising in the shadow of our flag'.

Writing of the lands through which the river supposedly flowed, Garnier and his friends popularised the term 'Indo-China'. Although not their invention, it epitomised their thinking. It would figure in the titles of the expedition's official report, of Garnier's personal account and of Louis de Carné's. 'Indo-Chine' might be unknown to its inhabitants, but the adoption and promotion of the term by the French awarded to the lands along the Mekong a new and convincing territorial integrity. Better still, it defined this integrity in terms which other European powers would understand. The region was no longer to be regarded as some hybrid borderland between other people's empires in India and China proper. As Indo-China, it was an arena for colonial endeavour in its own right. Indeed, in Garnier's fevered imagination it would be to France an 'India-and-China' in one – compensation for past disappointments in both, and equivalent to either in prestige and potential. It would also be a sensational assertion of France's revival under the 'Second Empire', and might one day become the 'jewel in the crown' of French possessions, indeed 'le perle de l'Empire' as later writers would put it.

The river offered some grounds for taking the idea of 'Indo-China' seriously. Its basin evidently embraced most of the lands that comprised the south-east Asian peninsula, and its course would be found to thread through them. Like the hanked necklaces nowadays being hawked in every Cambodian market, the looping Mekong strings together cultural souvenirs of unmistakably Indian provenance with jade-and-porcelain reminders of China, both being interspersed with filler-beads of dark wood and chunky silver from the intervening lands.

Angkor is Indian – or Indic, a word implying linguistic association rather than any aggressive acculturation from India. Debate rages as to the primacy given by its builders to Buddhist as opposed to Hindu cults (or, indeed, whether they should be deemed mutually exclusive); but the aesthetic of Angkor, the iconography, the scale and the building techniques all find parallels in the Indic monuments of Indonesia and take their inspiration from India itself. Also Indian are the Angkor scripts, indeed the Khmer script in use today and even the name 'Cambodia' (or 'Kampuchea' as those traditionalist sticklers in Pol Pot's Khmer Rouge regime preferred); both words derive from Kamboja, a place name and lineage bestowed on several remote kingdoms in ancient Sanskrit literature.

To archaeologically inclined empire-builders like Lagrée and Garnier, Angkor's Indian associations were as exciting as its scale. If for no other reason than to spite Britain's pretension to a monopoly of all things Indian, they found the site a mouthwatering experience; and they did not doubt that it would soon be restored to Cambodia – and so come under French protection.

From their base in Angkor Wat, which Garnier immediately dubbed 'the Buddhist Nôtre Dame', they explored Angkor Thom, or 'Great Angkor', the nearby palace-city. Even the lugubrious de Carné was mildly impressed, although still determinedly downbeat. It was all very remarkable, he thought, but where were the people, their history, their literature? 'The ruins of a monastery mouldering in the bosom of an English wood . . . move us more deeply.' Mouldering English monasteries being the lowest form of what was recognisable as civilisation, Angkor was off the scale; it was just too much, too barbaric, too dead.

To the more fanciful Garnier it was more like a living fairytale. The city's towered gateway with its myriad stone faces put him in mind of *The Thousand and One Nights*. They rode towards it on elephants through trees of Brobdignagian proportions and over a riverwide moat by the so-called 'Bridge of Giants'.

You can still do this. The elephant-ride costs ten US dollars and the steel tubing of the howdah is reminiscent of a prison cage. But at least for elephants, the traffic is stopped and the gateway's images may be examined at leisure. Alternatively you can just donate a fistful of Cambodian riels to the mahout; for that, you gain merit and the elephant gets a banana.

Crammed into one of the puffing little *canonnières*, the French explorers had taken two days to sail from Phnom Penh to Angkor – one to navigate the Tonle Sap river which connects the Mekong to the Great Lake and another to cross the Great Lake itself. Nowadays the whole trip takes five hours in an eighty-seater river-cruiser offering live karaoke, iced beer and chronic sunburn on the cabin roof. All boat journeys in Cambodia take five hours. Promoters have latched onto the idea that five hours is an acceptable journey time for foreigners, distance and horsepower notwithstanding.

Given a run of 270 kilometres, the Phnom Penh–Angkor cruisers go some way towards discrediting the idea that Cambodians have no sense of urgency. Snug at the apex of a surfer's dream wave, they slice through the cat's cradle of fishing lines along the Tonle Sap river, casually capsizing sampans and dousing innocent bottoms in slatted riverside toilets. Acres of water hyacinth are no impediment; they hightail over them like heifers on spring pasture, pausing only to reverse engines and disentangle propellers before making a three-hour dash across the choppy seas of the Great Lake itself. Big barn-like wats, startled from their morning meditations beneath a stack of upturned roofs, whiz past in a blur of maroon, gold and whitewash; corrugated towns peek from the towpath through a curtain of sugar palms; a hazy escarpment to the north interrupts an otherwise unpunctured horizon. Opinion rates the voyage an adventure, not a cruise.

At thirty knots it is quite impossible to ascertain which way the Tonle Sap river is flowing. For most of the year it definitely runs into the Mekong; but in June, when the expedition sailed up it, it was definitely running out of the Mekong. Garnier would confirm as much on the return journey. The Tonle Sap river is in fact that rarest of fluvial oddities, a river that flows both ways.

As the only link between the Great Lake and the Mekong, it is about eighty kilometres long and, where its course is defined by embankments, as wide as the Thames at Maidenhead. It is not deep, but like the Great Lake itself it supports what is said to be the richest freshwater fishery in the world. Fishing rights operate like logging rights and are no less controversial. Auctioned by the government, they make a substantial contribution to the national exchequer but occasion bitter accusations of corruption. Additionally successful contractors, in an effort to recoup both their bids and their bribes, are inclined to flout the regulations against electrocution-fishing and the use of explosives. The losers, apart from the fish, are inevitably the local fishermen, who nurse an abiding sense of injustice. Unpopular concessions require the protection of armed guards, and as catches decline, violent affrays are of frequent occurrence. These may have an international dimension. As in the timber trade, foreigners are well represented, notably the Vietnamese whose cross-eyed trawlers still monopolise the offshore waters of the Great Lake just as they did in the 1860s.

Legally hauled from the weedy depths by line and net, trap,

trawl and scoop, the silver bounty is notable for its variety as well as its quantity. Here are found fish that shoot down insects with missiles of mucus and others, much appreciated by the Mekong expedition, that attain the size of boats. There's a carp that gets drunk, a perch that climbs trees, and a black catfish that, alone and mainly at night, goes walkabout down dusty lanes. There are also, say the experts, quite a few species that have still to be identified and literally hundreds that may already be extinct.

In season, when the water level is at its lowest, catches are landed by the boatload, manhandled by the bucketload and distributed by the tractorload. At one-off markets in waterside villages buyers and vehicles from all over Cambodia converge. A festival air prevails at these gatherings. The rice spirit flows, clean shirts and brightly coloured blouses glisten with sequin-like scales, and fishy swains find fishy brides amid mountains of silver pungency. Carted home, much of the product will be pounded, salted and putrefied into fish paste, an essential ingredient of south-east Asian cuisine and, for most of the population, their principal source of protein.

Without the river and the lake, the Cambodian diet would not be deficient just in protein; it would be deficient, period. Rice is the staple food and, here as in the Delta, rice does best where an inundation of nutrient-rich water can be relied on. This is what the shuttle behaviour of the Tonle Sap river so obligingly provides. The Great Lake is served by no major rivers of its own. During the long dry season between October and June it shrinks, falling by six metres and losing more than three-quarters of its surface area. The Tonle Sap river drains it into the Mekong like any other tributary; evaporation also claims its share. The first rains in early June make little difference. The lake would in fact never recover its volume were it not for the much faster rise of the Mekong.

By mid-June the Mekong at Phnom Penh is edging up by half a metre a week. The Great Lake now being lower, the Tonle

Sap river goes into reverse. Instead of being one of the Mekong's feeders, it becomes one of its branches, drawing off its current and so replenishing the Great Lake. By mid-July the Mekong is up several metres, and by late August it is in full flood, bursting not only its own banks but also those of the Tonle Sap river and the Great Lake. In a hydraulic feat quite as wonderful as the Delta's 'diurnal tides', much of Cambodia becomes a vast reservoir enriched by all those suspended phosphates and nitrogens.

The rice farmer is ready with his seedlings. As the rains cease, the Mekong falls. Now lower than the Great Lake, it retracts its floodwaters; the Tonle Sap river starts to run back into the Mekong; and the Great Lake begins to recede. As it does so, the Cambodian heartland re-emerges as a sparkling Atlantis of vaguely concentric paddy fields. From the dry stubble of what was the lake's outermost rim, the sun-ripe gold of harvest shades inwards to the lime green of a mature sowing and then the tender lemon-grass of wispy seedlings protruding from the water's edge of the still-receding lake.

Thanks to this phenomenon, plus the potential for a second harvest in the winter months, Cambodia reaps all that it needs and conveniently does so over an unusually long period of the year, thus releasing a large section of the population for other activities. It has always been so. The wealth which made Angkor great and the surplus labour which made its monumental extrava-ganzas possible are commonly ascribed to this same freak of nature. Had Lagrée and Garnier paid closer attention to the behaviour of the Mekong and Tonle Sap rivers, they might have anticipated the most likely answer to the conundrum of how an otherwise unfavoured jungle kingdom could have attained such magnificence. They might also have drawn a valuable lesson for future French empire. The Mekong's importance lies in its role as a provider, not as a highway.

It has ever been so, but it may not remain so. In Phnom Penh and Saigon today's hydrologists wax paranoid about the changes being wrought along the river's middle reaches in Laos and Thailand, and especially along its upper reaches in China. The blasting of the riverbed to improve navigation, the construction of dams for hydro-power and irrigation, and the relentless deforestation of the whole basin could easily spell disaster to the hydraulic economies of Cambodia and the Delta. If the Mekong rises too high or too fast, people drown. If it rises too little or too late, they starve.

The situation is believed to be critical. Lights burn late, and long reports get written, in the Phnom Penh headquarters of today's Mekong River Commission. A multinational watchdog concerned with the river's 'sustainable development', this organisation publicly endorses many of the ambitious projects that its advisers privately decry. The contradiction between alleviating national poverty by large-scale development schemes and endangering individual livelihoods, usually those of subsistence farmers and ethnic minorities, by the fallout from these same schemes is proving difficult to reconcile. Dazzling projections and dire warnings emanate from the Mekong River Commission as erratically as they did from its near-namesake, the Mekong Exploration Commission of 1866.

Pacing the galleries of Angkor Wat, Francis Garnier made the length of its outer wall 3.5 kilometres, estimated that there were 1800 pillars in the temple itself, and scampering up its central tower, counted 504 steps for a measured height of sixty metres. The pillars were mostly single blocks of sandstone, each weighing up to four tons. 'Perhaps nowhere else in the world', he wrote, 'has such an imposing mass of stone been arranged with more sense of art and science.' To technical skills in the cutting and manoeuvring of megaliths that rivalled those of the Pyramids was added the spark of sheer genius. 'What grandeur and at the same time what unity!' he exclaimed. France, 'to whom Angkor should belong', had here a quite spectacular opportunity to proclaim its intentions in south-east Asia. He echoed *le Commandant* Lagrée's sentiments in looking forward to the day when the site would be reclaimed for Cambodia, and he called on archaeologists, artists and historians to petition the French government to undertake a wholesale restoration.

These hopes would eventually be realised. The fretted towers of Angkor Wat – nine in total but five in angled profile and three per exterior façade – would be restored to Cambodia and become its national symbol. Looking like an unfolded paper cut-out, their silhouette is today everywhere – on postage stamps, official letter-heads, ministerial car plaques, TV news logos. Cambodians seem quite oblivious of the embarrassing fact that, but for the much-maligned French, the site itself might still be in Thailand. For it was thanks to the French authorities that Lagrée's designs on the site would bear fruit. In 1907 Angkor and the 'lost provinces' would be wrested from Bangkok, studied, partly restored, and impressively landscaped as per Garnier's plea.

By the 1980s the towers of Angkor Wat also featured on the national flag. 'The blood-red flag above the towers is raised, and will lead the nation to happiness and prosperity,' ran the national anthem. This was doubly ironic; for at the time the Cambodian nation, still traumatised by the rule of the Khmer Rouge and ravaged by famine, knew neither happiness nor prosperity; and Angkor itself had again slipped beyond Phnom Penh's control. Indeed Angkor and the 'lost provinces' had been re-lost, being now held by the outlawed Khmer Rouge who, with the connivance of Bangkok and the support of the Western powers, formed part of a national front at war with the Phnom Penh regime. Even as Angkor Wat's profile fluttered on the blood-red flag, the towers themselves were reportedly being vandalised and their statuary sold off on the international art market.

Crises of national identity are to Cambodia much as floods are to the Delta. They well up with such depressing frequency that one is inclined to accept them as a condition of the country's existence. Independence Day is celebrated on 17 April; there is also a National Day on 7 January. But what these dates memorialise is a vexed question; there are just too many liberationist contenders in Cambodia's modern history. Independence could refer to Lagrée's rejection of Thai suzerainty in 1863, to the French emancipation of the 'lost provinces' in 1907, to the demise of French rule in 1955, to the overthrow of the US-backed Lon Nol regime in 1975 (the right answer, incidentally), to the overthrow of the Chinese-backed Pol Pot (Khmer Rouge) regime in 1979, or to that of the Vietnamese-backed Heng Samrin regime in 1989. Other possible candidates, already discredited and now ripe for demonisation, are the UN-backed administration of the early 1990s and the elected coalition of the mid-1990s. Only the Hun Sen regime, which overthrew the last-named in a 1997 coup, has definitely to be excluded on the grounds that, although often vilified, it has yet to be overthrown.

With such a sustained record of liberating itself from tyranny, Cambodian nationalism ought to command widespread respect. Yet the suspicion lingers that Cambodians have been forever redeeming themselves not so much from foreign aggressors as from fellow Cambodians. Bangkok, Paris, Washington, Beijing and Hanoi have found collaborators rather easy to come by in Cambodia because there is no consensus about what being a Cambodian means. Even Pol Pot's sui-genocidal Khmer Rouge could claim to represent an indigenous tradition. They traced the roots of their revolution not simply to someone else's little red book but to supposed Angkorian traditions of mass mobilisation and draconian discipline in the pursuit of an ideologised utopia.

Of neighbouring Laos as late as the 1950s it was said that most people who lived there had no idea that they belonged to a state called Laos. Cambodians were no doubt better informed, but not therefore more involved. As Lagrée and his companions would be delighted to discover, the region was woefully lacking in those structural elements – centralised administrations, respected institutions, shared interests, recognised frontiers – which underpin statehood and steady other national mansions. Like inland Africa, inland south-east Asia had plenty of political building timber but, as the twentieth century dawned, it had yet to evolve a stable and convincing architecture. Cambodia was still waiting for the French to reclaim Angkor and the 'lost provinces', without which it was like a Scotland minus the Highlands. As for the anthropologists' paradise which is Laos, it was not until the mid-twentieth century that most of its hundred-odd – and some of them very odd – ethnic groups would even be identified.

Yet international opinion as represented by organisations like the League of Nations and the UN made no allowance for such delinquency. Existing states were meant to correspond to coherent nations, and those that did not, supposedly soon would thanks to the process called 'nation-building'. Hence the credit for the survival of a country like Cambodia – or the insinuation of one like Laos – belongs less to the strength of its nationalist sentiment and more to a benign, if alien, world order which decrees that all existing states are inviolable. Whether they are viable is another matter.

The symbolism of Angkor relies heavily on Indian ideas of a formalised cosmos in which the earth, the oceans and the universe are organised and harmonised round a central axis, a hub. This axis was represented two-dimensionally as the concentric rectangles (or wheel-like circles) of a mandala, and three-dimensionally as a conical mountain, the mythical Mount Meru. Meru's elevation idealised the symmetry and hierarchy of a universal order to which human society must aspire and legitimate authority conform. The spatial arrangements of each of Angkor's monuments, and above all their soaring towers, demonstrated how the authority of the Khmer kings was both cosmologically ordained and divinely favoured.

In lands as flat as the Mekong Delta, natural hills might also be co-opted into this grand scheme of environmental protocol. A *phnom* is a mountain. The *phnom* in Phnom Penh is barely as big as the stupa which crowns it, but Phnom Krom at Siem Reap is a respectable hill and has no rival on the circumference of the Great Lake. Crossing the lake all boats, coal-fired *canonnières* or turbo-charged cruisers, steer for Phnom Krom. It flanks the estuary of the stream which leads up to Angkor, and somewhere near its base (precisely where depends on the height of the lake) the cruisers disgorge their passengers.

Here, in 1866, the officers on *Canonnière 27* had bivouacked for the night. Next morning they had risen early to scale the *phnom*; and on its summit, confronted by their first Angkorian monuments, Lieutenant Louis Delaporte had taken out his sketchpad to begin the pictorial record of the journey.

Besides *le Commandant* Doudart de Lagrée, surveyor/hydrologist Garnier and political officer de Carné, the expedition's senior personnel included three other officers. Two were naval surgeons with specific responsibilities. Dr Clovis Thorel was in charge of botanical observations and discoveries, and Dr Lucien-Eugène Joubert of geological and mineralogical data. Official French expeditions tended towards the multi-disciplinary. No field of enquiry was to be neglected, and the resulting concourse of *savants* could resemble a symposium on the march. Napoleon Bonaparte had set the standard. His 1798 invasion of Egypt had been accom-

panied by such an impressive array of archaeologists, agriculturalists, historians, irrigationists, surveyors, draughtsmen and natural
scientists that its report attained encyclopaedic status, with no
fewer than twenty-three monumental volumes – the famous
Description de l'Égypte. The Mekong Exploration Commission's
remit was less ambitious. In somewhere as *inconnu* as Indo-China
it was concerned more with economic and political potential, with
investigating what might be made of the place rather than appropriating whatever might already exist.

In addition to their scientific researches, Drs Thorel and
Joubert would find their medical expertise much appreciated, and
likewise their easy-going temperaments. Both were in their thirties, so older than the others (bar Lagrée) and perhaps less excitable. Thorel had been in Annam for five years and had some
experience of working with its *montagnards,* or hill tribes. Joubert,
though a more recent arrival, had been in Africa and had lately
undertaken a geological survey in upper Senegal. He could claim
a basic expertise, otherwise in short supply, in what would now
be called 'survival skills'; as the tallest and physically most
robust, he would also attract local attention as the 'Jumbo' of the
party.

Finally there was Lieutenant Louis Marie Joseph Delaporte.
'As draughtsman and musician he principally represented the artistic aspects of the expedition.' So put, Garnier's introduction of
Louis Delaporte seems to imply reservations about the necessity
for a violinist-cum-illustrator, especially one whose few months
in the colony had been spent laid up with fever. Although he was
supposed to assist with the survey work, Delaporte's inexperience
and general levity at first went down badly with 'Mademoiselle
Buonaparte'. Elsewhere we learn that Delaporte's naval prospects
had been blighted by an untreatable disposition towards seasickness and, more generally, by 'a great dislike of the sea'. He was
evidently someone who had joined the navy to see the world, but

not in ships. After some grim months in the north Atlantic he had hailed the leafy *arroyos* of the Delta with relief and there began sketching. His work attracted favourable comment. Although Lagrée had someone else in mind as his draughtsman – and Garnier perhaps anyone else – Admiral de Lagrandière had chosen Delaporte.

Nothing if not resilient, Delaporte would rise above such things. In a coloured version of the group photo (on which he presumably painted in the colour), his chestnut trousers invite more comment than his outsize head. Other portraits show a head so disproportionate as to suggest deformity. He looks a bit mad. But what is more significant is the fact that of Delaporte there are indeed other portraits. Against the odds, he and he alone was destined for a long and distinguished career as an *explorateur*. It began at Angkor, to which only he would ever return, and it would continue amongst Angkorian archaeology, of which he would become the outstanding champion of his generation.

As for the Mekong journey, it is largely thanks to Delaporte that it still has any popular resonance at all. His written contribution to the official report and to Garnier's personal narrative would be much the most readable, vivid and sympathetic of all the writings on the expedition. He wrote with the observant eye and the kindly heart of a genuine enquirer. Still more memorably, he drew with the genius of a considerable artist. His pictures, worked up from sketches made throughout the course of the journey and then engraved as plates for the various published accounts, have since achieved a much wider currency. Not exceptional are the fifty-five Delaporte plates which, unacknowledged and extensively recaptioned, illustrate Ross Colquhoun's 1885 book *Amongst the Shans*. As 'period prints', Delaporte's drawings now hang in upmarket hotels from Hong Kong to Bangkok, feature in tourist brochures, grace many a calendar, and have been reliably reported adorning the nether regions of a Kunming massage parlour. Siem Reap's newly opened Foreign Correspondents Club has a few Delaporte prints hanging amongst its press photos; the town's grandly restored Grand Hôtel d'Angkor has whole walls of them.

In the days before photography became an easy option for the traveller, no expedition was better served by its artist. Like Garnier's writings, Delaporte's pictures would capture the exoticism of the whole enterprise and especially that interplay of innocence and menace, of moments of serenity between eruptions of madness, which became the received image of the Mekong. Long before Conrad and Coppola, before Pol Pot and the Khmer Rouge, Louis Delaporte created the idea of the river at the 'heart of darkness'; and to see the Mekong today is to look through eyes on which this idea, his image, is indelibly imprinted.

Phnom Krom was a case in point. Near the summit of the hill beside the Great Lake there stands today the most rundown wat in Cambodia. Mangy dogs scratch and snarl in the shade of its *sala* (the raised and roofed assembly room). An updraught from the lake eddies around the deserted courtyard, lifting the dust and wrapping an amputated tree in bandages of shredded polythene. The prayer hall is locked, information unobtainable. Most of Cambodia's monasteries were sacked by the Khmer Rouge, and this one looks as if it has yet to be reconsecrated. But a little further, a little higher, and seven centuries earlier, the hilltop cluster of Angkorian stupas provides instant reassurance to a Delaporte disciple.

Clearly his upriver pictures with their naked savages and their jungle fronds of wallpaper intricacy owed something to artistic licence. Rhinos rootling through an abandoned palace, and elephants crowding the rock-strewn riverbed, were what nineteenth-century romantics expected. Dr Thorel teetering through the forest canopy in search of orchids was what his employers expected. For the exploding cataracts and the sheer Niagaras, as for the forest

Delaporte's drawing of the three stupas of Phnom Krom.

cathedrals and the obelisks of rock, allowance has also to be made. The river couldn't actually be that fast or the trees that vast. Delaporte was exaggerating.

But not apparently with the ruins of Angkor. The three stupas of Phnom Krom are still much as he drew them. A tree has disappeared, and another has grown where there had been none. The stupas (Buddhist memorial monuments, also known as *chedis*, *chortens*, *dagobas*, *thats* or *topes*) look more precarious, and some of the masonry is missing. So is the stone Buddha figure that Delaporte had found lying in a bush. Otherwise all is exactly as depicted in 1866.

It is the same at Angkor Wat and Angkor Thom, at the Bayon and at the Bakheng (another hilltop site). To the casual observer the buildings look practically unchanged. Allowance has to be made only for the sometimes artful composition of the picture and for later site clearance of some of the more riotous vegetation. In all other respects the fidelity of Delaporte's drawings of Angkor cannot be faulted.

This seemed to raise an intriguing question. Perhaps artistic licence was not in his repertoire. As the draughtsman for a scientific expedition, accuracy should have been paramount. Perhaps the elephants and the orchids, the lowering forest and the raging river were not exaggerations at all. Being on guard against his 'heart of darkness' image did not mean discounting it altogether. Perhaps upriver the gorges were still as grand, the waters as wild, and the menace as tangible as his pictures suggested.

Regardless of their accuracy, what makes Delaporte's drawings so appropriate is their apparently prophetic quality. In 1866 Cambodia's nightmare – 'the horror . . . the horror' evoked by Conrad and echoed by Coppola – had yet to materialise. It burst upon the country a hundred years later in the Khmer Rouge's reign of terror. Although the hell lasted less than a decade, it left such a reek of pain that today even the place names – 'Svey Rieng', 'Kompong Chhnang', 'Stung Treng' – sound like agonised utterances hissed through the gritted teeth of the dying. Actual shrieks and screams were strictly forbidden in the interrogation cells. To discourage reactions so reactionary, there was always another tweak in the torturer's repertoire. Men protested their pain, if at all, with a click of the tongue and guttural retchings. Dying, too, was a hushed affair, rarely worth a bullet; and contrary to received opinion, much of it was not even intentional.

'Fried frog and chips'? Or 'virgin pork uterus in sour sweat sauce'?

The menu in today's Café Kampuchino in Siem Reap reads like a witchdoctor's shopping list. Cambodia's culinary ingenuity was legendary long before the Khmer Rouge; it extends to various sorts of rat, bat, toad and snake, some of the larger, scrunchier insects, and assorted innards and extremities from more familiar animals. No great courage is required to order these things. Like heavily advertised promotions the world over, they are never available. 'No have,' says the waiter, scrutinising the *carte* as if he has never seen it before. 'Bat no now,' 'Entrail finish,' 'Frog tomorrow.' The list of fare is in fact a wish-list. Only rice or noodles with vegetables and a few proteinous trace elements can be guaranteed. As for the more delectable sections of, say, a chicken – the bits between its feet, its beak and its parson's nose – they never appear. What happens to breast, leg, wing and wishbone is one of the inscrutable East's best-kept secrets.

In the 1970s, participants in the socialist experiment pioneered by the Khmer Rouge were reported as being reduced to scouring the rice stubble for edible bugs and devouring any vertebrate in its entirety. From the killing in the Killing Fields not even butter-flies were exempt. Lice were reportedly prized fare in the death camps. Cambodia was starving; and during its 'holocaust' far more died from malnutrition – and the reduced resistance to malaria that resulted – than from the better-documented incidence of torture, strangulation or a blow to the back of the head at the edge of a pre-dug grave.

The Khmer Rouge called their collective and depersonalised leadership the Angkar, which is usually translated as 'the Organisa-tion'. Organisation was precisely what it failed to provide. Allied to a lethal ideology, it was sheer inefficiency that turned the country into an abattoir. Although the numbers are disputed, the human death toll ran into seven figures; so, at the time, did the country's total population. But a tragedy on such a scale will ever be incompre-hensible if reduced to newsworthy trivia about people eating bugs.

For about nine years (1970–79) – five in partial control of the country and four in power – the Khmer Rouge set about the

killings in the fields and the torturings in the camps with a ferocious intensity. Society had to be cleansed of those elements
tainted with the 'bourgeois criminality and debauchery' of previous
regimes. Cambodia must start again from 'year zero', building a
socialist utopia based on the labour of the masses divided into
agrarian communes. No wages would be needed; the Angkar would
provide food according to need from the collective pool. State
centralism was designed to protect the masses from exploitation,
not to appropriate the fruits of their labour. And as dictatorial
regimes go, that of the Khmer Rouge was indeed a model of
incorruptible probity. Its leaders lived simply, extravagant consumption was unknown, and the revolution itself was subjected
to relentless and mind-numbing analysis. The scrutiny, like the
savagery, was always devastatingly sincere.

But in this excess of method lay utter madness. During a
speech delivered in 1977, Pol Pot could congratulate 'the great mass
movement' on having liquidated 'the exploiting classes' while
in his next breath calling for a population of 'fifteen to twenty
million'. Having decimated the nation he demanded that it double.
Years of civil war had already traumatised the country. US bombing had perforated the paddy fields and destroyed embankments,
like those along the Tonle Sap river, by which floodwater was
funnelled to crops. The ground fighting had dislocated vital distribution systems, like that of the Tonle Sap's yield of fishy protein.
Hundreds of thousands had flocked from the countryside to
Phnom Penh for sanctuary. When the bandana-ed cadres entered
the city in April 1975, they found a vast population that had become
entirely reliant on US-aided food imports. These now ceased forth-
with. Evacuation was the logical response.

The failure was not of logic but of logistics. In the absence of
transport, shelter, medical facilities or adequate food, the evacuees
were marched into the wilderness and there marooned to die of a
combination of overwork, undernourishment and malaria, or to be

systematically liquidated as scapegoats for the regime's rank incompetence. Countryman killed countryman, neighbour neighbour, and cousin cousin not in the cold conviction of a racial holocaust but in a fight for survival born of mutual destitution and paranoia.

It ended when in 1979 the Angkar was ousted from Phnom Penh by a Vietnamese invasion that imposed its own regime under Heng Samrin, a Hanoi puppet. Seeking to legitimise itself, the new regime lit on the idea of publicising the atrocities of its predecessor. Former interrogation centres were reopened as tawdry holocaust museums; mass graves were exhumed and the bones, after being sorted into skulls and limbs, exhibited by the nearest roadside. As journalists began to trickle back into the country, Cambodians were encouraged to recall the horrors they had somehow survived. The blame was laid squarely at the door of the leadership as each witness duly told of siblings, parents, friends who had died at the hands of 'Pol Pot and his clique'. But in reality the killers too were siblings, parents, friends. Thirty years later the survivors and their tormentors still live side by side in the same villages.

Downriver in Vietnam neither better times nor worse block the historical perspective. There the war with the US retains its immediacy, rumbling on not with bursts of resentment or hostility but in a wave of officially sanctioned nostalgia for a time of simple truths and inconceivable sacrifice. Army and air force museums compete for the nation's affection with war crimes monuments, 'War Remnants' museums, theme-parked bunkers, downed aircraft doubling as climbing frames, and whole bazaars devoted to recycled armaments and US military memorabilia. With a reverence that would not be misplaced in the Uffizi, schoolchildren join veterans to study the photos – torture cages, dead and disfigured American airmen, defoliated villages, raddled call-girls. Thirty years on, and the war is still paramount in the national psyche. As a defining moment in Vietnamese history the fall of Saigon in 1975 ranks with the fall of the Bastille in French history.

But upriver in Cambodia memories of the carpet bombing initiated by Nixon and Kissinger have been swept under mats stiff with fresher bloodstains. Some of the craters left by the B-52s are now fishponds; others, after serving as receptacles for the harvest of the Killing Fields, have been reopened as genocide sites. Pol Pot's pogrom obstinately blocks the historical perspective. 'Year zero' remains the psychological backstop of modern Cambodia's calendar, and today's government ministers, some of them tainted with Khmer Rouge associations, others with Vietnamese collaboration (and Prime Minister Hun Sen with both), naturally stall over bringing the killers to justice. They also agonise over the nation-building role to be accorded to the death camps and the mass graves. The exhumed skulls are still stacked by the roadside like bleached watermelons; but the visitors are mostly foreign tour groups and the souvenir potential is limited. Pol Pot is dead, but life does not go on.

The unbearable burden of recall placed on survivors of a conventional holocaust would be a relief to the survivors of a self-inflicted genocide. With no one to blame but themselves, Cambodians seem still to teeter on the edge of a pre-dug grave, restrained only by the presence of international agencies and the promise of foreign investment. The trees trill with the deafening protest of unseen insects. The earth smells of blood. Seeing the country as other than the site of a holocaust proves nigh impossible. A 'heart of darkness' horror occludes the charm; and the innocence of a natural paradise is irretrievably tainted by the horrors of its fall. As for the dozy colonial outpost that was Phnom Pehn whence in 1866 the Mekong Exploration Commission ventured into the unknown, it simply beggars conception.

Though Louis de Carné characterises the expedition's stay at Angkor as a week of 'painful trips and incessant study', to Francis Garnier it had been more like a holiday. He would later complain that the time might have been better spent chasing up supplies and intelligence and preparing the subordinate members of the expedition for the rigours ahead. Instead, they pursued their individual interests. Lagrée archaeologised, Joubert geologised, Delaporte drew, Garnier mapped and de Carné moped. Only Dr Thorel did nothing; supposedly the best acclimatised of them all, he was the first to go down with dysentery. The others nursed him as best they could while they took the measure of one another. A routine of sorts was established in which each day ended with a round-the-campfire discussion on some weighty, if not philosophical, matter.

On 1 July they struck camp and headed back to the Mekong across the Great Lake and up the Tonle Sap river. This time it was definitely 'up' the Tonle Sap river, because Garnier noted that the waters had so risen during their absence that Kompong Luang, where Lagrée had his house, had become an island. Just above Phnom Penh, and perhaps where today the river-cruisers tie up, the little gunboats were moored and the expedition's stores stowed aboard one of them.

To the heavy cases of instruments, preservatives and drawing materials, and to the decidedly generous quantities of flour and biscuit (five hundred kilos) and liquor (766 litres of wine, 302 litres of brandy) was added the wherewithal for defraying expenses. Cash came in gold bars, gold leaf, Mexican silver dollars and Siamese silver ticals to a total value of thirty thousand francs. The trade goods included bolts of velvet, silk and cotton, glass trinkets, an enormous quantity of brass wire and a selection of pistols and rifles. The brass wire was reportedly in great demand upriver, says de Carné; the guns were 'a purely speculative investment'. At a rough calculation, the total displacement must have been around five tons, a hefty load for a *cannonière* and way beyond the capacity of most local craft.

Properly speaking, the river at Phnom Penh is the Mekong itself. To the French, though, this particular three-kilometre-wide reach was always Le Quatre-bras. 'The four arms', or crossroads, corresponded to the junction of the four rivers: the Mekong itself which comes swinging down from the north, the Hau Tien which exits east, the Hau Giang (Bassac) which exits south, and the Tonle Sap which comes and goes somewhat north by north-west.

Poised on the bank of such a vital confluence, it is curious that Phnom Penh had only just been selected by King Norodom as his capital. Lagrée liked to think it was French protection that had emboldened the king's move from his less accessible abode at Udong, and certainly the new site could be comfortably commanded by a *canonnière*'s cannon. Whether this was meant to reassure His Highness or to restrain him was debatable. A new palace was being built on the waterfront (where it still is), and the expedition's send-off celebrations seem to have doubled as part of the dedication ceremonies. A sweltering evening of speeches, toasts, light refreshments and leaden jokes was cheered, though scarcely enlivened, by the appearance of gold-girt beauties performing the statuesque posturing which is Cambodian classical dance. The Frenchmen lusted dutifully, then fidgeted involuntarily as they melted into their dress uniforms.

Departure came as a relief. As they cast off, the French flag was run up the tiny mast of Lagrée's *canonnière*. The other *canonnière* fired its single gun four times by way of salute, and on the command of a whistle – these things were strictly regulated – the crews cheered in unison *'Vive l'Empereur,'* then, after another blast of the whistle, *'Vive le Commandant de Lagrée.'* It was midday on 7 July 1866. There was no answering salute from the shore. The cheers died on the waters with the finality of what was indeed the last farewell. 'A few moments later,' says Garnier, 'we sailed alone on the vast river.'

THREE

To the Falls

'The highest point previously fixed by the French on the Great Cambodia River [i.e. the Mekong] was Cratieh, about 280 miles from the mouth. Beyond this a long succession of rapids was encountered, occurring in a scarcely inhabited region of splendid forest which separates Laos from Cambodia.'

SIR RODERICK MURCHISON,
President of the Royal Geographical Society, May 1869

ABOVE PHNOM PENH the river is at last the Mekong proper rather than one of its deltaic necks. Low-lying islands of unremarkable verdure clutter the stream and conceal its full extent; in Garnier's day they were planted with cotton from which King Norodom derived a sizeable tax yield. Beyond them, knee-deep in bamboo fronds and badly in need of a hairbrush, spindly sugar palms reel across the floodplain like pin-men with hangovers. Untroubled and still unconfined, the Mekong wallows, buffalo-brown in a swamp of green, as if reluctant to reveal its majestic proportions in such disrespectful company.

More interesting is the traffic. Smaller, slimmer launches than the Angkor cruisers today swoop upriver to Kratie, bus-stopping at riverside pontoons to offload passengers and take on hardboiled eggs. Sampans and the occasional rustbucket recall the Delta; but both are here upstaged and outpaced by the first pirogues. In October, as the annual water festival in Phnom Penh draws near,

Launching a racing pirogue.

pirogues predominate, darting out onto the river like agitated crocodiles. From bays and side creeks, from round the next bend and behind the last island, they nose into midstream, an Oxbridge armada not of rowing eights but of paddling eighties. The climax of the water festival is the boat races, and to that end competitors practise hard and then make their way downriver.

Most waterside villages, and quite a few nowhere near the river itself, participate. Each has its long racing pirogue and each racing pirogue is propelled by anything from twenty to a hundred paddlers ranged along its length in file. Many boats sport flags with their crews attired in identical bandanas, like cadres of some Khmer Rouge water fraternity. Others, clearly scratch outfits, have yet to master a stroke or merit team status. Adding much to the hilarity as well as the hazards, supporters offer abuse and encouragement from an accompanying flotilla of listing workboats and redundant ferries. Nowhere else, and at no other time, is the river so animated. The pirogues, sensationally tapered from hollowed-out tree trunks, skim between the sky above and the sky in the water, prows raised like fabulous sea-serpents.

Steaming upriver in July, with the rains growing heavier by the day, the Mekong Exploration Commission missed this spectacle. But come October they would find themselves at Bassac (now Champassak) in lower Laos and would there witness the same festival with equivalent boat races. Again Delaporte would be vindicated. He duly drew the scene: and but for the spectators, who seem somewhat underdressed and anthropologically over representative, he again took few liberties. Two of his most reproduced prints depict, respectively, the river races in the morning and the fireworks at night. In each there is much, perhaps too much, livestock and vegetation. Would not the pigs have taken their dustbath in the shade, or the elephants have been stampeded by the fireworks? But to carp at this is to nitpick, just like the mother cradling her child in the foreground. Delaporte's pirogues are superb; profiled against the great white river they are aligned like words in an unknown script, random runes adrift on an empty page.

Kompong Cham, the first port above Phnom Penh, is today notable as the hometown of Prime Minister Hun Sen and as the site of a brand-new bridge. The two things are not unconnected. Kompong Cham roots for Hun Sen and Hun Sen rewards Kompong Cham. The country's strongman is as locationally linked with its most impressive piece of civil engineering as are the two sides of the river by the bridge. This is, in fact, the only bridge across the Mekong in Cambodia, and as is the way with highstriding spans of gleaming ferro-concrete, it makes the river look misleadingly manageable. Having passed under it with eyes shut, a Mekong-lover may be excused for passing over it in silence.

In the 1860s there were no bridges over the Mekong anywhere, and this remained the case for more than another century. In

Chinese Yunnan, where the river is called the Lancang, a rickety Meccano construction reportedly replaced the ferry in the mid-twentieth century; but below that, for over three thousand kilometres, the river was unspanned until 1994. It was as if, in the United States, there were no way to cross the Mississippi south of Minneapolis. The engineering was not the problem. Few rivers so obligingly constrict themselves. Bridges were not built because the traffic which might use them did not exist.

Amongst the world's major rivers the Mekong, though neither the longest nor the largest, still enjoys the distinction of being the least utilised. No great ports disfigure its shores. Phnom Penh and Vientiane, though national capitals, scarcely qualify as cities; the towns are few and mostly disappointing; and the villages keep their distance, preferring the seclusion of a sidestream or the security of adjacent hill and forest.

In English, rivers are usually masculine and often geriatric – 'Ol' Man River' or 'Old Father Thames'. *Fleuve* in French is also masculine. But it was *rivière*, a feminine noun denoting a youthful river indirectly connected to the sea, which slowly gained currency among the personnel of the Mekong Exploration Commission. Their river was unquestionably female. Clad in virgin forest, she suffered no bridges across her bosom, no promenades along her brow nor trade routes down her limbs. Beguiling, wanton and capricious, in a pre-feminist era she conformed to every bearded bachelor's fantasy of a wild maiden from the hills.

For this apparent neglect of commercial grooming there are sound practical reasons, the first of which was about to confront the Mekong Exploration Commission. Above Kompong Cham the islands of greenery compose themselves and rejoin the shoreline. In the dry season, their place midstream is taken by shoals of the finest sand on which the skeletons of mighty trees lie stranded. Propped on tangled limbs, the trees recline on the sandbars with feet in the air like giants on holiday. But in July, with the river rising, the giants launch themselves into the flood, a hazard to diminutive gunboats. More worryingly for the expedition, glistening gobs of muddy foam accompanied the trees and, drifting erratically with no apparent regard for the current, told of sub-surface disturbance and turbulent times ahead.

Low hills loomed simultaneously through the mist to the north. Excluding solitary outcrops like Phnom Krom, the hills were the first hint of higher ground. The landscape had at last acquired a horizon and the Delta a conclusion. To the Commission the prospect imparted a new sense of direction and purpose. This was quickened by the changing shoreline. Almost imperceptibly the river had settled between natural margins. Just low sandy ledges, they were the sort of cliffs on which thrift might thrive and sand-martins nest. Though unsensational, to new arrivals from the Delta they were another welcome novelty. After five hundred kilometres of welling, slopping, brimming confusion, the river had recognisable banks.

They soon grew higher. On the second day the expedition reached Kratie and had to climb from the landing stage up a long flight of muddy steps to gain the palm and bougainvillea parkland on which the village was scattered. Here they halted for a week. Though barely thirty-six hours into the voyage, it was time to trans-ship.

The new boats were dugout canoes, and although they had evidently been pre-ordered, they needed to be substantially customised for the conditions ahead. Meanwhile the five tons of baggage had to be carefully sorted and, not for the last time, ferociously reduced. 'It foreshadowed the utter destitution which awaited us further on,' noted the rueful de Carné.

This transfer, so soon after leaving Phnom Penh, raises questions about just how much Lagrée and Garnier already knew of the river ahead. Was it really about to take them by surprise? Or were they rather better informed than they pretended? If nothing was known of its navigational properties, why had they anticipated the need for canoes? Yet if canoes were inevitable, why had they burdened themselves with such an impossible quantity of luggage? And why, as the downpours of June were succeeded by the deluges of July, were they tackling the river at the height of the rains, the least comfortable season for travel and the surest for contracting malaria?

While they unpacked and repacked, the *canonnière* took its departure. Last letters home were hastily written and entrusted to the crew. As the gunboat pulled away, the six explorers felt as if they themselves were being cast adrift. Their last link with all that was French and familiar steamed out of sight round a bend in the river, leaving them to a silence broken only by the whine of mosquitoes. Kratie had nothing to offer. They lodged in a hut through whose roof dripped the rain. It was 'a completely isolated village . . . with no commercial trade of any kind', according to Garnier. The only way home was now the way ahead. 'Henceforth France was before us, not behind us,' wrote de Carné. 'Our sights were set on China.'

But Lagrée, with the wisdom of years and the economy of the sore-throated, sounded a note of caution. Between Cambodia and China lay more than sixteen hundred kilometres of river attended, no doubt, by a like number of perils and disappointments. Excitement was premature, he croaked, if not downright dangerous; for was not 'enthusiasm near neighbour to despair'?

Above Kratie leggy trees of impressive height and symmetry take up position along the river's bank like spectators awaiting a naval review. The mud-thick flood, over a kilometre wide, nuzzles their roots and tugs at their dangling lianas but concedes nothing to them in scale. During the few months of the year in which navigation onwards to Stung Treng is possible, the little white passenger launch looks like a bathtime accessory as it skims through the frothy suds. In a setting so grand something more palatial seems called for – a Mississippi paddle-steamer, perhaps, with the orchestra playing, the tables set, and Scarlett O'Hara on the topmost deck against a blood-red sky.

This is not altogether fanciful. To patriotic French explorers the Mekong also brought to mind the Mississippi. Primed on colonial history, Garnier rarely missed a relevant parallel, while Louis de Carné's diplomatic training lent an international dimension to his political horizons. In the early eighteenth century Louisiana had been French. It had been named in honour of Louis XIV, and its port of New Orleans had developed to provide continental access by way of the Mississippi. Subsequent French losses in the New World had been as much a matter for patriotic regret as those in India. To redress them, the Second Empire had just wished Maximilian on the Mexicans. And now, with the delicious complementarity which so appealed to Gallic logic, Saigon and the Mekong were supposed to afford that exclusively French access to the Asian interior which New Orleans and the Mississippi had promised to the American interior.

That was the theory anyway, and although it was about to be seriously compromised, the dream of one day being able to paddle-steam into the heart of the continent would not readily be relinquished. In the wake of the Mekong Exploration Commission a succession of pounding little vessels would, over the next fifty years, try and generally fail to force a passage upriver, prompting all manner of bizarre technological solutions, most of which would also fail.

The slim launch which today plies, conditions permitting, from Kratie to Stung Treng is the unworthy inheritor of this dream. A twenty-first-century apology for nineteenth-century presumption, it addresses the increasingly angry flood with circumspection, swooping across its troubled surface in search of sheltered water and unimpeded channels like an ice-queen on a busy rink. Hastily the luggage is lashed beneath plastic tarpaulins; passengers are ordered inside and the cabin door sealed. The turns become sharper, the engine noisier. Condensation streams down the windows as if the exertion were too much. But wiping away the trickles makes no difference. The waves thrashing against the hull on the outside preclude visibility. It is like being marooned in a storm-tossed diving capsule.

Although not the ideal way of experiencing the Mekong's first rapids, the voyage compares favourably with a week of wet boating at the height of the monsoon. For the same run the expedition had secured a fleet of the dugout canoes which they called *radeaux*. The word translates as 'barges', but they were really modified pirogues. Closely related to those now reserved for racing, they were destined to become painfully familiar. Though their numbers would be reduced from the initial eight, this mode of transport would remain the same until the expedition abandoned the river altogether. Boats and boatmen would be frequently changed, a cause for endless delay and no little grumbling, but the style of boat and the method of propulsion would be much the same throughout.

Delaporte's sketches faithfully portray the design. To the basic hollowed-out tree trunk, some twenty to thirty metres long, was added a roof made of hooped bamboos thatched with palm fronds which extended from stem to stern and made the boat look like a large waterborne caterpillar. This canopy was supposed to afford shade and shelter for the squatting passengers but was never quite high enough for comfort and nowhere near waterproof enough to keep out the monsoon.

More bamboo poles of much larger diameter were lashed to the gunwales in bundles to form a semi-submerged platform which ran the length of both sides and met at either end in a poop.

Bamboo trunks being hollow, these side projections acted as flotation chambers, adding some much-needed buoyancy and stability to the overloaded canoes and acting, in effect, like the outriggers of a trimaran. The poop aft was where the helmsman rigged his steering sweep, that where the bamboos met at the bow was where the lookout sat. More importantly, the whole platform arrangement served as a walkway for the six to eight circulating boatmen. Down one side they punted, following their poles from stem to stern, and up the other side they panted, poles aloft, to start all over again.

More correctly this was not in fact punting but 'piking'. Since the current in open water was far too strong for heavily laden craft to be paddled against, propulsion on the middle Mekong depended entirely on purchase. The poles were strictly pikes, because they were tipped with a piece of ironmongery which combined a boathook with a sharp spike. Progression entailed warping along the most convenient bank, either by spiking rocky interstices and tree trunks or by hooking onto roots and branches, then pushing or hauling on the pikes as the boat slid forward beneath the retreating feet of the pikers. Handling the pikes required the skills of heavy-duty crochet and involved reading the bank as much as the water. Locomotion, in other words, owed more to jungle craft than to nautical skills. They were literally climbing the stream. From one point of purchase to the next the men pulled and shoved the boats upward as if the current were gravity and the river a hill.

This rotational system [says Garnier of the piking] *can impart to the pirogue the speed of a walking man provided that the pikers are capable and the bank to be followed is straight and unimpeded. The skipper must devote his full attention to keeping the boat's helm into the current, or rather, slightly inclined towards the bank. Should he let the stream*

catch the other side, the boat will come across and he must
make a full circuit before he can hope to bring it back into the
bank again.

De Carné, less nautically inclined, took a more human view of
this unconventional form of propulsion. For eight hours a day, he
writes, the 'unhappy Cambodgians [*sic*] revolved around us with
the docility of those blinkered horses used for turning wheels'.
Any slackening brought threats of a beating from the skipper. Yet
the boatmen, who had been snatched from their fields and their
families to work unpaid under their *corvée* obligations to the king,
showed no signs of resentment. On the contrary, they remained
'good-natured, resigned and often almost cheerful' – which was
more than could be said for de Carné himself.

I was leaving civilisation behind and entering on a savage
country; I had passed at one step from a steamship to a canoe.
The roof being too low to let me sit up, I had to stay half
lying down; and the rainwater accumulating in the bottom of
the boat continually invaded my person.

The skipper fussed over him whenever he could, 'for I was a great
lord in his eyes'. But the roof continued to leak and the only baler
was a scoop formed from a banana leaf sewn together with rattan.
Technology, like civilisation, was becoming a thing of the past.
All that remained of the nineteenth century was packed away in
their luggage or their heads. Otherwise they were adrift in a deep
green version of the dark ages.

To most of them the scenery was the great consolation. There
were no villages and no sign of man, but the trees were truly
magnificent and the river was again studded with islands between
which the current dashed through dozens of channels and rocky
defiles. These formed a series of treacherous cascades which Garnier dutifully recorded as the Sombor, Somboc and Preatapang

rapids. Each made 'a great thundering sound', says de Carné, but progress proved possible thanks to the trees and shrubs whose roots clawed to every visible surface and whose branches waved excitedly in midstream. The latter reminded de Carné of drowning sailors. As the only landlubber he greeted *terra firma* at each day's end with undisguised relief.

> *Come evening we cut down trees, cleared the soaking under-growth, and finally got fires going. Everyone exerted himself and dinner began. It was usually a frugal affair – but some-times sumptuous if the hunters had been successful – and always very cheerful. For dining room we had the forest; herds of wild boar had often to make way for us. Our bedroom was the damp and narrow jail of our canoes. A cicada followed us relentlessly from campsite to campsite and at the same hour emitted its single, long-drawn note, as if to set the pitch for all the local musicians of these sombre palaces of verdure.*

Garnier was less enraptured. The rain and the mosquitoes made sleep impossible and, more worryingly, his well-laid plans for the river were being dashed to bits by every cascade. At Kratie he had been bitterly disappointed when the captain of the *canonnière* had refused to go any further. Steam-powered or not, the little gunboat was reckoned too old to take on the rapids and too precious to be risked. That meant a postponement of the titanic contest between technology and nature which he anticipated; but it did not consti-tute a defeat. Around the Sombor rapids he was cheered to find 'an easy passage' by which steamboats might indeed, when the river was in spate, progress – provided their engines were up to it. 'The navigability of the river, which at the beginning of the journey was the most important point to research, had been ascer-tained up to this point without fear,' he crowed.

But the Somboc rapids proved much more challenging. Here

The Preatapang rapids.

the current was estimated at eight kilometres an hour, the sounding lead gave a depth of only three metres in the main channels, and all of these were choked by submerged rocks and trees which would be fatal to a steamship. By following the east bank closely and by dint of a week of Herculean labours, they somehow surmounted these hazards and entered the broader, calmer waters of the river's confluence with its Se Kong tributary just below Stung Treng. Evidently the main current followed the opposite bank through the even more dangerous Preatapang rapids. Garnier reasoned that the river there must be deeper and, however impetuous, therefore more practical for steam-powered vessels with greater draught than a pirogue. To investigate he crossed to the west bank to return alone downstream and take another look.

The river was here five kilometres across and, where it was not interrupted by islands, 'as wide as if not wider than the great rivers of America'. On the other hand it was considerably faster.

They were racing along even when the paddlers (downstream it was easier to paddle) paused to consider the approaching cloud of spray. This heralded the dreaded rapids of Preatapang. Garnier ordered the paddlers to shoot through them. They refused. A bribe was offered and willingly accepted but still they veered away from the main flood. Garnier expostulated, swore, then pulled a pistol on them. It was 25 July, his twenty-seventh birthday; perhaps he felt lucky. His courage would never be questioned but his reputation as a far-seeing navigator was in serious jeopardy.

As is the way with solitary excursions, the hair's-breadth escapes now came thick and fast. At gunpoint they entered the raging flood. It was here running at an *irrésistible* ten kilometres an hour and his paddlers were gibbering with fear, though whether from the gun-toting antics of their diminutive master or from the rapids themselves is unclear. They dodged floating tree trunks the size of whales, rode the white waters in a cloud of spray – 'the noise was deafening, the spectacle hypnotic, [but] it was too late to turn back' – and then slalomed through a flooded forest with the river running at what Garnier now estimated to be an *incroyable* seventeen kilometres an hour.

It was altogether an unmissable experience. In a single day he had shot downriver a distance which it had taken the expedition six days to ascend. But so what? He would rather have been flushed with triumph. Excitement merely signified failure. For Preatapang, however spectacular, spelled death to navigation. As he now despairingly conceded, 'the future of rapid commercial relations (of which I had happily dreamed the previous evening) by way of this vast river, the natural route from China to Saigon, seemed to me seriously compromised from this moment on'.

It was not quite the end of the dream. Perhaps a channel could be cleared round the rapids; and perhaps, although Sombor looked most practicable when the river was high, Preatapang would be navigable when it was low. There was always hope. Nemesis was being deferred, fended off with the push of a pike like another arboreal torpedo. But not for long. And not, as it would appear, unexpectedly.

Although accounts of the expedition are reticent on the subject, no forensic skills are needed to deduce that the Mekong above Phnom Penh was neither as mysterious nor as navigationally promising as Garnier, especially, had made out. After all, the French, including Lagrée, had been in Cambodia for three years. They can hardly have failed to notice that precious little trade came downriver, and that none of what did (principally forest produce) originated from further up than Stung Treng. Nor can they have been ignorant as to the cause. Several French prospectors and traders had already been to Stung Treng. Some had probably been beyond. And in the previous year Lagrée himself had been as far as the Sombor rapids.

It had been soon after this excursion that, on meeting Admiral de Lagrandière in Saigon, the question of the Mekong Exploration Commission had come up 'out of the blue' and *le Commandant* had accepted the leadership with that conspiratorial laugh. Knowing perfectly well what to expect – namely that the river was almost certainly unnavigable for anything but pirogues, and that even they could force the rapids only when it was in flood – his 'Why not?' began to make sense. The whole thing was indeed a joke. Garnier might be obsessed with the Mekong's hydrography – that was his job – but the more cynical Lagrée had long since acknowledged that the river itself was a *canard*. As elsewhere in the world, geographical enquiry was being used to lend scientific respectability to what was essentially a political reconnaissance.

Hence, too, the otherwise inexplicable decision to launch the expedition at the height of the monsoon. Everything had been timed to place the party in the vicinity of the well-attested rapids when the river was at its highest and the rapids, hopefully, deep enough to be negotiable. The two weeks wasted at Angkor and on the Tonle Sap had been by way of marking time while the river rose. Not without interest, Garnier had been recording its further rise ever since. And the three weeks that they now spent at Stung Treng were because the river was still rising, a vital consideration when, by all report, their only hope of progressing further lay in cresting the next obstacle on a veritable *tsunami*.

What they knew of the river above Stung Treng in Laos may have been less credible than what they knew of it in Cambodia. But it was not inconsiderable. In the 1670s Geritt von Wuystorff, an agent of the Netherlands East Indies Company, had travelled upstream from Cambodia to the Lao capital of Vientiane. He had later written a brief account of his odyssey, and this was known to the members of the expedition. It told of astounding cities in the midst of endless forest, of barbaric tribes and impenetrable mountains, and of colossal waterfalls and all-devouring whirlpools. That was the sort of thing one expected of seventeenth-century travelogues. But it was not necessarily a fabrication; and rereading it in the light of their own discoveries, de Carné would ask, not unreasonably, 'how anyone who had read the Dutchman's report could ever have held out any hope of the river proving navigable'. The 'anyone' he had in mind was, needless to say, Francis Garnier.

More significantly, among those unsung individuals who comprised the Mekong Exploration Commission's subordinate staff and escort, there was at least one man with direct experience of the middle and upper Mekong. The Commission's supernumeraries numbered sixteen and had mostly been inducted in twos, like the animals into the ark. There were two French sailors, two French soldiers, two Filipino soldiers (survivors of the Spanish contingent which took part in the original conquest of Saigon) and two interpreters (originally three, but the Cambodian one had been quickly dismissed, Lagrée himself having a good knowledge of the Cambodian tongue). There were also perhaps eight 'Annamites', Vietnamese auxiliaries, who figure so little that most of their names are not certainly known.

Wherever born and of whatever race, some of these men enjoyed French citizenship. Gallicisation by assimilation was one of the hallmarks of French colonial policy. They were not treated with the contempt habitually reserved by Anglo-Saxon explorers for their non-commissioned subordinates and 'native followers'. In the true spirit of liberty, equality and fraternity they participated in the intelligence-gathering as well as the dogsbodying.

This would be especially true of the man recruited as the expedition's Lao interpreter. To the French he was known as 'Alévy', that being an alternative name for the place of his birth, a town otherwise known as Chieng Hung, Xieng Hong or now Jinghong. 'Alévy' therefore came from the upper Mekong, from a minor principality which was then regarded by the British as one of the Shan states and by the French as one of the Lao states but which is now part of Chinese Yunnan.

Indeed Alévy was himself either a Shan or a Lao, or by some accounts a Thai or a Dai. The imprecision is not important since the Shan, Lao, Thai and Dai languages are practically the same, and all who speak them are generally considered of the same ethnic stock. In a region as little known as inland south-east Asia, different names for the same people, like different names for the same place, stemmed from the different perspectives of those who first enquired about such things. Thus the British in Burma might call someone a Shan who to the French in Saigon was a Lao, to the Chinese in Yunnan a Dai, and to the Siamese in Bangkok a Thai.

As well as sharing a language, these people were, and are, all staunch Buddhists whose menfolk may spend some years as monks. The Lao interpreter Alévy had done just that, but instead of staying put in Jinghong he had travelled from monastery to monastery through most of Laos over a period of several years. He therefore had first-hand knowledge of a long sector of the river which was of consuming interest to the Mekong Exploration Commission. Whether he had actually followed the river on into Cambodia is not sure. But he certainly knew southern Laos, a long riverine strip between Thailand and Vietnam which, during the 'Secret War' of the 1970s, the CIA would inevitably call 'the Laotian panhandle'. He must, then, at least have heard tell of the pan-handle's, and south-east Asia's, two outstanding natural wonders, the Four Thousand Islands and the mighty Falls of Khon.

Sadly, little is recorded of what transpired during those intense debates round the campfire which seem to have been such a feature of the expedition. Perhaps Alévy's itinerary was unknown to the French at this stage; perhaps his views were too unwelcome to be credited; perhaps he kept his mouth shut. For to Lagrée and his companions, as they waited in Stung Treng for Garnier to return from his Preatapang excursion, the Falls of Khon and the Four Thousand Islands seem to have been just rumours unsubstantiated with any useful detail.

Unearthing reliable information about these wonders of nature is even today strangely difficult. One guidebook dismisses southern Laos as notable only for being the last hangout of two endangered species, namely the Irrawaddy freshwater dolphin and the twentieth-century hippy. The dolphins live below the Falls; they numbered eighteen at the last count. The hippies live above the Falls and may be even fewer, although the migratory habits of both make the figures suspect.

Another guidebook devotes most of its two thousand words on the region to a horrendous account of the leisure complex –

five-star hotels, golf courses, landing strip, helipad and highway – which Thai developers have dreamed up for the Four Thousand Islands. As with Cambodia's new bridge at Kompong Cham, the contract involves a Prime Minister (and subsequently President), in this case of the Lao People's Democratic Republic (LPDR), whose home and power-base are in the region. Lest anyone doubt the connection, he rejoices in the name of Khamtai Siphandon, *si* being four, *phan* a thousand, and *don* islands. Mercifully Mr Four-Thousand-Islands and his Thai accomplices have lately been stopped dead in their bulldozing tracks by Asian recession and the tourism crises of the early 2000s.

Guidebooks are generally better on the practicalities of travel, although on the crucial matter of the Cambodian–Lao border they again disappoint. In the nineteenth century Stung Treng was in Laos. The Mekong Exploration Commission had thus left King Norodom's kingdom and French protection while piking up from Kratie. They noticed the difference when in Stung Treng the village chief stalked away from their introductions with lordly indifference. A giant 'with an interminable neck and a face made stupid by opium' according to de Carné, he offered only a pig by way of a present and showed no interest in assisting their progress with new boats or boatmen. The last Frenchman to visit Stung Treng had evidently abused the local hospitality. It took all of Lagrée's considerable tact, plus a generous outlay in trinkets, ticals and brass wire, to win him round. 'Thus', says de Carné, 'did we set foot in this terrible Laos.'

Nowadays Stung Treng is in Cambodia, having been detached from Laos by the French during the nibbling advance into Indo-China which the Mekong expedition would prompt. The town is in fact the last outpost in Cambodia, a distinction to which its status as roadhead, riverhead and dead end ought to lend a raffish appeal. Yet its present-day population is not much greater than the eight hundred souls recorded by Garnier and, though of

vaguely colonial aspect, it exudes only mind-numbing inconsequence. So ill-served is it by either river or road that the traveller's
satisfaction in having got there is instantly curtailed by worries
about how to get away.

Activity, such as it is, revolves around the muddy landing stage
at the water's edge and the petrol station above it – a weed-ridden
dump of forty-five-gallon drums in the centre of the town square
where the fountain might once have been. A busy weekday in
Stung Treng may include a speedboat departing for Laos in the
early hours, a quick turnaround for the Kratie launch in mid-
afternoon, and a sunset visitation by a vintage truck so strung
about with cranes, winches and hawsers that it, too, appears to be
in the habit of progressing more by purchase than drive.

The frontier has moved eighty kilometres further north. It
now crosses the river, which is here several kilometres wide and
jumbled with islands, just below the Falls of Khon; and it does so
obliquely, so that the west bank is still in Cambodia while the
east bank has become Laos. Knowing the whereabouts of the
border post is somewhat critical, not because the formalities count
for much but because this whole no-man's land is heavily unpoliced
by itchy-fingered 'guards' with AK-47s. Deployed to protect
unauthorised logging operations, they notoriously fail to distinguish between snooping officials and lost travellers.

For the record, then, the border crossing is at a spot called
Voen Kham where a tranquil arm of water glides through the
forest, so separating the east bank of the river, which is now Laos,
from the nearest of its many islands, which are still Cambodia.
Fish-eagles wheel overhead mewing their contempt for international convention. The Cambodian frontier post is in a clearing
on the island; with its ladders and walkways it might appeal to
Tarzan as a treetops domicile. The Lao post, located on the mainland opposite, occupies a rickety shack beside the flagpole at the
top of Voen Kham's single street. Like most Lao properties, the

Doudart de Lagrée (*above*) commanded the
Mekong Exploration Commission with weary
aplomb. The dynamism and the drama were
provided by his frenetic deputy and eventual
successor, Francis Garnier (*right*).

Can-tho (*above*), today the largest town in the delta, fronts the Hau Giang or Bassac river. One of the Mekong's nine mouths, it forks from the Hau Tien branch at Phnom Penh, where pirogues (*below*) first make their appearance.

In Vietnam shoppers in sampans visit barge-based stalls in the delta's floating markets (*above*); in Cambodia tree roots are streamlined by the current (*below*). What de Carné called 'the extreme individuality of the river' dictates the patterns of life.

The Mekong Exploration Commission rode on elephants into Angkor's Bayon over the 'Bridge of Giants' (*above*). The study and conservation of Angkor afforded a pretext for French intervention. Louis Delaporte's careful depiction of a ceremony in the Nong Khai wat (*below*) hints at a more personal interest in Buddhist ritual.

The Falls of Khon on the Cambodian–Lao border were found to be sixteen kilometres wide, much divided by rock and jungle, and totally unnavigable. On the left bank the Papheng Falls are the most accessible section (*above*); on the right bank Delaporte encountered tigers near the Salaphe Falls (*below*).

To circumvent the Khon Falls,
seven kilometres of railway
track were laid between the
bottom of the falls and the top.
The last train ran in 1940.
Only the loading gantry on
Deth Island (*above*), a bridge,
and a sad little locomotive
(*right*) survive.

Boatman and petrol-pump attendant in the Siphandon ('Four Thousand Islands') region of southern Laos. Outboards have now largely superseded paddle and pike. Cultivation is still extended into the riverbed as the water level falls during the dry season.

'Heaven meets Hades round every bend in the river.' Long before the Mekong became tainted with war and insurgency, its unpredictability was unnerving. Members of the expedition plunged from lyricism to lugubrium as clear water broke into yet more rapids.

shack is on stilts. If not eating within it, the immigration staff may be found dozing in the darkness beneath it. Allow a few minutes for them to tumble from their hammocks and retrieve their uniforms.

The expedition, already in Laos and untroubled by such formalities, tackled this section of the river with different misgivings. Stung Treng had shown them no favours. It had rained every day and most nights. They built an oven to make bread but it was flooded before they could light it. The flour was anyway ruined by the damp. Worse still, 'legions of invisible insects' had eaten through the barrels containing their liquor stocks. A thousand litres of fine wine and *eau de vie* trickled away in a single night. De Carné, who had rightly anticipated a lightening of their load, could scarcely credit that it had happened so soon and so unmemorably. 'From this last disaster we were barely able to decant a few bottles of wine for the sick and the little flour which was essential for making the quinine pills which we were all already taking daily.'

Quinine was the recognised treatment for malaria, or what they called 'typhus fever'. Although ignorant of the role played by mosquitoes in spreading the disease, they knew that it was associated with foetid air and swampy surroundings and that the middle Mekong in the monsoon provided near-perfect conditions. In fact, by the time they left Stung Treng to resume the voyage, nearly all of them were suffering the first pangs. They were also nursing their first casualty. Francis Garnier's narrative abruptly stops after his return from the excitement of the Preatapang rapids, because it was he who was afflicted. 'A rather serious indisposition . . . suddenly turned into an alarming illness and from this moment I lost all memory of what happened . . .' No longer able to write, speak or stand, he drifted into a deep and delirious coma, was carried aboard the boats, and in the opinion of Thorel and Joubert, the two doctors, might soon be expected to fill the expedition's first grave.

Thorel himself had recovered. Stricken by dysentery at Angkor, he had been too ill at Kratie to move, yet had staged a remarkable convalescence on the sodden floor of his pirogue as it was piked through the rapids. Now as they pushed through flooded forest towards the Falls, there was much to take a naturalist's mind off the state of his bowels. The *yao*, a colossal *dipterocarpus* whose silvery trunk soars for thirty metres before it ventures forth its first branches, was the tree from which pirogues were hollowed – initially by controlled burning, then by whittling. Like the umbrageous tamarind whose shelter offered the only respite from the rain, the *yao* has an extensive root system and stands its ground well while the floodwaters tug at its ankles.

Other trees are forced to compromise. Some teeter proud of the flood atop fin-shaped pedestals formed by their exposed roots being swept by the force of the current into fantastically fluted curtains. Yet others, mostly bamboos and palms, have been uprooted and ride along on the current bolt upright, like atolls on the move. With their rootbowls acting as keel and ballast they buck and twirl in hope of a friendly eddy to waft them to a sheltered beach.

And still, on the wallowing pirogues, the teetering trees and the sodden explorers, the rain fell. One night, while parked up in a sidestream, they were overwhelmed by a flash flood. They heard it coming but were too tired to turn out and investigate. A wall of water, four metres high, swept down the creek and continued over the boats, engulfing their inmates and all the stores and equipment. 'The disorder was unspeakable,' says Delaporte who, with Garnier still unconscious, had assumed the role of the expedition's official chronicler; 'anguished cries were heard, and the pirogues crashed against each other or were hit by tree trunks uprooted by the water. Luckily the danger soon passed; and luckily all the barges had been anchored to some roots or rocks.' It was too dark and wet to do much about the damage. They wrung out their clothes, emptied their boots, baled out the boats and crawled back inside for a moist doze until daylight,

On 17 August, three days after the expedition had left Stung Treng, the sun reappeared. They climbed a small hill in the evening to watch it set, and as it did so the boatmen drew their attention to a distant rumble that was just audible above the wind soughing in the forest. It was not another flash flood. 'It was the sound of the great falls of Khon,' says Delaporte, 'one of the grandest marvels which a traveller can see and the goal of our voyage for months.'

Next day they were back on the river early. Still hugging the east bank they piked through a maze of channels, often having to hack through fallen trees to avoid venturing into more turbulent waters. *In extremis* these torrents had to be crossed by sending over men in canoes with rattan ropes and then hauling the big pirogues through the flood. The boatmen were performing heroically, rising to every challenge. For them the danger was nearly over. Their stint would end when they reached the Falls, the noise of which was now making itself heard with greater power, noted Delaporte.

The thundering seemed to spread along a great front. Delaporte estimated it at more than ten kilometres wide. It is in fact about sixteen kilometres, and it is caused by a curtain wall of castellated rock, heavily camouflaged with vegetation and slung clean across the jungle plain between two low ranges. The river, meandering south with the prospect of Delta delights ahead, collides with this obstruction and its flood buckles, spreading along the base of the wall to its full width and backing upstream to a considerable distance. Outcrops of rock and hill isolated in this turbulent expanse at the top of the Falls comprise the Four Thousand Islands. At the height of the monsoon many of them would have been submerged and could only be guessed at from the trees protruding from the water.

As the pent-up waters rise, they scale the wall to squeeze

frantically through every fissure, erupting between the castellations and tearing at the vegetation. The Falls of Khon, though sixteen kilometres wide, are thus far from a continuous line of falling water. Literally thousands of spurts and cascades, some of colossal volume and with a sheer drop of up to twenty metres, others of lesser magnitude and broken into a succession of stair-like falls and water-slides, combine to form a panorama of chaotic industry in the midst of virgin forest. The dawn of creation springs readily to mind. Here thick brown lava hurtles down bare rock in a foam-flecked eruption; there plumes of spray tell of another deluge behind the next tree-crammed islet; and on the horizon, rainbows flickering in clouds of water-mist indicate more falls. Weeks are needed to explore this mapmaker's nightmare; but with the height of the river fluctuating by as much as a metre a day, such is the variable configuration of land and water that any map needs instant revision.

> *Finally* [continues Delaporte as they edged nearer to the Falls] *we entered a narrow torrent, progressing from tree to tree, from rock to rock. The torrent became ever narrower; the noise rose; then in front of us a beautiful sheet of water fell foaming amidst towering rocks.*
>
> *We were anxiously wondering how our skilful boatmen proposed to tackle this dangerous passage when luckily, round a mass of greenery, our barges landed on a very small beach in the basin that lies at the foot of the falls. We had arrived at the island of Khon which gives its name to these falls.*

The whole sixteen-kilometre spread is known as the Falls of Khon, but each of the principal waterfalls has its own designation. Hard against the east, or Lao, bank – and thus conveniently placed for easy viewing by bus-borne visitors – the Papheng Falls thunder sensationally into a rock-choked amphitheatre commanded by

The Papheng Falls.

viewing platforms and a Pepsi-Cola sign. Khon Island, perhaps the largest of the stepping-stone bits of *terra firma* interspersed across the Falls, lies further east. It must, then, have been the cascade now known as Sompaphit which halted the Mekong Exploration Commission and below which, beside the pool still beloved of those eighteen dolphins, they beached their pirogues and landed their stores.

The boats returned downriver; they would reach Stung Treng in as many hours as it had taken them days to ascend. Garnier was still delirious. Mercifully, perhaps, he was thus spared the spectacle which in the minds of his companions effectively extinguished any lingering hopes of vessels ever being able to sail up the river. What he had called 'the most important point to be ascertained' was utterly refuted by the Falls. No ship, however powered, could force a passage. (Recently even a hovercraft was defeated. In a trial run it apparently managed the rest of the river but had to be ignominiously transported round the Falls by road.) As de Carné baldly stated at the time, 'these cataracts offer an insurmountable obstacle to steam navigation'.

Yet Garnier would refuse to be beaten. When later filling in this hiatus in his account, he was evidently so desperate to disguise the truth that he prevaricated. The impression given – and that generally accepted in later works – is that the expedition actually ascended the Falls. On the island of Khon, he says, 'a transshipment' took place. They transferred from one set of pirogues to another; and since there is nothing about an overland journey in between, one presumes that the transfer took place on the same spot. The matter of the river's navigational potential was thus left wide open. And in due course the notion that the Mekong Exploration Commission had indeed surmounted the Falls would lure to disillusionment and even death a succession of hopeful navigators, puzzled engineers and reluctant labourers.

In fact, as de Carné makes clear and Delaporte confirms, the explorers disembarked at the tail of Khon Island and did not re-embark until they emerged at the head of it. They found men and a bullock cart to transport their luggage, plus the comatose Garnier; and they tramped from the island's southern tip at the base of the Falls to its northern tip at the top of the Falls.

'It was much easier to cross the island on foot, and take new boats on the other side of the cataracts,' says de Carné. 'We first climbed a narrow path in the forest,' says Delaporte, 'then we followed a muddy path through the rice fields which leads to the village.' Ban Khon, the village, was (and still is) above the Falls. It was from there that they resumed their ascent of the river by boat. Garnier would later return for a thorough examination of the Falls, but his narrative of their 'ascent' went unrevised. It was not a case of his being in malarial denial at the time. He was just a poor loser.

FOUR

Unbuttoned in Bassac

'Statements about the navigability of the river have been so constantly reiterated by persons who wished it to be navigable that,
when they obtained command of it in 1893, most Frenchmen
believed they had obtained a navigable waterway into Yunnan.
Not only is this not the case, but it does not even form a highway
for their own Lao acquisitions.'

H. WARINGTON SMYTH,
Five Years in Siam, 1898

THE ABSURDITY OF SAILING UP the Falls of Khon is
obvious to anyone who reaches the place. Although not as
high as Niagara, they are just as steep, just as impracticable. Later
writers, who on the strength of Garnier's account assumed that
the Mekong explorers had actually piked their pirogues to the top,
seem to have inferred that his *'cataractes de Khon'* were just another
set of rapids. With three such rapids behind him, and more to
come, Garnier's reticence over Khon became understandable. His
narrative was already awash with white water; for sparing the
reader more of the same his chronic indisposition provided a
perfect excuse.

Following his later visit, Garnier did write cryptically of 'the
unique features' of the river at this point. He was especially
impressed by the overall width of the *cataractes*, the grandeur of
individual *chutes* (falls), and the sheer desolation of the whole

scene: 'in this gigantic landscape everything exuded unimaginable power and assumed crushing proportions'. He could recall nothing remotely comparable in descriptions of any of the world's other great rivers. But he then further confused matters by insisting that, somewhere along the sixteen-kilometre precipice of *cataractes*, shipping lanes did indeed exist. There were, he says, 'channels of which the locals take advantage to make the descent in boats after having unloaded them'; hence the river was 'practicable for barges in every season between Phnom Penh and Bassac'. These channels changed with the state of the river; some remained dry for several months in the year. But 'a little dredging and some quays would', he ventured, 'be sufficient to improve the passage'. Alternatively a canal could be cut along the edge of them. The west bank looked the most promising for this purpose, and he strongly urged its early acquisition by France.

To this day fishermen inspecting their traps edge their little dugout craft behind the curtains of the cascades in defiance of the bucking, boiling maelstrom around them. With a rope, a boathook and a semi-aquatic paddler, a canoe can go pretty much where a dolphin can. But pirogues, let alone steamers, whatever the state of the river, are a different matter.

All of which was painfully apparent to other members of the Mekong Exploration Commission in their more candid moments. 'At Khon there stands an absolutely insuperable barrier in the actual lie of the land,' writes de Carné.

> *The truth at last began to force itself on the most sanguine among us. Steamers can never ply the Mekong as they do the Amazon or the Mississippi; and Saigon can never be united to the western provinces of China by this immense riverway . . . However magnificent, it* [i.e. the river] *seems to be only an incomplete masterpiece.*

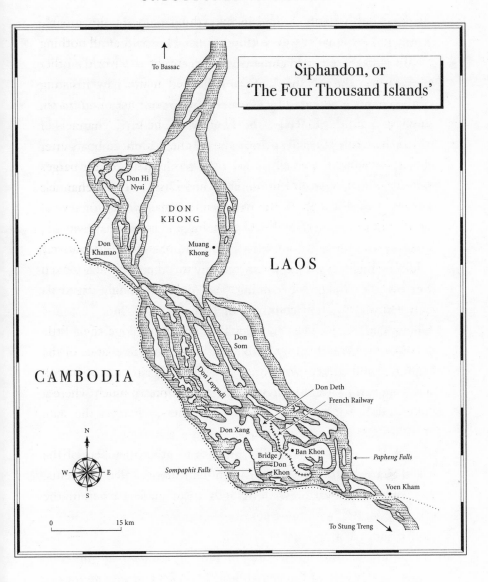

Siphandon, or 'The Four Thousand Islands'

Yet bright ideas, like small canoes, can be surprisingly resilient. Misled by Garnier and unacquainted with the actual terrain, promoters would launch a series of voyages and surveys in the 1880s. The Sombor and Somboc rapids would be dotted with channel markers and partially cleared in 1884, Preatapang in 1887, and the Khon Falls themselves were closely examined thereafter.

In 1890 there would come word of the discovery of a navigable passage near the west bank of the Falls, which may have been one of the channels reported by Garnier. Excitement mounted. In the same year Auguste Pavie, the man who would do more than anyone to realise Garnier's dream of a French Indo-China, passed down the Falls in a small pirogue. 'With the help of cables, and not without danger or considerable difficulties', he was told that larger pirogues also made the passage. True, this was in the height of the monsoon, and such boats travelled only downstream and unladen. But the news created a sensation in Saigon. The governor of the by then rapidly expanding colony was especially excited. He foresaw the Mekong becoming 'the main point of connection between the different countries of French Indo-China [Cochin-China, Cambodia, Laos and Tonkin], which will be able to communicate with each other through it'. Further trials were urged, commercial contracts were drafted, and specialised steamers for a Mekong flotilla were sought. Belatedly it looked as if Garnier's hopes might yet be realised.

The 1880s in south-east Asia were a time not just of rapid French expansion but of significant British expansion. Partly panicked by rumours of a Franco–Burmese treaty, the British invaded Upper Burma, overthrew its King Thibaw and in 1886 annexed his kingdom. This more than doubled the size of British Burma and made it contiguous to both British India in the north-west and China in the north-east. In the latter direction the Shan states, feudatories of the erstwhile king of Burma, extended as far as the Mekong and beyond, where they shaded uncertainly into the Lao states. The British now claimed suzerainty over the Shan states and thus took a giant stride into a part of inland south-east Asia on which French sights were already set. On the upper Mekong a tricky political obstacle would thus be interposed between the formidable physical obstacles confronting hopeful French navigators.

This lent greater urgency to the establishment of a commanding French presence wherever possible on the river. Not even painful revelations about the newly discovered passage round the Khon Falls could dispel it. Twice in 1891 and again in 1892 and 1893 diminutive steamships attempted the impossible. With engines roaring and boilers near bursting, with hundreds of men hauling from the rocks on ropes and others pushing from the decks with pikes, the steamers addressed the Falls. One, like a salmon to its spawning ground, allegedly wriggled up a narrow water-slide to within fifty metres of the top before the attempt had to be abandoned. Though the ships were of little more than one metre's draft and fourteen metres long, they all either grounded or were fouled by floating timbers. A more ingenious solution was required. Specialised steamers were still the answer; but they would have to be very specialised, in fact portable.

Two such vessels – steam-powered gun sloops not much bigger than *canonnières* – were constructed in France, shipped out in kit form, assembled in Saigon, and in 1893, as the *Massie* and the *Lagrandière*, they reached Khon. There, like the pirogues of the Mekong Exploration Commission, they were beached at the tail of the island and unloaded. Then they were completely dismantled and the sections manhandled onto flatbed trucks for which temporary rails had been laid across Khon Island. Only manpower was available to haul the trucks; and unfortunately the track proved too short. Rails from behind had to be uplifted and then relaid in front. Painfully slowly the bits of boats edged through the forest and across the paddy fields to Khon village, there to be again reassembled and finally relaunched above the Falls.

The twin vessels continued upriver to the next obstacle. In 1894 they reached Vientiane, and in 1895 the *Lagrandière* under Captain Simon sailed past Luang Prabang and, in an attempt to reach the Chinese frontier, got as far as the Tang-ho rapids. Like the Mekong Exploration Commission before him, Captain Simon here conceded victory to the river. The presence of a gunboat on the upper Mekong duly impressed the British; in fact it would contribute to a major war scare. But it was otherwise a mixed triumph.

Warington Smyth, the expert on diurnal tides who in 1894 was nearing the end of his 'Five Years in Siam', thought the French were deceiving themselves. So much had been expected of the Mekong that when a vessel at last made it up to Laos they imagined, says Warington Smyth, that they had 'a navigable waterway into Yunnan'. In fact it was not even a navigable waterway through Laos. As the river fell, the *Lagrandière* became marooned at Tang-ho until the following year. Far from commanding the Mekong, the gunboat had become its prisoner; and the same could be said of the *Massie*. Neither vessel, even empty, ever re-attempted the Falls of Khon or sailed again on the lower river to the Delta. The *Lagrandière* eventually went down with all hands when it struck a rock at Tha Dua just south of Luang Prabang; the fate of the *Massie* is unknown.

According to a contemporary report, they had only managed to reach the middle river by a *prouesse d'acrobatie nautique*, a 'feat of nautical acrobatics'. The difficulties encountered and the expense incurred were so great, said the report, as to render any similar *tour de force* out of the question for commercial operators. No less appalling, though unmentioned, was the loss of life, especially among the Vietnamese labourers impressed into service for the transit of Khon Island at the height of the malaria season.

But the presence above the Falls of two vessels, however small, did provide an incentive for new solutions. Warington Smyth suggested a tramway round the Falls, or a canal with locks. He reckoned the construction of either would satisfactorily cripple the French economy, costing about the same as the Manchester Ship

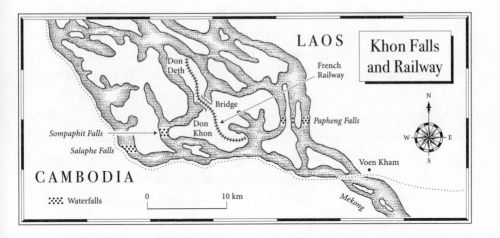

Canal yet never carrying more than one ten-thousandth of its tonnage. French opinion favoured a railway along the lines, as it were, of the four kilometres previously laid for transporting the two gun sloops. In 1897 a new track of narrow gauge was laid across Khon Island and a game little wood-burning locomotive was somehow landed and launched upon it. Laos had acquired its first – and last – railway.

Thanks to this innovation, ten years later the transit of Khon Island had become something of a formality. For Marthe Bassenne, a doctor's wife who published an account of her 1910 river trip from Phnom Penh to Luang Prabang, it merited only a paragraph. Porters were waiting at the tail of the island to stack the luggage on the railway trucks. The passengers piled on top, balancing themselves as best they could. The trucks had no seats, no sides and no shade.

The train, struggling and grating amid the clashing sound of steel, hauled us across the island, which is covered by teak trees and bamboos whose branches brushed our faces. The temperature was very high and the sun, filtering through the trees, roused noxious fever-vapours from the tangled undergrowth.

Sweat caked my hair under my sun hat; the heat burned my arms through my clothes; and the mosquitoes took advantage of my predicament to attack me as they pleased, all over the hands and face . . .

At Khon village, passengers transferred to the *Garcerie*, a steam launch which had been hauled up the Falls in bits, like the gun sloops. A creditable thirty-two metres in length, it could carry a hundred or so passengers but was too cumbersome to be man-oeuvred in the narrow waterways between the four thousand islands except when the river was in flood. To eliminate this prob-lem, in the 1920s the railway was extended to Don Deth, the next island above Khon, and gantries with steam-powered cranes were installed at the two termini. Another three kilometres of track were thus added and, more notably, were connected to the existing line by a fine stone bridge with three handsome arches.

Nearly a century later, the bridge still stands, a proud and preposterous colonial extravagance among the Four Thousand (otherwise unlinked) Islands but a boon to the children of Deth attending the village school on Khon and, to foreigners, a strangely tranquil and reassuring presence. Around its piers a dappled stream should glide and beneath its parapets arms of ivy should trail. It seems misplaced amid the ravaged forest, the thundering waters and that palpable sense of an all-crushing nature on the rampage.

The last train ran in 1940. During the Second World War the jungle encroached even faster than the Japanese. The line fell into disrepair and was never reopened. No doubt the colonial authori-ties were relieved to be rid of it. Used only for the few months when the rapids below Khon were high enough for navigation, the Lao State Railway with its seven kilometres of track and its single locomotive had never generated sufficient traffic to justify its existence.

Bits of uplifted track still lie among the paddy fields, spanning a ditch or fencing a pig-sty. The gantry on Deth Island rears from the palms like a giant's gibbet. And just off the main path on Khon (there are no roads on the islands), beneath an acacia, perched on two rails and neatly fenced lest perhaps it make a run for it, there still sulks the sad little locomotive. Stripped of any attachments that might be remotely useful, it looks very small indeed. Grass grows freely about its underparts, and the two large apertures in the cab through which the driver once peered down the track lend it a hangdog expression. Had rust not sealed the firebox and the boiler long since burst, the temptation to feed this most baleful of tank-engines would be overwhelming.

It was while camped on Khon somewhere near the site of the future bridge that in August 1866 Francis Garnier staged a miraculous recovery. With the river revealed as unnavigable, had its principal promoter died here it seems probable that the whole expedition would have been aborted. The brief written instructions issued by Admiral de Lagrandière for the direction of the expedition were of little help in this situation – or indeed any situation. The Commission was supposed to 'determine geographically the course of the river by a rapid reconnaissance pushed as far as possible, to study the resources of the countries, and to find by what means the upper valley of the Mekong may be commercially linked with Cambodia and Cochin China'.

But if ships could never use the Mekong, there was not much point in exploring the river geographically. It could never become a commercial artery of empire, and only Garnier was intrigued by its mysterious provenance. Had the expedition been aborted, French ambitions in south-east Asia would have been urgently redirected elsewhere – as indeed they were when the Commission eventually reported. Arguably, turning back would have been the better, as well as the easier, option.

But it so happened that the demise of hopes for the rampant river coincided almost exactly with the revival of hopes for the ailing Garnier. Soon after the departure from Stung Treng, he had suffered one of many delirious fits and somehow thrown himself overboard. Rescued by his despairing companions, he was stripped, dried and restored to his sick-berth, apparently beyond treatment. Yet he would later ascribe to this impromptu ducking 'the wholesome reaction which broke the fever'. Throughout the four-day voyage to Khon he had remained comatose. Then, Lazarus-like, on the island itself he began to stir again; a glimmer of consciousness returned.

> *The first almost clear recollection which I recall after this dark interlude of nightmares and delirious images from the past is a calm and smiling tropical landscape. Beside a confined and torrential river, not far from a dazzling cascade which the sun's rays envelop in a sparkling mist, a few huts are scattered . . . Some pirogues are moored in front of the houses, and about thirty natives come and go carrying boxes and bundles. Among them, overseeing and directing, I recognise most of my travelling companions, who give me a smile and a word of encouragement. Someone places me in a hammock and . . . I experience the acute thrill of finding myself alive.*

In fact, after a twelve-day coma, it took several weeks for him to recuperate; his journal would not be resumed until after they left Khon in late August, and he would still be convalescing when they reached Bassac in mid-September. But as his strength slowly returned, so did his resolve. If, as seems likely, it was during the long halt at Bassac that the decision to go on was finally taken, one may safely assume that Garnier had a major part in it.

Meanwhile his companions made the most of their eight days on Khon Island. *Le Commandant* Lagrée, throat-sore and care-worn, busied himself with highly speculative calculations of the distance yet to be travelled, the number of months it might take, and so the permissible rate of consumption for their cash reserves and their much-depleted stores. His air of intense preoccupation discouraged interruption, and with Garnier, his trusted little deputy, silenced by fever, few orders emanated from the expedition's high command. The other four men were thus left to their own devices.

The two doctors diligently pursued their specialist responsibilities. 'From morning till evening ... Dr Thorel made abundant collections of the most varied plants,' while 'Jumbo' Joubert, in between looking after the sick, undertook excursions with his geological hammer. Although their scientific contributions were acknowledged, Thorel and Joubert played a modest part in the conduct of the Commission and their personalities remain indistinct.

That left the two youngest and, in many ways, most interesting members of the party. Louis de Carné, the caustic observer from the Quai d'Orsay, was still being cold-shouldered by his companions. Additionally, he was now 'racked by creeping and persistent fevers' and had yet to discover his own field of interest. At Khon he took it easy. It fell, therefore, to the misshapen but irrepressible Louis Delaporte, artist, musician and (during Garnier's illness) official chronicler, to shoulder the burden of exploration. This meant conducting perilous reconnaissances amongst the Falls. His sketch of the Papheng waterfall, 'the second largest and the most picturesque', was made from the branches of a tree which commanded both the fall's twenty-metre drop and its one-kilometre width. Beneath him, as he drew, lay the carcase of a crocodile which had been pounded to death on the rocks.

The two-kilometre-wide Salaphe Falls on the other (west) bank proved more difficult. With a guide Delaporte was paddled across the river above the Falls and landed on a forest-choked island, through which they scrambled towards the deafening roar. They were halted not by the expected precipice but by an assault of leeches, 'some fine like needles, others bigger, sometimes reaching a length of six or seven centimetres'.

When we approached, they got up straight on each dead leaf, on each blade of grass and from all sides, and so to speak jumped in our direction . . . After a few moments I had become the prey of dozens which vied in climbing up my legs to make me bleed . . . It was useless to stop. For every leech I brushed off, ten new ones climbed aboard. Nearby was a big tree; I ran; I shinned up it, and when I was out of their accursed reach, I undressed and pulled them off one by one . . . My belt had not stopped them from climbing higher. I found one that had slid up to my chest.

The excursion was aborted, and a few days later a second attempt was made by island-hopping across the Falls. Too water-lashed for leeches, although much more dangerous, this approach necessitated Khon's strongest swimmer plunging into the intervening cascades with a rope which, secured to the opposite bank, served as a lifeline for the rest of the party. The constant swimming and wading prevented Delaporte from taking his sketching materials; stripped to a loincloth, it was all he could do to hang on to the rope. He would be obliged to recreate his view of these crossings, and of the Salaphe Falls themselves, from memory.

At last they slithered over boulders, pushed through a screen of lianas and branches, and, as the rumble became a terrifying thunder, 'found ourselves right in front of the waterfall'. As far as the eye could see, thick brown torrents exploded into frothy abysses. It was like a storm-tossed sea breaking on a rocky headland. Mud spouts shot into the air, spume wafted as from a cauldron, and downstream the furthest horizon of the river was still a deep blanket of glistening foam. The rocks to which they clung streamed with water and, under the impact of the nearest fall, seemed to shake themselves like a dog emerging from a swim. As each wave receded it left a tideline of 'branches, alligators, and big fish which had carelessly allowed themselves to be taken and smashed by the rocks'.

Delaporte wondered if such a sight had ever before been witnessed by Europeans. He recalled a description of the falls on the Rhine, and concluded that they would 'look like a small disturbance, scarcely worth a second glance' by comparison. In terms of average annual volume, the Khon Falls are in fact the third largest in the world and, when in flood, probably the largest. Niagara has about a quarter of their volume, the Victoria Falls only an eighth.

Above the deafening roar of perhaps ten million gallons per second bounding into the lower basins, conversation proved difficult. To get Delaporte's attention, his guide tapped him on the shoulder and pointed excitedly. Fresh pug marks were clearly visible in the silted sand and led to a nearby thicket. 'We judged it prudent to go back without delay,' says Delaporte. Tigers infested the islands. They moved among them with the ease of otters, gorging themselves on the prey trapped in their forests or beached on their rocks. It was a predicament that, unarmed, barely clothed and far from footsure, Delaporte and his men readily recognised. In some haste they re-enacted their hand-over-hand progress back through the cascades. A fortnight later Delaporte's arms still ached from the wrenching of the current.

On 26 August, with Garnier definitely on the mend, the Commission resumed its voyage upriver in a new fleet of pirogues. They had been sent downstream at Lagrée's request from Khong, the largest of the Four Thousand Islands, their chief settlement, and subsequently the root cause of much semantic confusion. Thanks in large part to sloppy editing, most published accounts of the river, including those of the Commission's staff, manage at some point to confuse Khong (or Kong) Island with Khon (or Khone) Island. Khon's Falls unfailingly become the 'Khong Falls'; the modest rapids below Khong are mistaken for the mighty falls below Khon; and misunderstandings about the river's navigable potential are thereby compounded, not to mention casual enquirers being hopelessly misled.

According to de Carné, 'Khong' or 'Kong' Island has further significance in that it is responsible for the '*kong*' in 'Me-kong'. He says that the '*Me*' means 'sea', and so the whole means 'the sea of Kong'. Others, including the know-all Warington Smyth, insist that 'Me-kong' is actually an abbreviation of '*Me-nam Kong*', or 'the great river of Kong'; and that since the original phrase from which Europeans adopted the name was probably Thai, the '*kong*' must refer not to Kong Island but to Chiang Khong, an important town and port on the Thai bank several hundred kilometres upriver in the Golden Triangle. However this may be, all agree that 'Mekong' is a linguistic nonsense used exclusively by foreigners. No one living along its banks has heard of the word in any other context. In fact, they presume it to be French or English. For them the river needs no name and has none. It is simply 'the river'.

From the northern end of Khon Island (Don Khon) to the southern end of Khong Island (Don Khong) is a distance of about thirty kilometres, but from Ban Khon (Khon village) to Muang Khong (Khong town) it is more like fifty kilometres. The pirogues took two days, piking and paddling up one of the half-dozen main channels into which the river is here braided by the mass of islands. Unlike the flooded forest and the deserted shorelines below Khon, above it the Four Thousand Islands supported a considerable population. The maze of waterways bristled with the protruding stakes of fish traps. Homesteads hiding in the verdure were betrayed by a stub of pier sticking out from the riverbank or by an explosion of naked children cascading into the water from an overhanging tamarind. Butterflies the size of bats yo-yoed round their pirogues like gulls about a fishing smack.

Here, as in the Delta, the arms of the river provide both fish and farmland. Annually, as the water level falls, the steep banks are reclaimed, cleared of tree trunks and other detritus, and terraced into carefully tended vegetable plots which descend into the riverbed as the season advances. Courtesy of all those upriver nutrients, by April the stream slides through a horticultural parade ground of massed lettuces, staked beans, stockaded maize, drilled carrots and apologetic tomatoes. Water buffalo ambling down for their daily ablutions require firm policing.

The chief – or lesser king – of Khong turned out to be an octogenarian who was so deaf that 'to keep him abreast of the conversation a servant had to be continually writing on a board that was held up before his eyes'. Happily this handicap hampered neither his geniality nor his curiosity. The expedition had never been made so welcome. His gift of an ox – and their first *filets mignons* since Phnom Penh – was especially appreciated, though no more so than the trinkets and ticals dispensed by Lagrée. Surely the Buddha himself must have been born a Frenchman, said the old chief as he admired a length of brass wire and bemoaned the poverty and simplicity of his own surroundings. The explorers might go anywhere on his island – and did so, despite the hundreds who assembled to observe their movements and inspect their possessions. De Carné, evidently enjoying a respite from his fever, admits to reciprocating this curiosity, particularly in respect of the ladies of Khong. Most obligingly they disrobed and bathed within a few metres of the expedition's camp. 'They were not a little forward and soon became familiar, even flirtatious, with the men of our escort.'

To farewells that were all the fonder for these happy liaisons the expedition took its departure from Khong on 6 September. Lagrée rewarded the old chief with a silver watch, a gesture that the disapproving de Carné likened to presenting a monkey with a coconut 'which he turns and turns without knowing how to open it or what use to make of it'. In de Carné's journal the prejudices of extreme youth and undoubted privilege all too easily found blunt expression. Though the most observant of local society, he would be the least tolerant, freely disparaging the appearance, race, faculties and honesty of almost everyone they encountered.

On the other hand, it was Lagrée's policy always to be as generous as possible. Although there was no obligation to give the boatmen a wage or to pay for the hire of their boats (both being a form of feudal service due to the local chiefs), he invariably did so. Word of this surprising conduct was already preceding the Commission up the river. By easing future procurement, it would prove a sound investment. More significantly, it was also intended to secure the good reputation of France. If the expedition was to have any political consequences, it was vital that the peoples along the river learn to value French civilisation and respect French visitors. Harsh conduct and hard bargaining, like that meted out by earlier prospectors in Stung Treng, only soured the chiefs and alienated their subjects. The cordiality of the Commission's reception at Khong had convinced Lagrée that no freebooting Frenchmen had yet reached the place; and he left it confident that the next French agent would be no less welcome than he was.

The same happy state of affairs would pertain at Bassac. Above Khong Island, the river reunited its streams for the first time since Kratie and subsided into a respectable flood. It was about one and a half kilometres wide, free of obstructions and flowing due south. Pirogues could here be paddled. In six boats, with fifty paddlers to a boat, they shot upriver in racing formation. The route was obvious and the boatmen accustomed to it. Lagrée and his men had only to lie back and point out their preferred campsite.

Evidently officials from Bangkok regularly passed this way. Laos, in the person of chiefs like those of Khong and Bassac, was known to acknowledge Thai suzerainty, and the Commission had accordingly armed itself with letters of introduction from the Siamese/Thai court. Ironically, even shamelessly, the explorers were travelling as honoured guests of an administration whose conduct over Cambodia they deplored and whose authority in Laos they must contest if a case were to be made for the French control of the Mekong. In the Lao states, therefore, friendly receptions were good in that they revealed a local disposition to a more lasting French presence, but indifferent receptions were also good in that they advertised local contempt for directives emanating from Bangkok. Either way, Bangkok's rule was discredited and the actual status of Laos thrown into doubt – a condition in which, so far as the rest of world was concerned, it would remain indefinitely.

President John F. Kennedy is said to have been responsible for the twentieth century's disparagement of the kingdom, now repub-lic, of Laos. Pressed in the early years of the war in Vietnam to provide an explanation of what the CIA was doing in neighbouring but neutral Laos, Kennedy feared that domestic opinion might baulk at American lives being risked in defence of a place that sounded like 'louse'; so instead he pronounced it 'Lay-oss', as in 'chaos'. Throughout the 1960s and into the seventies 'the chaos in "Lay-oss"' enjoyed an international currency that subsided only when US interest in the region itself subsided following the Communist triumphs of 1975.

To be fair, Americans were not alone in their ignorance of all that pertained to Laos. Was it one syllable or two? Singular or plural? Masculine or feminine? Concerning a land which only the French confidently called *Le Laos*, it could generally be said that those who knew what it was were not sure where it was, those who knew what it was and where it was were unable to define its international status, and those who knew none of these things did not care to ask lest they get the name wrong.

The award of a walk-on part in the Vietnam drama to an actor whose identity was so uncertain only aggravated existing confusion about the country. To its other discouraging attributes – impenetrable rainforest, interminable mountains, sparse habitation, bewildering tribes, negligible communications and an infinitesimal gross domestic product – was added an international obscurity that successive Laotian regimes of whatever ideological persuasion would do nothing to dispel.

Historically Laos is named after the Lao people, just as Thailand is after the Thai people. As noted, the Lao and the Thai are ethnically related, and their languages are so similar that Thai television channels are today the most watched in Laos. With minor exceptions, the Mekong currently serves as the common frontier between the two states. But now as in the nineteenth century, the river does not correspond to the ethnic distribution. The Lao have long lived on both banks of the Mekong, and more Lao still live west and south of the river in Thailand than east and north of it in Laos.

In fact in Laos itself the Lao, though the largest ethnic group, barely constitute a majority. Traditionally lowland farmers practising wet rice cultivation and a relaxed form of Theravada Buddhism, they may now be outnumbered in the country which bears their name by an exotic combination of indigenous forest peoples (Khmu, Lanten, etc.) and an even more confusing variety of recent and mainly upland immigrants from Yunnan (Hmong, Akha, Yao, etc.). All these peoples are comprehended by the term 'Laotian' but not strictly speaking by the term 'Lao', although in the country's official designation the issue is fluffed in favour of a wishful but misleading string of initials – LPDR, which in English stands for both 'The Lao People's Democratic Republic' and 'The Laotian Peoples' Democratic Republic'.

The golden age of the Lao had been in the mid-sixteenth century. From Luang Prabang, and subsequently from Vientiane, Lao kings claimed sovereignty over Lan Xang, a 'Land of a Million Elephants' (and nearly as many semi-autonomous *muangs*) which embraced most of what is now Laos plus parts of north-east Thailand. Lao historians emphasise Lan Xang's all-embracing sovereignty as proof of an ancient and respectable national pedigree; other historians make much of the semi-autonomous *muangs* ('provinces' or 'provincial power-centres') whose relationship with their sovereign was of a loose and indeterminate nature that did not readily lend itself to international notions of territorial control or political subordination.

Either way, over the next three centuries Lan Xang/Laos gave rather less than it got in an extended tug-of-war with its neighbours. Occasionally Lao forces encroached into districts under Thai, Vietnamese or Khmer rule; more often and much more disastrously, Thai, Vietnamese and Burmese armies marched into Laos.

In the 1820s, with Vietnam in turmoil and Burma preoccupied by the first British incursion, it had been the turn of the Thais to press their suit. Following a Lao attack, Bangkok's forces crossed the Mekong and stormed, ransacked and laid waste the Lao capital of Vientiane. Its famous Buddha image was appropriated and its population dispersed, many being settled in Nong Khai, a new town on the opposite (now Thai) bank of the Mekong. Similar resettlement led to the translation of many other Mekong townships to the right (west) bank with a consequent depopulation of the left (east) bank that is noticeable to this day. Beyond the river, Thai forces scarcely penetrated, but Thai diplomacy assured a transfer of allegiance by most Lao *muangs*, including the erstwhile royal capital of Luang Prabang, from Vientiane to Bangkok.

Thai authority in Laos was therefore very much in the ascendant when the Mekong Exploration Commission appeared on the scene. Bassac and Khong had been detached from Laos even earlier; Stung Treng and adjacent areas had been lopped off Cambodia to be similarly appropriated by Thailand; and only in the mountainous east and north of Laos were there still *muangs* that offered tribute not only to Bangkok but also to either the Vietnamese emperor in Hué or to imperial China.

It would be the French contention that in Laos, as in Cambodia, this Thai ascendancy over the east bank of the river was not a normal state of affairs but the product of recent and unprincipled aggression. It was historically unnatural, internationally unacknowledged and locally unpopular. Garnier would be the first of many to stigmatise Thai supremacy in Laos as 'suffocating oppression' and 'unendurable domination'. 'Liberating' the Lao was therefore a worthy cause; and if liberation could be realised and secured only by French intervention, so much the better.

On landing at Bassac (now known as 'Champassak'), Francis Garnier laid down an instant marker. The town, in a commanding position above a bend in the river, backed by enticing hills and blessed with a fine climate, was somewhere 'in which French influence must be most firmly implanted', he declared. Its young 'king' was just the sort of amenable and inquisitive Lao who would appreciate such a change and benefit from 'the civilising influence of France'. The king himself obligingly volunteered as much to Lagrée. Lagrée too then 'saw . . . an opportunity for a natural and legitimate retaliation against the government of Bangkok which France might take whenever convenient'.

The rains continued to fall, and the river to rise, until October. When the downpour stopped, young de Carné stepped outside their shelter at Bassac and knew how Noah felt when he emerged from the ark. Rejoicing in views hitherto hidden by the cloud, Garnier, Delaporte and Thorel paddled through the flooded fields and then clambered into the hills. They were keen, says Garnier,

The king of Bassac pays a visit to the expedition.

his sights wistfully set on the source of the river, 'to derive some encouragement for our future ascent of the Himalayan mountains and Tibet'.

The Bassac range, though steep enough, attains not half the

lowest altitude found in Tibet and bears absolutely no resemblance
to the howling wastes of the Himalayas. Here, as throughout
Laos, hills are more in the nature of perpendicular forests. When
ascending, the explorers hauled themselves up by hanging onto
the vegetation. Rather than trust to the hillside, they often found
it easier to climb a tree, travel along one of its topmost branches,
and with the help of creepers, rejoin the hill's precipitous rock-face
where the roots of another tree invited a repetition of the process.
In this arboreal progress the orchid-chasing Dr Thorel proved the
most adept, but even he failed to reach the top of the Bassac
range.

Clearly, though, the invalids were recovering. Garnier put it
down to the climate. With night-time temperatures falling as low
as 15°C, Bassac was the perfect place to convalesce. As well as
being strategically useful to France, he foresaw the place becoming
a health resort, an Indo-Chinese Vichy, to which those suffering
from the heat and dysentery of the Delta could repair for rest and
relaxation.

The Lao, though incorrigibly lazy, were better-natured than
the Vietnamese and less conservative than the Cambodians. Garnier found them 'an intelligent and gentle race ... their spirit
inquisitive and their religion tolerant'. The women – though he
hesitated to say so and wondered whether some allowance should
not be made for his 'long absence from France' – struck him as
especially 'gracious, indeed pretty'. Unlike the men, they did not
shave their heads but tied their long and 'always splendidly black'
tresses in a bun secured with a ribbon behind which fragrant
blossoms might be tucked. Below the waist they wore a short tight
skirt; above it nothing but a flimsy scarf that was draped 'without
much care being taken to cover the breasts'; its purpose, according
to de Carné, was simply to preserve the bosom's pallor from sunburn. Though Garnier and de Carné rarely agreed about anything,
on the subject of Lao femininity they spoke as one and unani-

mously applauded the 'liberal' customs that 'allowed plenty of indulgence for the weakness of human nature'. Among a people of such obliging disposition, not to mention their generally modest stature, little 'Mademoiselle Buonaparte' was beginning to feel at home.

> *A generous and luxuriant nature seems here to have inspired the most gentle and peaceful of customs. No violent or cruel excesses trouble the dreamy nonchalance of the inhabitants; caressed by the light of a tropical sun, the enchanting landscape bespeaks a tranquillity, an innocence, that is unique. All the hubbub, all the fracas of civilisation is stilled and dies away when you enter the region; nothing manages to disturb the absolute silence. The memory of it that one cherishes after returning to the hurly-burly of the outside world seems so strange, so remote, as to belong to a completely different planet, to another existence, and involuntarily makes one wonder about the transmigration of souls.*

To one who had just been snatched from the jaws of death the idea of reincarnation seemed especially apt. If not actually reborn, Garnier had at least been revived here. Ever after he would think of the country as a second home. 'I would like to live in Laos,' he would write shortly before his untimely death. 'With its silent, majestic forests, with its river forming great sheets of water reflecting the giant trees from which monkeys playfully dangle . . . it is anything but sad; Laos is wonderful.'

In effect the pioneer of the French colonial adventure was succumbing to a condition that would one day become endemic amongst his fellow countrymen in Laos. Ninety years later, in the last days of colonial rule, the British writer Norman Lewis found the French in Laos more enchanted than ever. 'This was the earthly paradise,' noted Lewis, 'the country that was one vast Tahiti, causing all the French who had been stationed there to affect ever after a vaguely dissolute manner.'

Laos became France's 'Happy Valley', a Polynesia with Buddhists, a Provence of doe-eyed sirens. Lewis was reliably informed that in this paradise no fruit was forbidden. The lonely *fonctionnaire* might admire a Lao maiden in the morning, be engaged by lunchtime, married by sundown, and tucked up in bed with her for dinner. The cost was trifling, the commitment negligible, the companionship priceless. More or less the same could be said of opium. Everyone 'went native' and most took a pipe or two. To the French – Breton or Corsican, Parisian or provincial – *le Laos* was no more a country than it was to the rest of the world; it was an unbuttoned state of mind, an elysium, a pipe dream.

Understandably reluctant to drag themselves away from the delights of such a place, the explorers stayed put at Bassac for all of three and a half months. It would not be the last such halt, and nothing perhaps better betrays the real nature of the enterprise. An expedition primarily dedicated to discovering the course of the river would have pressed on. Delay drained the common purse, and side excursions taxed the strength of the explorers; the ill-effects of both would prove their eventual undoing. But investigating the political and economic potential of the Mekong's basin was a very different proposition from resolving the mystery of the river's meanderings. Major tributaries must also be mapped, mineral resources explored, agricultural potential assessed, and political attitudes probed. It all took time; and so at Bassac they waited.

They waited for the rains to stop because they made travel so unpleasant; then they waited for the river to fall because high water, though essential for the rapids and the falls, would be an impediment in calmer reaches. Next they waited for the return of those who had undertaken satellite excursions while they were waiting; and finally, most of all, they waited for news from Cambodia.

At the last minute, directions had been left with the French officials in Phnom Penh for the forwarding of letters, newspapers, some vital instruments and hopefully a few delicacies. This had not been part of the original plan, but had become an attractive option when the expedition had departed Cambodia without its accreditation for China. A request for the necessary letters (in effect visas or 'passports') had already been granted by the imperial government in Beijing, but the actual documents had still to materialise. Orders had therefore been left for the immediate forwarding of the documentation as soon as it arrived in Phnom Penh; and Lagrée had been expecting it ever since.

When no courier overtook the Commission at Stung Treng, Khon, Khong or Bassac, he was near despair. If Laos had taught them anything, it was that they 'could not have advanced a step' without Siamese passports; and the same would be even more true of China. Garnier blamed the indifference of a supine administration. No one in Saigon or Phnom Penh took the mission seriously; the letters had probably been sitting on someone's desk. To intercept them, or otherwise expedite delivery, he agreed to go back downriver.

It was during this excursion that Garnier revisited the Falls of Khon and revised his companions' ideas on their unnavigability. But though he accounted his discoveries a success, the trip was otherwise a failure. He got as far as Stung Treng, only to be there halted by an unforeseen complication. In the course of the previous two months north-eastern Cambodia had erupted in revolt. A major rebellion against King Norodom and his French 'protectors' was underway. If the passports had indeed been overlooked somewhere, it was because the French authorities now had meatier matters to worry about.

The Cambodian rebels knew all about the Mekong Exploration Commission, indeed regarded its members as desirable hostages. Led by a claimant to the Cambodian throne who had escaped from French detention in Vietnam, they had almost caught up with the Commission before it left Khong and were now reportedly considering a raid on Bassac. The insurgents also held both sides of the river below Stung Treng. Communications with Phnom Penh were therefore interrupted. In effect the Commission was cut off from its base and marooned in lower Laos.

De Carné's earlier pontification about their only way back to Saigon – and so to France – being through China began to seem horribly prescient. At Stung Treng neither Garnier nor his interpreter could find anyone willing to run the gauntlet of the rebel-held river. He therefore headed back to Bassac. The most that could be said for his excursion was that it appeared to resolve the uncertainty about the expedition's future plans. Reassured by Garnier's optimistic reappraisal of the Falls, and now denied any easy line of retreat, the expedition could only advance.

That still left the question of the Chinese passports; Lagrée's legendary patience was about to be tested. But on arrival back at Bassac a shamefaced and empty-handed Garnier was relieved to find his superior absent. Only Delaporte and Thorel were in residence. He joined them in the exploration of Wat Phou, a nearby temple complex which spills down a steep hillside. More an architectural declivity than an edifice, it includes the extensive reservoirs, glorious statuary and challenging staircases so beloved of the Khmers. 'Late Angkorian', say the books, so confirming the verdict of Garnier and Delaporte.

A site of such sophistication in the wilds of lower Laos prompted thoughts both salutary and comforting. It was sobering to think that here, even more than in Cambodia, civilisation had so obviously regressed; but it was encouraging to find in Laos such persuasive evidence of an ancient empire to which the French increasingly regarded themselves as the successors. Wat Phou, like Angkor, must be protected. It was another good pretext for French intervention.

The rest of the party – Lagrée, de Carné and Joubert – had gone off to the east to explore the Se Don. A major tributary, the Se Don joins the Mekong at Pakse, which is today a large town a few kilometres above Bassac; it was built by the French and has a bridge courtesy of the Japanese and a pebbledash palace, c.1968, courtesy of the last ruler of Bassac (who was a grandson of the young chief who entertained the Commission). The Se Don and the Se Kong (the even bigger tributary which joins the Mekong at Stung Treng) drain and encircle a region known as the Bolovens plateau which projects westwards from the Annamite mountains, themselves the frontier between Laos and Vietnam. It was important to check whether either of these tributaries furnished an easier route from the French provinces in Vietnam into Laos, as well as to ascertain whether the Se Don's silver mines and the Se Kong's gold deposits were commercially viable.

This last was a job for the geologising Dr Joubert, of whom Delaporte drew a portrait sitting beside the first falls on the Se Don with geological hammer to hand. The picture is notable on two counts. It reveals 'Jumbo' Joubert's eccentric wardrobe, in this case a Lao silk jacket with anorak hood above shorts, fishnet stockings and canvas gaiters; and it introduces the expedition's first dog. Garnier also had a dog, a highly intelligent bitch called Dragon, possibly a pointer, on which he doted. Joubert's 'Fox' was probably the only other dog. He looks like a whippet and may have accompanied his master from west Africa. Less extrovert than the dainty Dragon, Fox would long survive her and become in the difficult months ahead the expedition's mascot and undisputed favourite.

Like a mirage, and much to Joubert's annoyance, the silver

Joubert and 'Fox' beside the Se Don.

mines above the Se Don vanished as they approached them. Confidently predicted by their escort one day, they were emphatically
pronounced non-existent the next. The expedition drew the obvious conclusion: the mines' whereabouts were being kept a secret
because of the value of their yield.

The gold was, at least, being visibly worked. Before homes
that resembled kennels in the bed of the Se Kong, wizened
womenfolk and naked toddlers panned silt. The return for their
labours was minimal and, melted into ingots, all found its way
into the Bangkok treasury. But it might be a different story if the
gold-bearing strata upstream could be located. 'Gold in abundance'
undoubtedly existed; they had it on the word of a respectable
Chinese merchant and, as de Carné added, 'God only knows what
a Chinaman would not risk to sniff out a profit.' The Chinese,
and the Lao, only desisted from actually engaging in the extraction
process because of the extremely unsavoury reputation of '*les sauvages*' who inhabited the region.

Sauvages is a word easily mistranslated. When rendered into
English as 'savages', it conveys a pejorative judgement of the
peoples so described and of those so describing them. But in

French the word is unburdened with such slights and simply indi-
cates peoples who are comparatively 'wild', 'free' or 'unsociable'.
The '*sauvages*' encountered by the Commission were the more
remote and often semi-nomadic inhabitants of the country. They
were the non-Lao-speaking (and non-Thai-, non-Dai-, non-
Shan-speaking) peoples of the forest and the hills who usually
engaged in slash-and-burn cultivation and to whom, subsequently,
terms like 'tribals', 'ethnic minority members' or 'micro-culture
members' would be applied.

In Vietnam the French knew such upland tribes as '*Moi*'. The
Lao, just as cavalier and indiscriminate in such matters, called
them *kha*, another pejorative term denoting 'slaves'. It is supposed
that in the distant past when the Lao first settled in the middle
Mekong, they may well have enslaved the indigenous Khmu,
Lamet and Lanten peoples. Happily Lao and *kha* now seemed on
better terms. Forest products were traded for salt and rice, local
hill chiefs played an important role in Lao rituals, and de Carné
had noted how most of the racing pirogues at the boat races were
manned by *sauvages*.

But the Bolovens region was exceptional and remained a no-go
area of sinister repute because there, to the horror of the explorers,
kha still meant 'slave'. Boatloads of slaves, mostly boys and young
girls corralled from the remotest uplands, were to be seen passing
down the Se Kong. For them paradise lay up in the mists of their
native hills, and the riverine Lao were a race of effete demons.
The usually snide de Carné was especially distressed by this first
revelation of the Mekong's darker side. A representative of the
Quai d'Orsay surrounded by sailors, he felt a natural sympathy for
other outsiders and would discover in the mountain and forest
tribes of Laos his own field of study.

*The unhappy captives seemed more crushed by their grief than
by the irons that held them ... Immovable in their narrow*

floating prison, letting their sad gaze wander as it might, they showed in their bearing that nobility which hopeless misfortune, profoundly felt, everywhere imprints on the human figure.

In the seventeenth century the slave trade, like that in spices, had provided a dynamic for European expansion. But by the nineteenth century it was evident that the returns obtainable from participating in the trade could be dramatically exceeded by those to be made from suppressing it. In Africa especially, the British and the French now saw the suppression of slavery as a Christian duty that justified all available means, including military intervention and political appropriation. Precious metals, strategic advantage, archaeological conservation and public health might provide incentives for French intervention in Laos. The abolition of slavery provided an imperative.

Although de Carné was troubled by the fact that most of the slaves were destined for 'a market at Phnom Penh under the shadow of our flag', this was no reason to hang back; for it must not be forgotten, he lamely added, that as yet France was 'only the protecting power in Cambodia'. Garnier, too, was troubled by this anomaly. But unlike, say, Dr Livingstone, he clearly saw the abolition of slavery not as an end in itself but as part of the imperialist mission.

The suppression of the slave trade [in Laos] *is the most urgent of measures and the one that most concerns the dignity of France ... The immediate results of abolishing this odious traffic will be the raising of moral standards, the development of the resources and security of the area, and an increase in the prestige of Europeans.*

With so many excellent reasons for a French move into lower Laos, Lagrée, de Carné and Joubert completed their circuit of the

Bolovens plateau and headed back to Bassac well pleased with their work. The sight of Garnier standing among the welcoming party was also good news until he revealed that his mission down-river had in fact failed. For de Carné, receiving no letters or newspapers from home was 'a serious disappointment'. It was, though, as nothing compared to 'the disaster' of the Chinese pass-ports. Their non-arrival 'compromised the success of the whole expedition'. Lagrée, only lately recovered from his first bout of malaria, weighed the options in dismay.

To go on without the passports would almost certainly mean being turned back as soon as they reached the Chinese frontier. This would preclude the exploration both of the upper river and of the all-important commercial potential of Yunnan. It would also mean a long and arduous retreat through Laos and either Tonkin (northern Vietnam), Thailand or Burma. According to Lagrée's painstaking calculations, their resources in cash and trade goods would not stretch that far. At their present rate of progress – about a thousand kilometres in six months – they were reluctantly coming round to the idea of being away for at least two years. In China they could expect help from the scattered French missionary houses and from the credit enjoyed there by Europeans. But else-where they were on their own and utterly dependent for carriage and cash on their limited resources.

On the other hand, they could not now return through Cam-bodia. The situation there was unclear. Phnom Penh appeared to be completely surrounded to the north. Garnier wanted to try again, this time taking an uncertain overland route west from the river and then south to Angkor. But even if he made it, Angkor might now be cut off from Phnom Penh; indeed Phnom Penh itself could have fallen to the rebels.

As Lagrée wrestled with the problem, they paid their farewells to Bassac. The young king remained obliging and hospitable to the last; so did his subjects, especially the women. They had given their visitors a grounding in Lao customs and culture that would serve them well in the months ahead. The boat races had been the highlight and had been sketched by Delaporte with particular care. Other festivities – weddings, funerals, a weird courtship display, a wrestling match, various royal rituals, and the religious comings and goings of Bassac's sixteen monasteries – had so punctuated their stay that they ceased to snipe at Lao lethargy. 'The time did not seem long,' says Delaporte, 'because there was so much to do.' A society so frantically busy with ritual could ill afford to work.

In return for all this entertainment, the explorers had demonstrated their marksmanship, paraded their trinkets and prescribed for the sick. Garnier explained the finer points of astronomy as he made his observations, Dragon performed her repertoire of canine tricks, and Delaporte drew countless portraits. He also dug out his violin for the first time. Of an evening he would serenade his colleagues from under a nearby tamarind tree, though to mixed effect. Familiar airs, he explains, induced only homesickness. It was the Lao who were the most appreciative. Although 'La Belle Hélène' left them quite cold', more melancholic tunes 'greatly impressed them', the slower and sadder the better.

The young king himself came down to the river to see them off. Overwhelmed with parting presents that included a silver-plated rifle and portraits of Louis Napoleon and his consort, he was genuinely sad to be losing them. 'He made himself the mouthpiece of the regrets of his capital,' says de Carné. Meanwhile the entire population quietly lined the bank above. Dotted among the palms and the bamboos, they stood quite still and, without waving, 'for a long time gazed after the barges carrying their visitors to distant shores'. The vast silence of the river once again engulfed the explorers. It was 25 December. Their first Christmas on the river passed unremarked and uncelebrated.

FIVE

Separate Ways

'During our long march we requested hospitality in more than a hundred pagodas, and whether we came alone or in a group, in good health or bad, whether we stayed a night or several, we always met with the same reception, the same kindness, the same welcome ... We often talked about this among ourselves ... and could not but recognise that when it comes to toleration, any comparison [with the European missions] is entirely to the advantage of the Buddhist priests.'

LOUIS DELAPORTE

IN ASIA AS IN AFRICA the European powers often disdained naked aggression in favour of a steady colonial creep. Empire encroached, rarely charging forward with guns ablaze but preferring to insinuate itself, like floodwater on the rise, querying a border here, claiming a forgotten precedence there, and then demanding substantial compensation for both somewhere else.

The Mekong Exploration Commission's long dalliance in lower Laos looked innocent enough. In 1866 France, with only a modest holding in the Delta plus protectorate rights over the now rebellion-racked Cambodia, was not obviously poised to overrun a vast, unknown and disappointingly inaccessible wilderness. Yet for doing just that in lower Laos, the Commission had compiled such a powerful array of arguments – moral, mineral, strategic, hedonistic, archaeological – that its acquisition quickly became a basic requirement of French policy.

The actual acquisition would take time. Those heroic attempts to steam up the Falls in the early 1890s would be conducted when the river at Khon was still not technically French. Not till late 1893 would the east bank of the Falls become so, and not till 1904 the west bank – and then only as part of a wider settlement (including the return of Cambodia's 'lost' provinces) that would follow tenser stand-offs elsewhere, all of them attributable to earlier advocacy from the Mekong Exploration Commission.

The loser in all of this would, of course, be the kingdom of Siam/Thailand. French colonial promoters supposed that in south-east Asia, as in sub-Saharan Africa, anywhere not already subordinated by their British (or Portuguese, Dutch, etc.) rivals was fair game. Thailand, therefore, was no more obviously excluded from French designs in south-east Asia than Laos or Tonkin (northern Vietnam). In fact those who, like Garnier, dreamed of an all-French Indo-China assumed that it must one day include Thailand. The Mekong would be to this new empire as the Nile to Egypt, its core and lifeblood, not its outermost limit. It followed that a broad swathe of eastern and northern Thailand would have to be incorporated into the French possessions. And this would in turn raise the inviting possibility of a further extension into the adjacent Menam basin, the heartland of Thai culture and production.

From neighbouring Burma the British would contest such ambitions. With an unassailable diplomatic position in Thailand and an overwhelming share of its trade, the British already enjoyed many of the benefits of a colonial relationship without the responsibilities and expense of colonial rule. Links with the Thai court were cemented by the professional services provided by, for instance, Warington Smyth as the kingdom's mineral prospector, or Mrs Anna Leonowens, the much romanticised royal nanny of *King and I* fame. Somewhat literally, Thailand was already tied to Britannia's apron strings.

Accordingly and in an unlikely role-reversal for the world's arch-imperialist, Great Britain would boldly uphold Thai sovereignty and stand forth as the champion of just the sort of intrigue-ridden 'oriental despotism' that usually incurred heavy censure and rapid emasculation. French overtures for a compromise involving the partition of Thailand between the two European powers would be firmly rejected. According to Whitehall, only the interposition between the British and French possessions of a fully 'independent' and 'neutral' buffer state could prevent a clash of the colonial titans. To this end, if no other, Thailand must be preserved.

And so it was. But the price eventually paid by Bangkok for retaining its independent existence would be the surrender of most of its Lao dependencies, including all those east of the Mekong. And thanks largely to the rosy views of the Mekong Exploration Commission, this retraction would be taken to an extreme in lower Laos. There, as well as the stone bridge at Ban Khon and that sad little tank-engine, the Commission's legacy still lingers on in a blatant piece of border engineering.

For a good fifteen hundred kilometres, and with only one other exception, Laos's present-day border with Thailand follows the course of the Mekong. But above Pakse, with a mere 120 kilometres to go before the river rampages into Cambodia, the border unexpectedly acquires a mind of its own. Deserting the middle of the river, it steers for the west bank, scrambles up it, and makes for a line of hills tending still further westward. By the time this final section of the Thai–Lao border meets the Cambodian border, it is eighty kilometres from the river. A jagged triangle on the west bank of the Mekong that might otherwise have remained under Thai rule has thus been, as it were, wrenched away from it and awarded to Laos, itself by 1904 under French rule. Predictably the triangle includes the still dreamy township of Bassac (now Champassak) and the Angkorian remains of Wat Phou (now a World Heritage Site), plus all of the Four Thousand

Islands (Khong and Khon among them) and both sides of the Khon Falls.

Just north of where the border strikes off on its own, the river is joined by the Se Moun, a west bank tributary from what is still just Thailand. Fifty kilometres up the Se Moun, the town of Ubon (now Ubon Ratchathani) was the expedition's next goal. In what was even then the first place with urban pretensions that they had encountered since Phnom Penh, Lagrée hoped for information on the river route to Vientiane, and Garnier for information on a land route back to Angkor, Phnom Penh and their Chinese passports.

The two-week voyage from Bassac to Ubon proved comparatively uneventful. Above where Pakse now stands, the Mekong narrowed to just two hundred metres yet was so deep that Garnier's seventy-metre plumb-line failed to find the bottom. Dr Joubert, their best shot, bagged a hare. It served all six of them as a New Year's feast, by which date they had turned into the Se Moun and encountered its first rapids. The boats had to be unloaded, the loads carried and the boats themselves dragged round the rapids. The whole armada then repacked for the short run up to another line of rocks and another portage. 'We passed from one year into the next, exhausted by our efforts,' says Garnier.

The news gleaned at Ubon was both good and indifferent – good in respect of reaching Cambodia, indifferent so far as the river was concerned. Carefully digested, it resulted in the division of the expedition's personnel into another three-pronged manoeuvre.

Garnier was again to attempt a dash back to Cambodia for the Chinese passports. A route to the south-west circling round the rebel-held territory in Cambodia was thought feasible for someone travelling light and at the height of the dry season. It would bring him down to the Great Lake near Angkor, from where the Tonle Sap river-route to Phnom Penh might still be possible. Having collected the Chinese passports, he was to return with all speed by the same trail, then follow the Mekong north until he eventually overhauled the main expedition. No one knew the time this would take, only that 'it would probably be quite long'. Lagrée and the rest, not without anxiety, bade him God's speed and farewell on 10 January 1867.

A week later they saw off Delaporte. Assistant hydrographer as well as artist, he was to take over Garnier's duties by voyaging alone back down the Se Moun to its confluence with the Mekong and then recommencing the ascent of the main river. Meanwhile the rest of the party, plus all the heavy baggage, would take an overland shortcut from Ubon to a place higher up the Mekong called Kemarat. There they would rendezvous with Delaporte and then continue along the river to Vientiane with many a backward glance for the returning Garnier.

These elaborate dispositions were prompted by a growing awareness that the journey was taking much longer than antici-pated. Originally they had thought in months; now they contem-plated years. Lagrée estimated that they would be lucky to reach Luang Prabang before the next rains in June. Luang Prabang was still five hundred kilometres short of the China border; and they would there have to sit out the rains, 'which seemed [says Garnier] to defer to the next dry season – for another year in other words – any serious exploration'.

Lagrée ascribed their troubles to the endless delays caused by having to commandeer new boats whenever they passed from the jurisdiction of one *muang* to the next. This happened at least twice a week and would, it appeared, become still more frequent in the months ahead, *muangs* being thicker along the banks upriver than down. The Thai letters which entitled them to this gratis transport were beginning to look like a mixed blessing. Gifts or bribes – the difference lying in the importunity with which they were solicited – had invariably to be paid to the local officials before river craft actually materialised. Even if Lagrée had not been in the habit of then rewarding every boatman, any saving in cash was negated by the time wasted in making these arrangements.

But if they were going to pay their way regardless, the obvious solution was to ignore their entitlement as per Bangkok's letters, hire their own transport for as long as suited them, and so evade the *muang*-to-*muang* changeovers. Lagrée liked this idea, and tried it. At Ubon he bypassed the local officials and let it be known that the expedition was offering attractive rates for porters and wagons willing to undertake the overland trek to Kemarat. No one applied. 'They seemed almost indifferent,' says de Carné, 'doubting, perhaps, whether our promises could be trusted.' Evidently the Lao laboured only when ordered to do so. Paid employment was a novelty with subversive connotations in that it was taken to mean that the foreigners had been refused official status. Such, sighed de Carné, was the reason for the Lao's chronic 'laziness', such 'the rudimentary state of civilisation in these parts'. In the end Lagrée was obliged to swallow his pride and go, tail between legs, to the 'king' of Ubon with his Bangkok letters. 'At a word from His Majesty' fifteen assorted ox and buffalo carts, fifty men and six elephants 'gathered as if by enchantment'.

Garnier, too, had fretted over the delays, but he blamed them on precisely this enormous carriage requirement. He thought the constant changeovers were a problem because of the excessive number of men, boats or wagons needed at each. The expedition, in other words, was far too big and far too encumbered. At Ubon, he says, 'I insisted to M. de Lagrée that we must reduce our staff and I offered to escort those laid off [back] to Angkor.' He was thinking especially of the French members of their military escort – the two soldiers and the two sailors. They had been recruited too hastily and showed little interest in the enterprise. In fact they were now proving a liability. One had run amok with a rifle in Bassac; crazed by alcohol and the attentions of a particularly determined lover, he had terrorised the place for several days and only been subdued with the assistance of the local militia. Garnier made it clear that he wanted rid of both him and his colleagues.

A less temperate leader than Lagrée might have taken exception to such implied criticism of his men from a hot-headed young lieutenant. But as so often over the ensuing months, *le Commandant* nodded a weary concurrence and offered no objection. 'Mademoiselle Buonaparte' had got her way; all but one of the troublesome 'other ranks' duly accompanied Garnier back to Cambodia.

Yet, even without them, without Garnier himself, without Delaporte, his sketching materials and the surveying instruments, and without the original wherewithal for a travelling bakery and a fair-sized cellar, the party still needed all of those fifteen carts, fifty porters and six elephants. Garnier was right. As Lagrée would eventually concede, the problem was not the men but the baggage – the brass wire, the silver ticals, the glass trinkets, the bolts of cotton. Slightly better progress was possible by curtailing the side excursions, scaling down the colonial survey to concentrate on the river, and spurning doe-eyed distractions in favour of sterner considerations, like cash flow and survival. But for the 'serious exploration' after which Garnier hankered, the only solution would be to abandon their baggage, travel light, and be prepared to rough it.

Once clear of Ubon, each of the expedition's three prongs enjoyed wholly predictable fortunes. Garnier sustained a personal tragedy, performed feats of endurance, took appalling risks, and invariably triumphed over every challenge. Delaporte, travelling in a succession of small canoes, surmounted a most turbulent section of the river, made friends everywhere, and clearly enjoyed himself. And the main party, with de Carné as chronicler, slogged glumly across a parched and wearisome landscape with little to be said for it – or of it.

'Everything was dry, withered, burned up,' recorded de Carné. Though it was still January (and so five months ahead of the monsoon), 'all nature seemed to be sighing for the rains'. Dust thickly powdered the leaves of the stunted trees and was so deep underfoot that the wagons sank to their axles and the buffaloes to their bellies. The lighter ox-drawn carts did better, but they too had to be exchanged for more porters at one of the inevitable changeovers. Now with a pedestrian following of around two hundred, the expedition forged on through a baked desert of rice stubble. The heat was unbearable, the water undrinkable. Only the elephants met with general approval. They were mainly for riding and, though changed frequently and far from comfortable, were slightly kinder to stiff Gallic joints than the springless carts.

When after ten days they neared the river, Lagrée and his companions sighed with heartfelt relief. It was like passing into a different world. The shade of the forest closed around them, its trees as majestic as ever and its foliage a symphony of eye-soothing greens. The river itself, here comparatively docile, greeted them with cool breezes and open vistas. Its damascened waters were now familiar, its gurgle reassuring and its northward course full of promise. While the elephants gorged themselves on bamboo, the men did likewise on luscious mangoes. De Carné, though no lover of boats, hailed their first pirogue like an old and incorrigible friend. By common consent the passenger's half-sitting, half-lying posture, though once deemed so excruciating, was infinitely preferable to being jolted to jelly on the back of an elephant or broken to bits on the bed of a cart.

At Kemarat, Delaporte awaited them. The local chief had been primed to expect important visitors, and a large *sala* (pavilion) had been constructed for their reception. Had the village possessed a red carpet, it would undoubtedly have featured in Delaporte's

Delaporte greets Lagrée and the other members of the expedition at Kemarat.

finished painting of the occasion – an unusually grand tableau which might have served nicely for the meeting, five years later, of Stanley and Livingstone.

[Mounted on the elephants] *the retinue made a dazzling entry amidst the assembled population. Dr Joubert was in front, carrying in his arms his poor dog Fox, who was sick and emaciated. Then came Dr Thorel and M. de Carné, rifles over their shoulders. Our Annamites* [Vietnamese] *and Tagals* [Filipinos] *marched happily on foot, their bags and rifles on their backs. Finally the only remaining Frenchman of the escort,* matelot *Moëlho, a loyal and courageous Breton, pre-ceded* le Commandant *de Lagrée . . . We exchanged cordial handshakes and quickly told one another of the principal events of our different journeys.*

In this exchange of travellers' tales, Delaporte undoubtedly came off best. On the Se Moun he had met a woman who had just been mauled by a tiger, his boatmen had started a forest fire which was probably still burning, fish had been so plentiful that they could be hauled out by hand – and all this before he had reached the Mekong itself, there 'to resume the exploration of one of its most extraordinary and dangerous sections'.

The reported difficulties of the rapids below Kemarat were what had persuaded Lagrée to strike out overland and so spare the main expedition more watery delays and upsets. Delaporte heartily approved of his leader's decision the moment his boat entered the main river. He was expecting surprises, but 'the reality would surpass my expectations'. Though still calm and unruffled, the flow quickly became constricted between near-vertical walls of rock. At one point it was barely 120 metres wide. Wondering what had become of a flood that was over two kilometres across at Bassac (and sixteen at Khon), Delaporte heaved his plumb-line overboard. He added further rope when it failed to ground, then tied on anything else he could find, including some coiled lianas that were lying in the boat. 'And still I had not reached the bottom.' He concluded that beneath his pirogue 'there was more than a hundred metres of water'.

In places the Mekong hereabouts is indeed deeper than it is

wide, a phenomenon not unusual among bounding mountain torrents but unheard of in the stately middle reaches of a mature
waterway. It was as if the river had grown tired of lying on its
back and had rolled onto its side, so burying its broadest dimension
and presenting to view only a slender flank. The impression was
sustained by the 'enormous fish' that also flopped playfully on
their sides just below the surface and 'spouted water when they
breathed'. They were possibly Irrawaddy dolphins, though the
species is now almost unknown above the Falls. Alternatively this
was the expedition's first recorded sighting of the truly enormous,
and now even rarer, *pa beuk*, the Giant Mekong Catfish.

Not unlike a denizen of the deep, at the head of this trench
the river itself seemed to come up for air, suddenly breaking the
surface with an explosion of white water. Evidently divided by an
island jumble of house-size rocks, the two descending arms here
reunited to form the first of what would be revealed as a series of
sensational rapids. They kept Delaporte busy for the next five days.
Taking his hydrographic responsibilities seriously, he criss-crossed
the torrents to take angles from both banks, to observe the sun at
midday for latitude, and to plumb the depths for navigational
potential. His only companion was 'an interpreter', presumably the
Lao ex-monk Alévy. Otherwise he relied on local boatmen whose
small canoes were easily hefted round the worst cataracts.

There was much to be said for this simpler form of travel.
Delaporte slept where there was cover and ate when there was
food. Game abounded in the forest. He saw deer, wild boar, 'wild
cows' (water buffalo?), alligators, and numerous kinds of monkey.
Early mornings were disturbed by the trumpeting of elephant
herds and nights by the growling of tigers. Although both were
best avoided, he confessed to being grateful to the tigers. Easily
scared, they often abandoned a kill almost untouched. The
expedition made many such finds, and frankly, says Delaporte,
'the big game we ate was more commonly killed by a tiger than

by ourselves'. With the possible exception of Dr Joubert, none of the explorers had much experience of rough shooting, nor did they 'possess the equipment of professional hunters'. 'Generally we just opened fire at anything that happened to cross our path.' Peacocks suffered most, they being large, slow and noisy enough to attract even an amateur's fire. Delaporte reckoned them good eating, and found their feathers prized by the womenfolk.

The distinctive feature of the rapids as he approached Kemarat was their whirlpools. He had never seen anything like them. They gouged deep craters in the current and were matched by humped blisters of up-swelling water. The whole river was heaving like a lunar landscape before the rocks cooled. Mostly the whirlpools formed beside and below the foaming rapids and continued on downstream in a regular sequence on either side of the main current, like footprints left by a water-walking elephant. The largest were several metres wide, with vortices equally deep. They would swallow a canoe without trace, and were carefully avoided by the large rafts of bamboos that were occasionally piked downstream. How a steam launch would fare amid them Delaporte could not imagine. But half a century later, when Marthe Bassenne rode the Khon railway and then continued upriver aboard the *Garcerie*, it was these hazards that constituted the highlight of the voyage. Khon's train ride had been worth only a paragraph in her journal; the passage of the Kemarat rapids ran to five pages.

Extra timber had had to be taken on board the *Garcerie* the previous day. At 3 a.m. Madame Bassenne was awoken by a frantic stoking of boilers. Deck passengers were ordered inside and told to keep very still 'in anticipation of a panic situation that might hurl them all to the same side'.

At 7 a.m. a shout was heard: 'The Rapid!' I ran to the front [writes Bassenne]. *Before us were walls of foam, snouts of rock and whirlpools that, in line ahead, blocked the current perpendicularly . . . The waves rose upwards, overwhelming us; water streamed over the bow; the lower bridge was swept away. Beneath us the current swelled like a heaving flank. To right and left, hollows were bored into the surface forming large bowls in which dirty crests of foam appeared to boil. Not once did the captain leave the helm.*

With engines straining, funnel belching, and the whole shuddering vessel tipped at an alarming angle, they inched through the barrier of rocks. The *Garcerie* righted herself and the engines slowed. They were past the first rapid.

Bassenne, her feet soaked by the inrushing water, 'complained a bit' and was shouted down by her fellow passengers. Then suddenly she was hurled to the ground by an almighty thud and sent rolling across the floor.

I cried out – and this time the locals did the same. 'Shut up,' snapped the Captain, 'it's nothing, just the slight caress of a rock!' We were in another rapid! Hopefully the leak wouldn't prove serious! . . . The rock was clearly visible on the left side just next to the boat. On the right we were on the brink of an immense whirlpool. We dared not advance, the situation was critical, the minutes long.

Reversing one of the engines, the captain slewed the ship away from the rock and somehow 'braced it against the edge of the whirlpool'. The manoeuvre worked, and they pounded on to the third rapid. There, possibly because the timber must by now have been thoroughly drenched by the splashing river water, the boiler pressure fell and the ship began to lose way. 'I noticed this by observing the reference markers on the bank,' says Bassenne. Lusty shouts of 'Go to it, stokers!' did the trick. The engine picked up and they nosed back into calmer waters.

The next rapids were not dangerous, merely 'delightful', in fact 'beautiful'.

And the scent, the sweet scent of Laos, reasserted itself as if to compensate for our day's exertions. Simultaneously a sensation of mystery, of intense, keenly felt melancholy descended upon us.

The *Garcerie* made it up to Savannakhet, the next town, but had there to be retired from service for repairs to the damaged hull. Marthe Bassenne's trip, its first run of the year, was also its last. Even in their heyday the timetable of Mekong sailings operated by the government-funded *Messageries Fluviales* would be a bad joke.

As for Delaporte, though less susceptible to the sweet scent of mystery and melancholy, he was rewarded for surmounting the rapids by the company of his colleagues and by a musical *soirée* in a nearby village. The Lao had a better understanding of music than either the Vietnamese or the Chinese. He sketched their instruments and contributed pages of musical notation to the expedition's journal. As 'duet for *clui* and *khen*' or 'tune with variations for *khen*', they made a change from Thorel's botanical cataloguing and Garnier's tabulated log of distances and bearings.

In all, two weeks were passed at Kemarat. Joubert went in search of some non-existent iron mines, Thorel concentrated on fruit trees and resins, Lagrée visited the *sauvage* tribes on the east bank, and de Carné tagged along with Delaporte as he completed his hydrographic work on the rapids and hung about the villages with his music-loving acquaintances.

They left on 14 February. Six pirogues carried them up the river, which was at first divided into many channels, all of them paddle-able, then melded into a gleaming expanse, more lake than river, that stretched away to the north as far as the eye could see.

'I shall not weary the reader with giving all the stations on our route,' says de Carné. Savannakhet on the east (Lao) bank and Mukdahan, its bustling ferry partner on the west (Thai) bank, did not then exist. In fact there were no towns and not many villages. Delaporte found consolation in the quality of the light. To an artist the 'unforgettable effulgence' of a tropical sun redeemed any natural monotony. It gave to the river the fascination of a countenance and to the vegetation a sparkle of wit. With the waters nearing their lowest, sandbars and lagoons fringed the steeply terraced banks, above which towered the interminable forest. 'Indeed,' wrote Delaporte, 'our whole odyssey could be said to be taking place in one unending forest. We entered it in Cambodia and we were not going to be out of it until we set foot in China.'

Every river has its less sensational reaches. The three hundred untroubled kilometres above Kemarat are as near to boring as the Mekong ever gets. For the same reason this section also rates as its most navigable. Here the *Messageries Fluviales*' timetable would actually mean something. 'Between Savannakhet and Vientiane' Marthe Bassenne would be pleased to learn that 'one can safely sail around the year by steamer.' One could also sail around the clock. With only brief refuelling stops, the *Colombert* (to which she had been transferred from the crippled *Garcerie*) ploughed on through the hours of darkness to complete the whole leg in two days.

Briefly in the early twentieth century, part of the river here performed the service for which Garnier had considered it intended, that of uniting the lands along its banks. Linking the capital of Vientiane to lower Laos, this section was always much its busiest. Yet ironically the same section is today one of its least frequented. Where barges might still be a sensible option for the transport of timber and rice, and where passenger launches might usefully ply the riverside towns, scarcely a vessel is to be found.

Not even the yellow speedboats that shatter the peace upriver are to be met with. Having failed so dismally to live up to earlier expectations, the Mekong has here been rewarded with enforced redundancy.

Among the several novelties – houses on stilts, beer in flagons, flowers in hair – encountered by anyone entering Laos today, those who do so at the Khon Falls also find a road. On landing at Voen Kham the newcomer rouses Lao Immigration from their day-long siesta, buys some *kip* (the well-named Lao currency) and advances into a prickly hinterland. The rutted track that supposedly skirts the impediment of the Falls seems to be going nowhere, and the impinging vegetation leaves only a narrow right of way that spiders span with webs of bungee elasticity. Because partially obscured by a curtain of bamboos, it is easy to miss the road sign announcing a T-junction. A clearing follows, in which, as unexpectedly as a low-flying jet, there swoops across the trail the mirage that is Route Nationale 13. A two-lane highway with a double white line down the middle, it shimmers in the heat between well-cleared verges. There being no suggestion of traffic, you turn left for Laos, right for Cambodia.

That was the intention, anyway. In fact, the right turn is not a serious option. Within less than braking distance the pristine tarmac slithers into a tangled wall of undergrowth and expires at the base of a stately *dipterocarpus*. Until Cambodia recognises roadbuilding as relevant to national reconstruction, there is no reciprocal highway to which RN13 can connect. The dead end could not be deader.

Turn left, on the other hand, and the RN13 – or 'Mekong Highway' – runs smoothly north, with only minor hiccups, for the eight hundred kilometres to Vientiane, plus a further three hundred to Luang Prabang. Though perversely numbered (or just superstitiously so, for thirteen is thought lucky in Laos), it is in fact the nation's number one artery, the only surfaced trunk road in the entire country, and a monument to the Lao People's Democratic Republic's proud surge into the twenty-first century. It was completed in 1999, from which date the utility of the Mekong as a means of limited communication may be said to have ceased.

All travellers, all freight and all livestock now go by road. Probably cheaper, it is certainly quicker. But the road is not a busy one. Laos, a country the size of the British Isles with fewer inhabitants than Scotland, has a small travelling public and a limited haulage requirement. Lumber trucks use RN13 only to get across it, then down to the nearest ferry to Thailand. Bottled soft drinks, audio-visual appliances, nylon fishing nets and earthmoving machinery enter Laos the same way.

RN13 is more symbolic than commercial. Like the defunct *Messageries Fluviales* or the valiant Lao Aviation, it serves received ideas about how an independent nation state ought to be articulated. Tour buses can now run from Vientiane to the Khon Falls without ever leaving Laos. In the other direction it is possible to ride on public transport from the dead end at Voen Kham past Pakse, Savannakhet and Thakhek to reach the capital in a single day. Throughout, the road runs parallel to the river, rarely actually skirting it but never more than a day's rough march from its eastern bank.

It also parallels, even parodies, the only other north–south road in Lao history. A more notorious trail, this snaked through the hills just fifty kilometres to the east. By demonstrating the possibilities of wheeled transport in an otherwise roadless region, it set a precedent for RN13 that spelled death to any other form of transport. Developed in the 1960s, and always more a network of tracks than a single highway, the Ho Chi Minh Trail was never entirely motorable, though everywhere lethal. In its heyday it carried much more traffic than has any subsequent road in Laos, including the RN13. Bicycles by the thousand jammed its slippery gradients; mountain caves became repair shops and service stations; motor vehicles could be backed up for weeks. Unlike the road, the Trail was emphatically not symbolic. Mostly it was invisible; officially it did not exist. But it was a lifeline for the Viet Cong operating in what was then the Republic of South Vietnam, and without it the Vietnam war might have turned out differently.

When in the mid-1950s the French withdrew from Indo-China (following defeat at Dien Bien Phu and a peace conference at Geneva), Vietnam was effectively divided into a Communist North and a non-Communist South. The dividing line was at the seventeenth parallel, which – as Delaporte had just deduced from his solar observations – crosses the Mekong about eighty kilometres north of Kemarat. Over the hills to the east Vietnam is here at its narrowest, a mere sliver about fifty kilometres wide between the South China Sea and the Lao border on the Mekong watershed. Easily monitored then, the dividing line and the Demilitarised Zone (DMZ) severed contact not only between North and South Vietnam but also between Hanoi and its guerrilla sympathisers in the South, principally the so-called Viet Cong. The only way to direct, provision, arm and reinforce the Viet Cong, and the only way for the North Vietnamese army to infiltrate the South, was to develop a clandestine supply route that bypassed both the DMZ and the hostile forces in the South. That meant trespassing into the territory of then neutral Laos. Hence Hanoi's decade-long insistence that no such trail existed.

In fact, during the late 1960s and early seventies over half a million combatants passed up and down the Trail – on foot, on bikes, in lorries, on stretchers. So did several million tons of armaments, munitions and provisions. The Trail was extended down to the Bolovens plateau for access to the Delta and Cambodia; elsewhere it was frequently realigned; and increasingly it was fortified with bunkers, artillery and anti-aircraft batteries. For over this route that did not exist, through a country that was not involved, there soon raged a war that was not acknowledged.

The logic of denial was faultless. Since the neutrality of Laos was solemnly guaranteed by international agreements, the only war there must be a civil war. Hanoi denied having troops in the country; Washington denied bombing them. Neither was a combatant in Laos, hence neither was accountable for the tens of thousands killed and maimed along the non-existent Trail, nor for the millions of tons of high explosives and chemical defoliants dropped on it. So emphatically was 'Lay-oss' neutral that neutrality became its best-known characteristic. A world ignorant of its geography and unsure of its national credentials knew only of its non-alignment. Indeed the country was so neutral – and the war there so not an international war – that campus slogans objecting to the US presence in Vietnam or the bombing in Cambodia never demanded that anyone 'Lay off Lay-oss'. It was a war so secret it evaded even protest.

Those who knew better said little. As the CIA took control of the unacknowledged operations in Laos, the Mekong towns on both sides of the river experienced an unprecedented boom. From Pakse, Savannakhet and Vientiane, as well as from various bases in Thailand, the reconnaissance and supply flights were non-stop. A surrogate army raised from the Hmong hill people of Laos's Xieng Khouang province had to be trained, armed and provisioned. In the neighbouring provinces of Khammouan and Bolikhamxai on the Vietnam border, news of enemy concentrations along the Ho Chi Minh Trail had to be relayed daily to the B-52s flying out of Guam and the Philippines.

Compared to the carnage in Vietnam itself or the post-war killing in Khmer Rouge Cambodia, the scale of the Lao tragedy was modest. Thankfully, the heaviest bombardment in history was visited on an elusive target moving through sparsely populated forest and mountain. The local inhabitants, mostly hill peoples, or *sauvages*, rapidly dispersed; and to an area still boasting more unexploded ordnance than anywhere else on earth, they have been slow to return. Later the US-funded Hmong (Meo) army with its coterie of maverick CIA advisers would also disperse. In 1973–75, deserted by the disengaging Americans and dislodged by the advancing Communists, the Hmong descended towards the Mekong. Resettlement elsewhere in Laos had been promised, but was not forthcoming. Faced with a choice between a Pathet Lao re-education camp and a Thai refugee camp, thirty thousand chose the latter and streamed across the river. Of those who safely made the crossing, many would eventually be resettled in the United States.

The heaviest casualties were sustained by the Vietnamese on the Trail itself. Yet the loss of life signally failed to interdict its use. Though bombarded and strafed, deluged with defoliants, detergents and bomblets, bugged by sensors, scanned by beacons and eventually assaulted by ground forces, the traffic on the Trail just kept on coming. By 1969 up to nine hundred sorties a day were being flown against it, but to little effect. The Vietnamese supply operation scarcely faltered. The war in the South was sustained thanks to the Trail, and the war with the Americans was won thanks to this sustained resistance in the South.

Air power had proved ineffectual. The runways bequeathed by the war would guarantee a future for civil aviation in Laos, but if a jungle trail could supply an army and unite a nation, there was no point in building railways or agonising over river transport. For the newly installed People's Government of the Lao Democratic Republic the priority would be roads.

It is thanks to this emphasis, as well as to the natural difficulties of the river, that the Mekong in Laos retains its untamed and untravelled aspect. Lagrée and his men would have no difficulty in recognising it today. Rejoining its course after some dusty overland excursion, they would still be rejoiced by its pristine verdure, awed by its silent grandeur and beguiled by its few peoples. Between Kemarat and Vientiane the forest is perhaps more patchy and the market gardening along the riverbed more intensive. But here too, as elsewhere, for endless miles, nature reigns unchecked. Lining the banks, thickets of bamboo cast their tendrils on the current like competition anglers. Wild banana plants crane to watch from a tangle of ferns, and the forest crowds them both, pushing to the water's edge in a collective mass that denies the identity of individual trees. In chaotic abandon foliage of infinite variety cascades from what ought to be the treetops – except that from the top of this wall of verdure rises a colonnade of trunks whose sky-spread branches eventually brace a whole new storey of airy leaf and errant creeper.

Seen from the other side of the river, the forest composes itself into the foreground of a still grander landscape of lumpy karst protuberances and tousled crags that extend untouched to a fairy-tale horizon. The skyline of Lakon (near Thakhek) seemed to de Carné to have been composed 'by some mad geometer'. No two hills are alike, 'each doing as it pleases without troubling about its neighbours'. Turreted towers jostle domed mausolea. Madcap gables frame sky-filled apertures. Festooned with vegetation, the fantastic shapes recall a lost city. Entering an amphitheatre of vertical walls, Delaporte reported 'embrasures, truncated cones, spires, rocks in the most bizarre forms, all fashioned by natural architecture and recalling the ornamentation of our old gothic cathedrals'.

In such surroundings the sunsets command awed reverence, and storms trouble the spirit like a *Götterdämmerung*. Today the only serious omission from the river of the 1860s is the soundtrack – the screech of peafowl, the trumpeting of elephants, the sharp bark of the deer and the groaning of tigers. In the last thirty years Laos is said to have lost an alarming 40 per cent of its primary forest, but in the process appears to have exterminated a near 100 per cent of its wildlife. The occasional eagle, the dart of a kingfisher and the pipe of a sandpiper are pitiful compensation.

Lagrée had seen a rhinoceros in the Bolovens region; the forest was everywhere alive with monkeys and squirrels; in the 'Land of a Million Elephants' family groups of up to twenty 'proboscideans' were an everyday hazard. Now even tame elephants are rarely met with. Tigers, rhinos and all manner of more exotic creatures may well survive, but only in the remotest of regions. The most likely places are said to be in the untrod forests of Khammouan and Bolikhamxai provinces along the Vietnamese border, in other words precisely the tracts crossed by the Ho Chi Minh Trail. The forest is evidently more forgiving than its inhabitants. The scars of defoliation have largely healed and the unexploded cluster bombs and personnel mines claim fewer limbs from cautious quadrupeds than they do from inquisitive bipeds. By keeping human settlement at bay, the lethal bounty of the B-52 may claim to have done its bit for wildlife conservation.

The Mekong Exploration Commission's closest encounter with a tiger came the way of Francis Garnier as he returned from his long detour back to Cambodia for the Chinese passports. Approaching a village at dusk in search of somewhere to sleep, he heard 'piercing cries'. He pushed on regardless and suddenly, 'just a few metres away', he noticed a violent thrashing in the foliage. A tiger bounded forth, and it appeared to be 'dragging along a child'.

Firing my revolver at the animal, crying out to my porters to throw down their loads and follow me, we all dashed in pursuit of the ferocious beast, shouting at it. A few minutes later we

Wild elephants bathing in the river.

came upon the child, which the animal, either frightened or wounded, had dropped in its flight. The child was four or five years old, and its continued screams afforded abundant proof of its not yet having breathed its last. I rushed to retrieve it and, turning it over and over, could find not a single scratch.

Naturally the parents were delighted and took the gun-toting blackbeard who had materialised from nowhere for 'some kind of death-dealing, life-saving deity'. He was instantly fêted by the whole village and gifted enough pigs and chickens to start a farm. 'They desperately wanted me to stay with them and promised me the freedom of the forest,' he says. 'I have often wondered since whether I did not let slip a unique opportunity of there living the good life in peace and happiness.'

A few days later he came face to face with a leopard up a tree. Unarmed, he retreated backwards towards his camp, moving very slowly and never taking his gaze from the cat, which followed him step for step. It was waiting for him to stumble, he says, but fled when it heard the voices of his men. These things happened to Garnier. They were not implausible. The solitary traveller was both more likely to surprise a wild beast and less likely to be able to muster any corroboration.

The excursion to Cambodia had tested him to the utmost. A marathon of endurance, it had been dogged by danger and marred from the start by a singular tragedy. Garnier could hardly bring himself to describe it. How, he wondered rhetorically, could he tell in sober prose of the ghastly event which had imparted to his solitary journey such acute sadness? 'It was the death of my faithful Dragon.'

So named after the gunboat on which she had been born off the China coast, Dragon cannot have been more than ten years old. But in the East the years could be as hard on dogs as on men. Dragon had given birth to several litters and had delighted the whole colony with her tricks. She was now, though, past the age when a five-thousand-kilometre walk in the woods held much attraction. She wanted only to while away her remaining years in the comfort of her Saigon home. The expedition was asking a lot of her, and her master knew it.

In Cambodia Dragon had begun to evince senile tendencies – 'she remained obedient but was no longer affectionate' – then suicidal tendencies. Either that or she was faithfully following her master's example. For like him, she repeatedly threw herself into the river and had to be fished out half-drowned and at great risk to her rescuers. The final straw had come when Garnier had broken away from the rest of the party at Ubon, and Dragon had had to part from her friend Fox. Fox, though presumably younger, had been a good ally and an attentive companion. Seeing Joubert, with Fox by his side, wave them off 'was too much for her', says Garnier. The following night Dragon curled up beside him in his boat as was her wont, gave him a few licks more than usually tender, and was gone by the morning. She was never seen again. Garnier prowled the banks of the Se Moun calling her name; enquiries were spread about the countryside. He could only suppose that she had drowned or been devoured by a tiger.

Grim-faced and grief-stricken, he had turned his back on the Se Moun, obtained ox carts for the baggage, and force-marched his men across a plateau. The plateau ended in a near-perpendicular drop to the Cambodian plain. It could only be negotiated by unyoking the oxen, dismantling the carts, and leading the former while manhandling the latter. No water, little shade and a merciless sun made for exhausting work, but once on the plain the going was easier. He resisted the temptation to inspect several unknown Angkorian sites and reached Angkor itself three weeks after leaving Ubon.

There the Thai authorities painted a grim picture of the rebellion in Norodom's kingdom. Many more provinces were by now affected, the Tonle Sap river was in rebel hands, and Phnom Penh itself had recently been besieged. Although troops sent from Saigon, aided by the game little *canonnières*, had since relieved the siege, Garnier would be most unwise to continue his journey, and the Thai governor could not permit him to do so. He, however, insisted. 'I had not come so far only to retrace my steps without obtaining the long-awaited mail.' He drafted a letter exonerating the Thai authorities and persuaded the governor to lend him 'a big strong barge'. No Cambodians were willing to man it, but from among the Vietnamese fishing fleet on the Great Lake he recruited a stalwart crew and sailed south on 3 February.

Next day 'we entered enemy waters'. He had equipped the barge with axes for cutting through any barricades and with guns for all the men. They were not needed. On the lake they bluffed the challenge of two warlike vessels; then along the Tonle Sap river, though they heard war drums summoning the rebel forces to resist them, 'by the time they had managed this, the current had put us beyond their reach'. This being the height of the dry season, the Tonle Sap river was running strongly towards Phnom Penh and the Mekong.

The French in Phnom Penh were as amazed to see Garnier as he was delighted to be there. He submitted a report on the Commission's progress and learned of the short Austro–Prussian war of 1866 which foreshadowed the greater Franco–Prussian tussle of four years later. Half the expedition's mail was still stuck in Saigon; so were the instruments he had requested. Such 'care-lessness . . . forgetfulness' he had come to take for granted. But at least the documentation from Beijing had arrived.

Just forty-eight hours after landing at Phnom Penh, while the town was engrossed in celebrating the Chinese New Year, Garnier slipped away again. He was back in Angkor by 13 February, and clambering onto the Thai plateau by the eighteenth. Travelling with a single Vietnamese servant, he dispensed with carts and resolved to walk the rest of the way, hiring porters as required.

Porters came in different guises. Beyond Ubon the harvest was in progress and only girls were available. A dozen of these damsels, 'eighteen to twenty years old', answered the call but seemed to treat the march as a picnic. It was, says Garnier, a particularly hot day; yet he wondered at their passion for swimming. At every spring and stream they downed loads, removed their *langoutis*, and 'in the garb of Eden bathed and showered without the least embarrassment about the foreigner observing their frolics'. Clearly a little miffed at this unconcern, he supposed that it had something to do with his abundant beard. Since only the most geriatric Lao patriarchs had any facial hair at all, the girls must imagine him to be 'at least a century old'. 'I never tried to disabuse them,' he writes, as if genuinely convinced by an explanation that was no less artful than the girls' nudity. He, like they, had an audience to consider.

He struck the Mekong where Mukdahan now is, and there at last found news of Lagrée and his colleagues. They had passed through ten days earlier. To recline in a pirogue after marching more than 240 kilometres in a week was bliss. Relieved in mind and body, Garnier could at last relax. The river here had already been surveyed by Delaporte. He simply sat back and savoured the welcome ahead. He had been away just over two months and had covered, he reckoned, 1600 kilometres.

On 10 March young de Carné was daydreaming in a shady pavilion above the river near Uthen. Still suffering from intermittent fever and the light-headedness which accompanied it, he had been excused the day's duties. The river ran broad and smooth as a mirror of steel; the sky, 'like a white-hot metal basin', burned his eyes. 'As always my thoughts had turned, in a kind of half-sleep, to France when suddenly whoops of joy told me that we were about to hear from it. M. Garnier had arrived.'

For once de Carné was genuinely pleased to see his tormentor. Here at last were the Chinese passports, a few letters from home, and the latest journals. Barely listening to Garnier's well-honed account of his exploits, his companions devoured their first news of the outside world in nine months.

The turmoil in Cambodia no longer concerned them; with the Chinese passports to hand, there was no need now to contemplate a withdrawal downriver. Rumours of strife in Yunnan were more worrying; if the valley of the upper Mekong had thrown off Chinese allegiance, the passports would be useless. But most ominous of all for patriotic officers was the Prussian victory in Germany. A 'near and terrible war involving France itself' seemed inevitable. The thought made them more homesick than ever. For de Carné, it was this news 'more than any other incident in the whole trying journey' – a bold statement given his declining health – that made him regret having joined the expedition.

Lagrée, as usual, kept his thoughts to himself. It therefore fell to Garnier to rally the party with the sort of exhortation he felt called for.

The passports from China that I had just obtained enabled us to prosecute the journey to the fullest possible extent. For the first time in three months we were finally all reunited around the chief of the expedition, full of energy and health [de Carné's malaria evidently did not count]. *After a long initial period of feeling our way, we would now proceed with the confident, precise and swift execution of the programme that had been proposed.*

Whether or not resented at the time, such presumption would later be held against Garnier. It was not for him to make good the taciturn and throat-sore silence of their leader. Nor was it such a good idea to tempt fate with confident talk of speedy progress.

SIX

❖

River Rivals

'The events in which I had taken part [at Paklai] gave me a chance
to devote myself to the common good and to sow without effort
the germ of an amiable disposition towards France in Laos. I
had not dared to hope for such a rapid outcome. It was ample
compensation for my rebuff in the direction of Tonkin; and I and
my men were more convinced than ever that, without serious new
obstacles, success lay within our grasp.'

AUGUSTE PAVIE,
A la Conquête des Coeurs

As if LAOS were not labouring under enough handicaps,
great uncertainty surrounds the spelling of its place names.
Nearly all are descriptive, and since many are therefore duplicated,
custom sanctions alternative Roman renderings for the same name
when it crops up in quite different locations. The spelling of
the eastern province of Xieng Khouang, for example, now clearly
distinguishes it from the western town of Chiang Khong, although
early visitors were given to understand that they in fact shared the
same name.

European attempts to Gallicise or Anglicise the names have
further compounded the uncertainty – so much so, in fact, that a
country which is often mispronounced now has a capital which is
invariably mis-spelled. Most modern maps show the city as 'Vientiane' (which for easy recognition is the form used here). But its
first European visitor, that seventeenth-century emissary of the

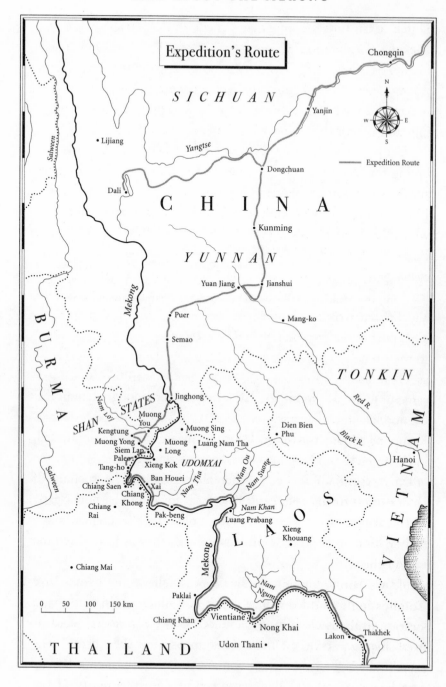

Expedition's Route

Expedition Route

Dutch East India Company, spelled it 'Win-kyan', while the Mekong Exploration Commission opted for 'Vien-Chan' (de Carné) or 'Vienchan' (Garnier). Some such spelling – 'Vian-chan', 'Vieng Chen' either hyphenated, as one word, or as two – is now making a comeback. It seems to be the LPDR's preferred rendering, and is probably as near the Lao original as any.

Yet well into the twentieth century English-speakers were still opting for 'Wieng-chan' (Warington Smyth, etc.), while French-speakers increasingly plumped for 'Vientiane' (Bassenne, etc.). The English language seemingly takes liberties with its 'v's and 'w's, while the French language has difficulties with the 'ch' sound. Because in French 'ch' is invariably pronounced as a soft 'sh' (e.g. *champagne*), some other combination of letters is required for a hard 'ch' (as in the English 'champion' or the Lao *'chan'*). Occasionally French writers adopted the Italian 'ci', as in 'Ciantaburi', a Thai port near Bangkok which would become of some importance to the French in the 1890s but which in English is usually spelled as 'Chantaburi'. More commonly the alphabetical pick-'n'-mixers came up with 'ti', 'x' or even 'tsi' for the hard 'ch' sound. Thus the Cambodian town that should be 'Kracheh' became 'Kratie', and Kompong Cham was often 'Kompong Tsiam'; all the 'Chiangs' in Chiang Mai, Chiang Khong, Chiang Saen, etc. became 'Tiangs' or 'Xiangs'; and Vian-chan became 'Vian-tiane', hence 'Vientiane'. Under French colonial rule, this last spelling triumphed; and when adopted by English-speakers it sounded like four syllables ('Vi-en-ti-ane'), a notable advance on the original two.

As the name of the place grew in the twentieth century, so would its configuration. But in 1867 the Mekong Exploration Commission found Vientiane as dead as Angkor. It was the one location in their whole itinerary, says de Carné, on which he had fixed his hopes of civilised living when he first joined the expedition. Yet all that awaited them was 'a heap of ruins'. Two centuries earlier the Dutchman von Wuystorff had found one of the most magnificent walled cities in all of south-east Asia. He was conducted upriver towards it in a fleet of royal pirogues and then paraded round it in a procession of richly caparisoned elephants, one of them reserved solely for carrying the vast ewer of solid gold in which his letter of accreditation was deposited. There followed a veritable 'cloth of gold' reception. The king's bodyguard consisted of three thousand warriors, and there seems to have been a like number of elephants in the manoeuvres laid on for the Dutchman's delight. All had been dispersed – gold, elephants, and people – when in 1827–28 the Thais overthrew the Lao monarchy and comprehensively sacked the city.

The annual vegetative explosions triggered by the monsoon had completed the destruction. Nature had erupted through paved courtyards, lifted timber floors, shinned up carved columns, prised off roof shingles and smothered the whole site in a green pillow of feathery foliage. As at Angkor it was now hard to tell whether the remaining structures were being supported by the trees, or the trees by the structures. Just three buildings were still recognisable: the That Luang, or 'Royal Stupa', venerated by the Lao as a national shrine and talisman (though minus the half-ton of gold with which it was plated in van Wuystorff's day); Wat Phra Keo, the royal temple where instead of the Emerald Buddha (now ensconced in Bangkok) sat a massive but disconsolate replacement swathed in lianas; and Wat Sisaket, from the floor of whose library the expedition scavenged a few fragments of palm-leaf manuscript.

In less than forty years a stately metropolis had crumbled into an overgrown rockery. De Carné ascribed this decay to the Lao's sense of insecurity. Their considerable skills had been lavished on the decoration of the buildings to the detriment of their construction. The Khmer, on the other hand, had trundled their megaliths for miles to make Angkor truly imperishable. It was as if 'the one people had no faith in their country's future while the other counted on centuries of power for it'.

Vientiane's Wat Phra Keo invaded by jungle.

These were sobering thoughts for would-be empire-builders. Vientiane might yet, they thought, be coaxed from its jungle slumber, and Laos reconstituted as a sovereign state, but not while its identity lay smothered under Bangkok's leafy embrace. If, though, it could be shown that any of the Lao *muangs* owed, or had once owed, some form of allegiance to a different neighbouring power, there might be grounds for contesting Bangkok's position. This, in fact, was a fairly safe bet in respect of somewhere ringed by the empires, some defunct but all formidable, of China, Annam, Burma and Khmer Cambodia. Lagrée had been instructed to make close enquiries about such political and tributary ties, especially in regard to any relationships between the Lao *muangs* and the Annamite, or Vietnamese, emperor in Hué. French colonial promoters already foresaw Hué coming under French protection; and that would in turn entitle France to resurrect, assume and pursue any Vietnamese claims in Laos – to the detriment, of course, of Bangkok's claims.

In their ascent of the Mekong, Lagrée and his colleagues had for this very reason directed most of their side excursions to the east of the river, and so towards *muangs* near the Vietnamese border. Disappointed in the Bolovens region, they had finally been rewarded up a feeder called the Se Banghien opposite Kemarat. There, reported Lagrée after a six days' absence, he had discovered that 'the whole region east of the Mekong between latitudes 16 and 17 [roughly the one hundred kilometres north from Kemarat to Lakon] had been under Annamite rule until 1834'. In that year the Thais had attacked and been repulsed by the Vietnamese but had returned 'soon after', overrun the area, and removed its Lao population. Tribal *sauvages* had since settled in their place, but 'in every village of the upper [Se Banghien] valley there was still an Annamite chief alongside the Laotian chief'.

> So [writes the prescient de Carné], *if in the course of time and events France should find herself heir to the claims of* [the Vietnamese] *government . . . she will not find titles wanting to establish her dominion over these vast tracts which European genius alone can make fruitful.*

In Lakon there was already a small community of Vietnamese fugitives. According to Garnier, they were extremely hard-working and were setting a splendid example of what industrious colonists might achieve; under French protection millions of their fellow countrymen could be expected to follow their example. Laos was to be transformed not by European genius alone but by every worker who proceeded from the overcrowded mouth of the Mekong to labour in the Lao wilderness. Ever bullish, the Mekong Exploration Commission was not just outlining the extent of France's future empire, but furnishing legal and practical tips on how it might be achieved.

Vientiane provided further hints of Hué's erstwhile influence. In 1828 the Lao king, after the fall of his capital, had actually sought sanctuary in Hué. Unfortunately he had been very quickly betrayed to the Thais, then very slowly killed by them. But this whole section of the middle Mekong so close to the Vietnamese border had obviously enjoyed close links with its eastern neighbour from time immemorial. It was accordingly earmarked by the Commission as being of pivotal importance in any future advance into Laos. So, indeed, it would prove; and so, a century later courtesy of the Ho Chi Minh Trail, would it prove to be no less pivotal for North Vietnam's advance into South Vietnam.

Political considerations apart, March and April 1867 brought the Commission only disappointments. The plight of Vientiane wrung from young de Carné another groan of world-weary *ennui*, while the departure of Séguin, their Thai interpreter, prompted a not unmerited racial outburst. Séguin, evidently a French citizen but of Franco-Thai birth and normally resident in Bangkok, had been abusing the authority of the Commission for months. He had seduced Lao girls and seized local provisions without making the payments appropriate to either transaction. He had no interest in the expedition, and his one professed ambition was to return to southern Laos, purchase a boatload of slaves, and realise a handsome profit back in Bangkok. The horrified Lagrée facilitated only his return. Séguin was arrested and handed over to the Thai authorities in Nong Khai for forwarding to French territory and a French court.

That left them with only one interpreter, Alévy, the Lao ex-monk. His conduct also left much to be desired; but it went uncensured because Alévy had contrived to administer his own punishment. When he emerged one night from the darkness dressed entirely in white and dripping with blood, Louis Delaporte had taken him for a ghost. Apparently he had been on a short visit to the monks at an important shrine north of Kemarat and was now returning, relieved of much guilt as well as all three joints of his left index finger. With a wife and family back in Phnom Penh, he had gone to seek forgiveness for several marital lapses in the course of the journey upriver. Absolution had been a formality; and by way of a penance he had been advised to do whatever his conscience dictated. It was then that he distinctly heard the Buddha advising the removal of a limb. He promptly repaired to a chapel and, according to Delaporte, 'there on a small altar, before an old statue of the Buddha, had hacked off one of the fingers of his left hand with a knife'.

Fortunately the wound was healing well. Alévy took this as a good sign and would soon resume his philandering, much to the annoyance of his masters. Instead of lopping off just a finger, de Carné thought he should have 'gone a bit further and emulated the example of Origen' (i.e. castrated himself). What with the earlier loss of their Cambodian interpreter, the disgrace of Séguin, the dismissal of three of the four French escort, and the release of one of the eight Annamite followers (because of an ingrowing toenail), the expedition had now dwindled from the original twenty-two to a more manageable sixteen. This thinning of the ranks was all to the good. It was offset, however, by a genuine disappointment: for the river was now leading them in the wrong direction.

Having obligingly conducted them due north ever since Phnom Penh, the channel of the Mekong above Thakhek had begun the first of its infuriating loops. Edging to the north-west, it had swung gently west, then south-west and, approaching Vientiane, due south. After Vientiane it briefly returned to a north-westerly bearing, then again twisted south-west, south and at one point even east of south. Instead of heading straight for China, they were being diverted towards Burma, then apparently redirected towards Bangkok or even back to Cambodia. It was as if the river had changed the rules of the game to become a snake instead of a ladder. After nine months of laboriously climbing the rungs of latitude from ten degrees north to nearly nineteen, they were now slithering back down towards the seventeenth parallel. Every minute of a degree lost would have to be regained, and every gruelling day spent sailing south meant another gruelling day sailing north just to make up lost ground.

As the river makes its first westward swoop, its pace quickens below densely wooded hills that press hard from the north. Here those giants of the tropical forest, the *dipterocarpi* and the *Lagerstroemiae*, made what would prove to be their final stand. Dr Thorel had identified twelve species of the latter and eight of the former. As well as supplying nearly all the lumber used in Laos, they furnished much of the oil and lac for which the south-east Asian mainland was as famous as its islands were for spices.

Less prosaically, these magnificent trees give to the forest both a collective architecture and an individual statuary. Fluted, flanged and buttressed, the great grey columns lift from the forest floor like elephantine legs. Skirts of undergrowth are left dangling round their ankles; cabbage-leaved climbers valiantly cling to muscular thighs, and inquisitive tendrils hitch themselves round an interminable waist. From there on up only tufted epiphytes clothe the naked limbs, bushing from a fork in the trunk or from the armpit of an outstretched branch like body hair. Trees so anatomically equipped command attention and cannot easily be denied a personality. They are as much fauna as flora.

Down through the hills on this bend in the river squirm two notable tributaries, the Nam San from the cloud-wrapped heights of Xieng Khouang and the Nam Ngum from the fertile floodplain north of Vientiane. Both river systems offered a promising access to the interior, and both have since been dammed for hydroelectric and irrigation purposes. The Ngum was Laos's first such project and the San (or Theun) is its latest, though by no means its last. Thanks to the waterworks and the site clearance, the giants of the forest are here now rarities. And thanks to the same waterworks, fishermen and farmers in Cambodia and the Delta have genuine cause for alarm.

Between Nong Khai, the Thai city in which Vientiane's defeated and displaced citizens had been resettled in 1828, and Vientiane itself, the valley opens out again. Just above where its first bridge, the Australian-built Friendship Bridge, now straddles the stream, the river is over a kilometre wide. Speedboats fly downstream, unzipping its silken surface as if it were a taut cocktail dress. When the water is at its lowest, long sandbars appear. It looks almost wade-able, and indeed waded much of it was by the fugitive Hmong in the pre-bridge 1970s.

For so-called 'stone age tribesmen', the Hmong had fought stoutly on behalf of 'Free World' values throughout the Vietnam war. Under CIA direction they had flown reconnaissance planes, defended US surveillance installations, kept infiltrators from North Vietnam at bay, and stiffened the otherwise ineffectual forces of the (non-Communist) royalist party within Laos. They deserved better than to be deserted by their American sponsors, then obliged to flee before the advancing Communists when the US began its south-east Asian disengagement.

From the uplands of Xieng Khouang the Hmong straggled down with their families to the river, and it was here, above and below Vientiane, that they surreptitiously paddled, waded and swam towards Thailand and an indefinite exile. A few precious belongings were towed on rafts, babies were perched on shoulders, heirlooms balanced on heads. Lacking the luck of the Israelites, they received no favours from the Mekong. As its yellow flood denied them the dry crossing so miraculously provided by the Red Sea, a once chosen but now unwanted people were left to fend for themselves. Some were drowned; all would be overwhelmed by a lifelong nostalgia for their lost highlands and their irrecoverable way of life. It was hardly surprising that many of their CIA sponsors felt as guilt-stricken as Alévy; or that one of them would later opt for a dazed and dark atonement among other *sauvages* higher up the river.

Sixteen kilometres west of Vientiane the rapids begin again. They continue, on and off, all the way up to Luang Prabang, a distance by boat of over four hundred kilometres. Route Nationale 13 here deserts the Mekong to find a more direct way north, but the river is not therefore busier with traffic. The odd speedboat skims from an unsuspected creek to disappear into the dense cover of the Lao bank; equally oblivious of international niceties, the occasional fishing canoe slips from the territorial waters of the LPDR into those of the kingdom of Thailand. In fact 'traffic', such as it is, now becomes an ambiguous term as it begins its mutation, ever so subtly, from noun to verb. The Golden Triangle may still be many days away, but the contraband connotations of 'trafficking' seem to have escaped downstream on the current and here become snagged, like the discarded flotsam of polythene packaging, in smugglers' coves composed of stranded tree trunks and hairy root bowls.

'Picturesque but wild,' reported Garnier, 'no dwellings, no trace

of man on the bank . . .' On both sides the hills boldly advanced
to the river and 'soon became mountains, pushing their roots of
ruddy rock into the bed of the stream'. Delaporte's sketchpad filled
up with wilderness views of a desolate torrent powering through
primordial jungle. The terrain was finally closing in, compressing
the river and hemming it round with ramparts of boulders chaot-
ically stacked beneath tumbled walls of vegetation. A wisp of
smoke high on the hillside betrayed the presence of tribal *sauvages*.
Though undoubtedly observing the travellers, the hill people
remained invisible to them. It was all mildly disconcerting, if not
yet menacing. At dusk the jungle pulsed with a buzzing, burping,
trilling cacophony interspersed with drummings and unexplained
rustlings. From the river, on whose sandbanks they camped, came
strange plops and sighs. Suddenly, as if by command, the whole
racket would stop, leaving a gaping silence spanned by the swish
and slosh of the waters that was even more unnerving.

The rapids were as treacherous as those in Cambodia, but
because the river was now at its lowest, much more difficult to
negotiate. It was seldom possible to use pikes; the water was too
far from the floodline and the purchase of roots. Garnier likened
the stream to a moat cut into the rock-strewn bed of the river and
running as much as twelve metres below its high-water mark.
Instead of being piked up the cataracts, the pirogues had to be
unloaded and then hauled through them at the end of rattan ropes.
In the absence of forest colossi like the *yao*, the boats were here
smaller, yet some of these portages lasted for days. Progress was
proving as slow as it was arduous. They were averaging only eight
kilometres a day – and most of those in the wrong direction.

Garnier was now walking barefoot, his last pair of shoes having
expired on the long hike back from Phnom Penh. His companions,
to conserve any still serviceable footwear, followed his example.
In the river's shadeless bed, they could at least see what they were
treading on, though the sharp rocks and burning sand were no

kinder to tender pink soles than the thorns and razor-edged sedges of the forest. Weakened by fever and dizzy with the heat, de Carné trudged on in a sweat-soaked trance. 'My ears rang, I looked without seeing, and I lost all sense of my existence. My legs worked mechanically with no mental input whatsoever.'

They halted at 'Xieng Cang' (Chiang Khan, or sometimes Muong Mai), another Thai township in which displaced Lao from across the river had recently been resettled. Here the news was again both good and bad. The bed of the Mekong was about to abandon its long east–west sidestep and, after a series of guilty wiggles, resume its northward trend. Apparently it held this bearing all the way to Luang Prabang. They were back on course for China. The appearance of pink-flowered oleanders and plum trees hinted at cooler climes. Garnier at last sniffed the long-awaited prospect of serious exploration. The river was dwindling to manageable proportions of between one and six hundred metres wide with a depth of ten to a hundred metres. His survey, already conducted without interruption for about a thousand kilometres from Phnom Penh, was finally getting the better of the wayward hydrography. Like a horse that had to be broken, the river was submitting to the bridle of plumb-line and the bit of his angled observations. Whatever its shortcomings as a highway, Garnier began to believe that the Mekong would as surely be theirs as the Niger had been Mungo Park's and the Nile was Samuel Baker's.

Or would it? At Chiang Khan, like a firecracker innocently rolled into the conversation, some Burmese traders made passing mention of another party of Europeans who were apparently descending the river. They were said to be English, there were as many as forty of them, and they were even now approaching Chiang Khan. They had come from Chiang Khong, five hundred kilometres upstream, and had already visited Luang Prabang. In effect they had thus pre-empted French hopes of claiming the middle river as their own discovery and its adjacent lands as their exclusive preserve. Much more numerous, better turned out, and more generously supplied with gifts, any such English expedition must shame the French endeavour and expose the presumption of its political ambitions. The southern section of the river, by virtue of Garnier's survey, had become what he called 'our indisputable property'. 'But it was hard for us who had hoped for larger discoveries and the more dazzling glory of penetrating into China . . . to be satisfied with a relatively trivial part.'

If it was the news of war in Europe that had devastated the diplomatically-inclined de Carné, for the empire-building Garnier it was this revelation about a rival for the river's favours that constituted the greatest disappointment of the whole voyage. So near, it seemed, so almost theirs, and yet so far. If only they had wasted less time at Bassac, if only the Chinese passports had not been held up, if only the expedition had been more adequately funded, if only they had not been at the mercy of the Thai authorities for transport, if only . . . if only . . . A few weeks earlier and they might have claimed the whole river. After nearly a year of anxious endeavour they deserved 'a harvest untouched by any other reaper'; yet now they must 'scrabble for grains of comfort through a crop already trampled by others'.

Lagrée, though no less disappointed, tried to rally his men. If the approaching expedition was indeed British, it could only have come from Lower Burma (the upper part of Burma would not be annexed by the British until 1886). The British explorers could not therefore have struck the river very far up, and surely not as far north as China. 'Well then,' declared Lagrée, 'if they have explored the middle course, we seek our revenge to the north. We continue to the river's source if that is the only way to eclipse their achievement.'

Garnier wholeheartedly approved. Geography was back at the top of their agenda and Tibet acknowledged as their ultimate objective. It was the sort of fighting talk he liked to hear. In fact, it is only in his account that Lagrée's words are actually heard. Given *le Commandant*'s later reluctance to make any commitment to the upper river whatsoever, they ring somewhat less than true. The normally taciturn Lagrée may, of course, have been bluffing in an effort to boost morale; to save his still troublesome larynx he may have been whispering so quietly that only Garnier heard him; or he may, in fact, have said nothing of the sort.

They left Chiang Khan with Garnier still in a fever of excitement over the imminent encounter with the British. De Carné looked on with an indifference that must have been no less infuriating for being wholly in character. 'A general who sees his battleplan undermined and the fight lost by an enemy manoeuvre, or an artist who recognises his own inspiration in the canvas of a rival, could not have been more cruelly disappointed,' says de Carné. He was writing of their shared sentiments but especially of the distraught 'Mademoiselle Buonaparte's'.

Putting a brave face on matters, they prepared to receive their rivals as best they could. They ransacked their larder and roasted a peacock. It was by way of paying lip service to the cordiality of Anglo–French relations, says de Carné, wincing nevertheless at what he deemed to be rank hypocrisy. 'For my part,' he continues, 'though I cherished no professional animosity towards the English, I joined in the general vexation, yet could not help smiling beneath my beard.'

De Carné was exercising a diplomat's prerogative. As for the officers of the expedition, they evidently shared a horror of the British that bordered on paranoia. While the peacock cooked, Lagrée and Garnier dashed off a *précis* of their progress and a report on their current predicament. These were to be forwarded to Phnom Penh either via the British, if friendly, or if not, via any surviving member of the Commission. French colonial interests had every reason to be wary of their worldwide rivals; and the French navy, in particular, nursed a deep resentment of its better-equipped, invariably victorious and altogether more illustrious royal British counterpart. Garnier was no exception. He consistently inflated the British challenge; and in Ubon and Nong Khai he had detected Albion's perfidious presence in every bolt of printed Manchester cotton offered for sale and in every bazaar-traded rupee used to buy it.

The proximity of the British in Burma and their domination of the Thai market seemed to Garnier a far more effective basis for political penetration than the Commission's scientific credentials. Indeed his anglophobia was commonly informed, though not necessarily tempered, by a grudging regard. London knew what it was about. It cut no corners, spared no expense, to secure its own interests and to bring the benefits of European rule to the world's less fortunate nations. Paris, on the other hand, dithered. Colonial endeavours were hostage to domestic politics; initiatives, like his own, languished for want of official backing; the fiasco over their delayed Chinese passports was typical.

Moreover the British understood the role of exploration. In Britain explorers were fêted by the establishment, knighted by the Crown, and lionised by the press not because they courted danger but because they were perceived as imperial flagbearers. They spattered the globe with geographical features named after Victoria and Albert, and they were not averse to dabbling, like Thomas Stamford Raffles at Singapore or James Brooke in Sarawak, in a bit of do-it-yourself empire-building. 'The more is the pity that I am not English,' Garnier would write after the expedition. 'I would then be someone of distinction and influence. [But] misfortune decrees I cannot just decide not to be French any more.'

Better informed than his colleagues about the modalities of British exploration, he longed to emulate giants like Richard Burton and John Hanning Speke, whose eagerly awaited confrontation over the source of the Nile had in 1864 been so dramatically aborted by the latter's death. Seven years later their shared sponsor, the Royal Geographical Society, would gather to honour Francis Garnier. He would attend in person, deliver a gracious speech when collecting his gold medal, and for once bask in the sort of adulation that was so notably lacking in France. Sir J.G. Scott, otherwise 'Scott of the Shan States' and the only Briton to rival his exploits in mainland south-east Asia, would call him 'the most gallant and talented explorer of the century'. The British understood his motivation, respected his achievements.

Garnier's earlier adoption of 'Francis' (instead of 'François') as his first name, and his later marriage to the daughter of an expatriate Scot, suggest further layers in this love–hate relationship with the British. For him, then, the imminent encounter on the middle Mekong was fraught with both political and personal significance. He was convinced that the approaching expedition was indeed British, and he insisted that it must be regarded as a direct challenge to what he called 'our own exploration of Indo-China'.

But not all his companions concurred. Still smirking into his big black beard, young de Carné watched mischievously as telescopes were trained and eyes strained for the first glimpse of Albion's armada.

A raft appears in the distance, gliding carelessly over the waters. Good eyes see Englishmen everywhere; they are pointing their fingers at us. The raft approaches. It hails us. It is a splendid floating house, with a verandah fore and aft, its height enormous, its proportions magnificent. What luxury! What comfort!

Behind it came another raft. Someone claimed that he could see an Englishman 'making his toilet'. The first raft glided to a halt upstream of them. Ill-at-ease, they stood to attention under a blazing sun – six dishevelled Frenchmen, ten assorted followers, and one small dog. At worst they braced themselves for a trial of strength that they could only lose, at best for a detestably patronis-ing encounter and an earful of Britannic pleasantries.

Although they were well aware of all extant itineraries in the region, neither Garnier nor de Carné felt inclined to make much of the fact that this section of the river had already been explored and so was not virgin territory awaiting either them or their approaching rivals. Indeed, it had been traversed by one of their own countrymen. Six years previously Henri Mouhot, the natural-ist who is best known for having penned the first description of Angkor's ruins, had travelled up from Bangkok, struck the Mekong north of Chiang Khan, and continued up its west bank to Luang Prabang, the home (since the sacking of Vientiane) of the Lao monarchy and the commercial hub of upper Laos. Thereabouts, in the course of several entomological excursions, Mouhot had died of what was probably malaria. But his letters, scientific notes and sketches had been collected. So had his journal, whose con-clusion, written in a pitifully failing hand, is one of the most poignant on record. After a succession of incomplete entries, the last one, dated 29 October, reads simply: 'Have pity on me, oh my God ...' He lost consciousness a few days later and expired on 10 November 1861.

To discover Mouhot's grave and memorialise his visit would be one of the Mekong Exploration Commission's priorities in Luang Prabang. But in this task the Commission again found itself embarrassed by the British. For Mouhot's visit could not be rated as a proof of French precedence in the Lao capital since, though indeed French, he had been travelling on behalf of two British organisations, the Royal Zoological Society and that *bête noire* of French endeavour, the Royal Geographical Society.

Mouhot, like Garnier, had received little encouragement in

Paris, had despaired of French patronage and had turned to London. He had taken up residence on Jersey, married a kins- woman of the great Mungo Park, and – horror of horrors – was reliably reported to have muttered his last recorded words in English. His itinerary was useful and his conduct had been exemp- lary; there would be some advantage in being able to claim him as a fellow countryman. But his name and his visit were of no value whatsoever in any stand-off with a British expedition.

As the first raft slid to a halt, de Carné, though short-sighted, could descry only Thais. One of them approached and declared himself an officer from Bangkok. The sense of relief occasioned by this news was short-lived. De Carné continues:

> [The Thai] *announces that the English follow close behind; that there are three of them; and that they are busy with the geography of the country. Smiles turn to grimaces. The second raft is on the horizon. The tension again increases. Keen eyes distinctly see the French flag floating from its roof. It is being flown out of courtesy. Courtesy comes easily to those who triumph.*
>
> *O, surprise. The French colours are those of Holland, identical to ours, of course, but arranged differently. The raft keeps to the middle of the stream, passes openly before us, and no European answers our signals. This is obviously a diabolically devious ruse born of typically British insolence. Disappointment gives way to boiling rage.*

With the full benefit of hindsight de Carné milked the occasion for all it was worth. Never again would he find his companions quite so ridiculous, never again would he find the energy to crow quite so lustily.

To act as go-between, Garnier was despatched downstream to where the new raft had halted. He returned with a business card. It announced not forty Britons, not three, not one even, but a single very frightened Dutchman plus a couple of half-Thai assistants and a crew of Lao raftsmen. All were in the employ of Bangkok. Mr Duyshart's card described him, in English, as 'Land Surveyor and Architect of His Siamese Majesty's Government'. He was conducting a survey of the river which was almost certainly prompted by that of the French themselves. Bangkok was availing itself of the right to map its own territories and Duyshart was simply one of the many Europeans in Thai employ.

Just as the Thai expedition's numbers and nationality had been grossly misrepresented to the French, so the Frenchmen had been described to Duyshart as sixty strong and at the head of a small Cambodian army. The Dutchman had deployed his rafts accordingly, hoping to burn the French encampment while ensuring an easy escape downriver ahead of his foe. Only the sight of the forlorn deputation on the beach, the absence of any hostile disposition and a whiff, perhaps, of roasting peacock had deterred him.

Duyshart was in a hurry to get back to Bangkok before the rains. He stopped for only a few hours, insufficient time for Delaporte to sketch those palatial rafts but long enough for a rapid mutual exchange of information. Garnier provided co-ordinates, bearings and distances for points downriver, Duyshart for points upriver. Thanks in part to Mouhot but mainly to Duyshart, the expedition would have a better idea of what to expect of the next five hundred kilometres than it had had of the previous thousand. Garnier's surveying responsibilities would thereby be eased, and the river's next great loop above Luang Prabang would come as no surprise.

On the other hand, the Dutchman's understanding of the situation above Chiang Khong in the now 'Golden Triangle' was deeply disturbing. Although he had not been there, he predicted almost certain death from the monsoon fevers in this most unhealthy part of Laos. Moreover the ascent of the river along the Burmese border was near impossible, and their Thai 'passports' would there be useless, in fact a liability. Law and order were non-existent in these unknown borderlands, said Duyshart, for as in China itself 'the populations were warring with each other'. If the Frenchmen had not already died of natural causes, they would surely be picked off by brigands or headhunted by *sauvages*.

With these cheery words, the flying Dutchman cast off and was swept downstream. The French explorers returned to their canoes to paddle to the next rapid, then haul their way up it. Garnier rated the meeting with Duyshart and the information obtained 'the most important events of our journey since our departure from Saigon'. But as yet he gave little credence to the reports of 'warring populations', while de Carné positively relished the idea of soon being no longer beholden to the Thai/Siamese authorities. 'We were at last about to see countries where they cut off Siamese heads. I may be accused of ingratitude but I confess I was delighted at the prospect.'

The next and, even on modern maps, the only place until Luang Prabang is Paklai. It had been visited by Mouhot who, coming from Bangkok, had here got his first sight of the middle Mekong. Though nearly fifteen hundred kilometres from the Delta, the river was 'much larger than the Menam at Bangkok', he reported. It came 'roaring' through the mountains 'with the impetuosity of a torrent scarcely able to keep within its bed' and slowed only briefly to swirl past Paklai, which was 'a charming town' of spacious houses and prosperous inhabitants.

The expedition begged to differ. De Carné thought Paklai 'a poor village'. Garnier found it 'rather different from what we were used to', since it was hemmed in by a 'harsher, darker forest' and had no fields and no coconut palms. The people partook of their gloomy surroundings and he dismissed them as unfriendly, a slur which, though undeserved, is still current. Because Paklai is roughly halfway from Vientiane to Luang Prabang, any craft today plying this section of the river usually halts here. A change of boatmen or boat may be necessary and, as Lagrée and Garnier had discovered, changeovers mean delays and additional expense. Across the language barrier these inconveniences may leave the visitor thinking he has been intentionally stranded, held to ransom, and fleeced – for all of which the 'pirates of Paklai' get the blame.

Ideally Lagrée would have liked to have hired the same boats and boatmen for the entire journey. Garnier seconded this, and bemoaned the official parsimony that made it impossible for the expedition to purchase its own boats. Both men, like the Mekong-mad of today, ignored the obvious objection – that the vagaries and navigational hazards of each section of the river are so extreme that none but local boatmen can be expected to know them and none but local boats can be assumed to be suitable for them. Nowadays a licensing system operates, with pilots and boatmen (mostly speed-boatmen) being restricted to specific reaches of the river. As ever, changeovers are tiresome but sensible and often unavoidable.

Still scarcely a town and as pleasantly remote as ever, Paklai stands above the river on its west, or Thai, bank yet is today nevertheless in Laos. Hereabouts, in other words, begins the only other sector of the river that has Laos on both banks; and just like that wedge of trans-Mekong Lao territory around Bassac, this anomaly is again a result of the forward policies that would be pursued by the French in the aftermath of the Mekong Exploration Commission.

The first French advance into the interior of Indo-China since that of Lagrée into Cambodia would be directed into Tonkin (i.e. North Vietnam) in the 1870s. It would owe a great deal to Francis Garnier and would be a direct outcome of the expedition's findings further upriver. Renewed in the early 1880s, the Tonkin offensive would result in the establishment of a protectorate over Annam and its emperor in 1883. The moment, foreseen by de Carné, when France would inherit whatever claims the Annamite emperor possessed along the Mekong in Laos had arrived. When the Tonkin initiative was checked by Chinese intervention, a second advance, no less informed by the findings of the Mekong Exploration Commission but more diplomatic in character, would specifically target Laos.

The man responsible for it, indeed the unacknowledged conservator, if not founder, of what is today the LPDR, would be Auguste Jean Marie Pavie. With Pavie, as much as with Garnier, would rest the fate of the Mekong. And it was at the remote township of Paklai that fortune would first favour Pavie's grand design for reconstituting Laos under French protection.

A slight but sturdy Breton with close-cropped hair and a walrus moustache, Pavie was the antithesis of the well-bred young officers of the Mekong Exploration Commission. Aged seventeen, after a rudimentary education he had signed on with an infantry regiment and then been posted to Saigon. At the time that Lagrée and his men were toiling up the river he held the rank of quartermaster sergeant but, on his own admission, suffered from a 'chronically timid disposition'. In the 1880s while medals were being won and reputations made in the Tonkin campaign, poor Pavie languished in an obscure tract of coastal Cambodia erecting telegraph poles. He possessed no obvious credentials as a diplomat or a scientist. As an explorer he betrayed only the most basic qualifications of abundant energy and a cast-iron constitution.

During twelve years in Cambodia, most of them passed far from Phnom Penh and without European company, Pavie learned the Cambodian language, studied the economy, history and geography of the region and dreamed of continuing the exploration inaugurated by Lagrée and Garnier. His popular account of his exploits would be titled *A la Conquête des Coeurs* ('In the Conquest of Hearts'), a presumptuous sentiment for an empire-builder but for Pavie a genuine one. He fell unashamedly in love with the people, identified with them, and to an unusual extent adopted their lifestyle. He never wore shoes and had no use for a uniform. Save for his droopy whiskers, beady eyes, battered straw hat and clay pipe, he was indistinguishable from his followers.

In 1882 he offered to undertake a mission to Luang Prabang with the object, urged by Garnier, of finding a practicable route from there into Tonkin. The job went to a Dr Neis, while Pavie was commissioned to continue his telegraph line through to Bangkok. Neis acquired a menagerie of exotic monkeys but failed to cross into Tonkin. In fact he managed only to antagonise Bangkok and to provoke the formidable bands of marauding Chinese who had taken refuge in the mountains of Tonkin and Laos following the suppression of southern China's Taiping rebellion. Arming the hardy peoples of Xieng Khouang, including the Hmong, Neis encouraged them to seek French protection against these Chinese 'Ho' (or 'Haw'). But he was in no position to deliver such assistance. When the Ho appeared, he fled down to the Mekong. Xieng Khouang was ravaged and, according to its next European visitor, 'the Haw then amused themselves by applying thumbscrews to persons who had been special objects of Dr Neis's generosity'. When, ninety years later, the CIA came bearing more arms and promises, the Hmong should have been warned.

Pavie finally got his wish to resume the exploration of Laos in 1886. Like Neis, he was initially commissioned simply to proceed up to Luang Prabang and explore all practicable routes from there across the mountains to Tonkin. He travelled north through Thailand with James McCarthy, a British surveyor in Bangkok's employ who had taken over from the flying Duyshart the mapping and monitoring of the Lao frontier. McCarthy, often accompanied by an escort under the command of Louis Leonowens, the son of *King and I* Anna, was extending a trigonometrical survey across the Mekong that originated in British India and already spanned

Burma. This, plus his nationality, excited French suspicions as much as Neis's and Pavie's activities excited British suspicions.

On the upper Mekong, as along the upper reaches of the Nile in Africa, the French and the British (through their Thai and Burmese surrogates) were by the 1880s playing a game of cat-and-mouse across the river. Because the British had just appointed a consul to Chiang Mai, the French had hastened to appoint Pavie to Luang Prabang. Every move had to be matched; wherever one went to ground, the other took up position. Since the cat must of course be Siamese, the mouse was French. It was really a variant of the Great Game, that interminable struggle between British India and Tsarist Russia for political and strategic advantage north of the Himalayas. Indeed on the British side, many of those who would find a discreet celebrity as explorer-spies in central Asia first snooped and mapped in south-east Asia. For the Great Game, this 'Lesser Game' along the Mekong was excellent practice.

McCarthy got on well with Pavie, who was 'always courteous' and a genial companion. When by mutual consent they parted it was because, as McCarthy delicately put it, 'continued association could have led to no good in any direction'. The game had its rules, and though each planned to observe the other, neither wished to be observed observing the other. Pavie reached Luang Prabang in October 1886 and pushed on towards Tonkin in early '87. He was halted near Dien Bien Phu, the remote township where in 1954 French rule would come to its inglorious end. The marauding Ho (Haw, or sometimes 'Flags' because each band of these Chinese freebooters followed a different coloured banner) barred his path. Indeed they were advancing. Lately worsted by a Thai expeditionary force that had taken hostages, the Ho were out to exact revenge on Luang Prabang itself.

Pavie scuttled back ahead of them. With just nine Cambodian followers, he could offer no resistance. From his camp across the Mekong downstream of Luang Prabang, he observed and waited.

The Ho entered Luang Prabang unopposed. They appeared to want only money and the return of the hostages taken by the Thais. On this understanding negotiations were opened with the old king of Luang Prabang and his advisers. Pavie and those who had already taken refuge in his camp remained suspicious; and to watch out for the king's safety, three of Pavie's most trusty Cambodians were sent back into the town.

In the early hours of 10 June, the Ho stormed the palace. All hell broke loose. A one-sided firefight raged through the streets; some of the town's most venerated wats were burned; and the population scattered. Most, including the king and surviving members of the royal family, made for the riverbank, piled into boats and shoved off into the current. Being June, the water was rising and the current fast. As day dawned, Pavie watched the approaching fleet through his field glasses, unsure whether it was Ho or Lao. The sight of his Cambodians, and then of the blood-stained Lao and their old king, reassured him. He too then ordered an embarkation and joined the downriver exodus.

> *The Mekong offered a strange and arresting sight; boats jammed with women, children and old men collided with one another; they were crammed with bundled matting, grubby luggage and baskets full of objects grabbed in haste, plus heaps of clothing that, thanks to an ill-timed shower, steamed under a blazing sun. Most of the rowers made little impression on the current and no one seemed willing to show the way through the approaching rapids. This was usually the job of the boatmen but today the boats happened to be laden only with families plus a good many folk, like myself, who were seeing this section of the Mekong for the first time.*

Pavie busied himself with the wounded and heard how his Cambodians had saved the king's life. The danger of pursuit was real; so they kept to the river despite the shortage of experienced boatmen. Pavie says nothing of their total numbers. Perhaps there were fifty boats – pirogues, canoes and rafts – and about a thousand fugitives. With the river running so fast, the pirogues should have been lashed round with bundled bamboos for greater stability; but there had been no time for such precautions. As the mass of tightly-packed craft slid towards the first of the great rapids, some were beached while their occupants went ashore to cut bamboos and size up the hazard. Most just raced ahead on the crest of the flood. Into the Keng Luong rapids they plunged en masse. It would have been better to go in single file, says Pavie, but it was impossible to impose any order. 'Each went his own way.' The women and children knelt in prayer as the boats spun between the rocks and 'plunged vertiginously'.

Suddenly our attention, though glued to the progress of our boat, was drawn despairingly to an isolated rock. Some women, really girls, having escaped the sinking of their pirogue, were pacing in every direction what little surface the rising waters had yet to cover. Looking for a way off or some means of escape, they were becoming frantic. Their hair streamed about them and, having at first thought themselves out of danger, they had removed their skirts and blouses to dry them on the rocks. I can still see them, three or four pale forms dashing over the black rock in the last rays of the setting sun, their clothes brilliant with colour. I hear, and will always hear, their heartbreaking shouts to the men and to the gods . . . Within an hour the rocks were covered with a sheet of water as level as a gravestone. A young mother, who alone had escaped by clinging to a dead tree trunk and being carried downstream, was running along the water's edge crying for her lost child.

Pavie was horrified. He had hitherto been treated with some sus-picion by the Lao, his presence even being blamed for the Ho's

Keng Luong, one of the rapids below Luang Prabang.

attack. But in disaster and grief he became one with the refugees, tending to the wounded, comforting the bereaved, rallying the boats. Continuing downriver, the survivors repaired to Paklai and there for two months, while the rains fell and urgent messages were sent to Bangkok, Pavie stayed with them. Every day at dinner the old king joined him for coffee. And whenever the question of returning arose, says Pavie, the king told his subjects 'that he took my advice, that I was his friend, their friend, and that they must each remember this'.

This rapport would transcend the relative rights of Bangkok and Hué in upper Laos and the conflicting allegiances of the Lao *muangs*. McCarthy had been taken sick and had returned to Bangkok. The Thai expeditionary force had retired for the rainy season; and the Ho, having ransacked Luang Prabang, likewise withdrew towards Tonkin. Pavie had the field to himself. Enjoying the confidence of the Lao court, he would return to Luang Prabang and from there, over the next seven years, would orchestrate the liberation of the Lao *muangs* from both Ho encroachment and Thai sovereignty, and so clear the way for a French protectorate.

Lagrée and Garnier never met Pavie. They might have disapproved of the man but not, surely, of his creation. Pavie, for his part, would be inspired by their adventure, ever mindful of their findings, and particularly grateful for the information acquired, at terrible cost, during the final months of the expedition.

For Pavie, Luang Prabang would become a second home, but for the Mekong Exploration Commission it was not much more than halfway. As the Commission laboriously worked its way up through those same rapids that Pavie would descend in such dramatic circumstances twenty years later, they appreciated only the importance of making a good impression in what Garnier rated the most significant 'city' since Saigon. Rifles were greased, medals polished, dress uniforms unpacked and brushed. Before rounding the last bend below Luang Prabang, they went ashore to wash and change.

When the city hove into sight on the opposite bank, its houses stretched along the river for three kilometres, and from across the water there came 'a confused hum'. To de Carné, heartily sick of the vast solitudes and empty forests, it sounded like music, 'a delicious harmony of human sounds'. They moored below the steep bank and, not apparently expected, sounded the gong which announced the arrival of an official. No one paid any attention. Their Annamite auxiliaries then went ashore and formed a guard of honour. In their dazzling white uniforms with a gold-embroidered 'Mekong' on their hatbands, the men looked superb. Lagrée and his entourage clanked past them, all buckles and swords. Still the usually inquisitive crowds failed to materialise. 'The people were too busy to notice our presence,' says Garnier. The expedition must indeed, thought de Carné, 'have at last come to a collection of houses and people meriting the name of a town'.

SEVEN

❖

Hell-Bent for China

'On 15 July 1910 the unlucky *Lagrandière*, descending from Luang Prabang to Paklai ... sank with aboard General de Beylié, the commander of the troops in Cochinchina, and Dr Roufiandis, chief of public health ... The vessel was engulfed by a whirlpool seven metres wide ... [and] sank in twenty seconds to a depth of eighty metres, where the explosion of the boiler completed the work of drowning.'

MARTHE BASSENNE,
Au Laos et au Siam, 1912

UNIQUELY, IT IS STILL POSSIBLE to imagine the Mekong Exploration Commission coming ashore at Luang Prabang. In the Delta all the towns have been recast in concrete to withstand the floods, Phnom Penh is unrecognisable from what it was thirty years ago, let alone a hundred and thirty, and Vientiane was of course rebuilt completely in the twentieth century. Only Luang Prabang preserves something of the picturesque aspect that it presented to the Commission in April 1867.

Seen from the river, the capital of northern Laos recedes shyly, like the hills which surround it, in a series of leafy terraces. April being a time of low water, the bottom-most terrace sprawls over sandbars and stagnant puddles at the river's edge – a tangle of snarling motorboats, grounded pontoons, precarious walkways, mooring ropes, houseboat washing-lines, stranded trees and abandoned fish traps. A canoe full of monks in barleysugar robes darts out from a landing stage like a hornet from its nest. Across the swiftly sailing stream, pirogues with outboards arc extravagantly towards a possible berth, there to swap their mixed salad of vegetables and villagers for a drum of diesel and the morning's shopping.

Rising straight as ladders from all this activity at river level, flights of steps scale the thirty breathless metres to street level. Here, across a not too busy road, verandahs and balconies gaze out through the palms and await the sunset. The buildings are low, mostly dilapidated colonial villas or two-storey shop-houses with more roof than floor space. Poultry scavenge inside and out; next door the breeze sets the coconut fronds clattering in a monastic courtyard. Save for vehicles instead of water buffalos, and but for a spluttering colossus of electrical switch-gear where there was once a mango tree, Wat Mai (the eighteenth-century 'New Wat') looks just as new as in Delaporte's painting. Its tiered pyramid of red roofs tipped with gold swoops down to brush the ground as if in deference to the neighbouring palace with its still holier Wat Ho Prabang. ('What ho, Prabang!' echoes the grateful returnee.) Round the corner a fishwife with a bath-size basin hacks a winged stingray into purchasable portions. Two markets are held each day, noted Garnier, one in the early morning, the other in the evening. And there are still two markets a day, the dawn one for raw produce, the dusk one for grills and confectionery.

Higher still, the midtown mass of Phousi, 'the Sacred Hill' that serves as the local Mount Meru, disguises both its craggy profile and its presiding stupa in woodland as dense as that which clothes the untamed hills in the distance. The Buddha's footprint and an adjacent monastery share the slopes of Phousi with a well-emplaced anti-aircraft gun. Now decommissioned, it pivots contritely amongst the pagoda trees (frangipani), a recent convert to non-violence and a sunny perch for small boys and large lizards.

From up here the configuration of the old town becomes clearer. De Carné described it as a rectangle with water on three sides. The Nam Khan, a tributary of the Mekong, advances casually from the east, but on meeting the base of Phousi, changes its mind and takes a teasing turn to the north. It continues to parallel the Mekong until the gilded shrines of Wat Xieng Tong deign to hallow their confluence. A raised promontory is thus formed between the two deep-set rivers, and this, about a kilometre long and a quarter of a kilometre wide, was de Carné's rectangle. Its extremity is actually pointed, and along with the gridiron street plan, led Norman Lewis to make a mischievous comparison with Manhattan Island. Wat Xieng Tong, humming with prayer, stands roughly where Wall Street would be; and Phousi's greenery corresponds to Central Park, with Wat Mai's concertina of rectilinear roofs nicely parodying the cylindrical look of the Guggenheim.

Higher up the Nam Khan, the fever-racked Henri Mouhot had penned that prayerful last entry in his journal before commending his papers to his servants and drawing his final breath. According to the Commission's informants, his body had subsequently been brought down the river and now lay buried beside it. But burial being an invitation to the spirit of the deceased to hang around and make trouble, the grave was located well away from the town. In fact it was only thanks to the high regard in which Mouhot was held that he had been buried at all, cremation being the norm among Buddhists.

That was six years before the Mekong Exploration Commission appeared, but Mouhot was still fondly remembered. People kept approaching the Commission's members with beetles and butterflies on the assumption that, like him, they must be interested in bugs. 'Unfortunately there was no entomologist among us and we often regretted this,' says Garnier. They were, though, interested in dogs, and especially so when 'with astonishment' they learned that Mouhot's King Charles spaniel still lived.

Well known to readers of his master's two-volume *Travels* as the adorable 'Tine-Tine' – his inseparable companion all the way from Jersey – here perhaps was a replacement for the late lamented Dragon and a playmate for the lonely Fox. An introduction was quickly arranged but, according to Garnier, did not go well. 'The ungrateful brute had become so friendly with its new owners that it showed us its teeth when it was brought before us.' Evidently six years was sufficient 'to erase all memory of the race to which its master had belonged'.

An audience with the king (the predecessor of Pavie's friend) also proved tricky and only took place after tense negotiations over protocol. As finally agreed, Lagrée was excused having to prostrate himself, the king rose to greet him, and armchairs were provided for his colleagues. These things were important if the local authorities were to gain a just impression of the might of imperial France plus, as Garnier added, 'some idea of the preponderant role she would one day play in this part of the peninsula'. The king nevertheless remained suspicious and 'uttered only monosyllables'. Garnier supposed that it must be because, considering himself semi-independent, he resented their Bangkok passports. Either that, he added, or it was because he suspected they were English.

Only in the matter of Mouhot's grave was His Majesty helpful. Permission was given for the erection of a commemorative monument which, designed by Delaporte and built with labour and materials provided by the king, was duly unveiled in a solemn ceremony attended by the entire Commission. The short but confusing inscription – 'H. Mouhot, May 1867' – referred not to the date of Mouhot's death but to the date of the memorial. Wondering which of them would be next to find a resting place in Laos, Garnier imagined the monument attracting the attention of every passing native and serving as 'a lasting reminder, both sad and touching, to the passage of foreigners in his country'. In fact the whole thing had disappeared by the time Pavie arrived twenty years later. He would have to rediscover the spot and repeat the memorial, a process which has been going on ever since. Today's stone is recent and almost certainly in the wrong place. On the banks of a flood-river on the edge of the fast-changing rainforest, human mementoes last no longer than canine memories.

The Commission's original plan was to stay put in Luang Prabang throughout the rains. That meant that, having arrived on 29 April, they would not move on till September. The most commodious lodgings they had ever enjoyed were specially erected for them, probably near where the town's covered market now stands. Joubert began a series of rambles in search of coal, a single lump of which had been found in a nearby monastery (its origin would remain unexplained). Thorel meanwhile botanised, and Delaporte embarked on a portfolio of drawings dedicated to the votive objects found in the innumerable wats.

The population, which they estimated at about fifteen thousand, was especially interesting. Since the sack of Vientiane, Luang Prabang supported the largest concentration of Lao anywhere in south-east Asia. Hitherto the expedition had known only the southern Lao, whose lackadaisical hospitality they had so enjoyed in Bassac. Here for the first time they met the northern Lao, a marginally more industrious and assertive people who occupied all the upriver valleys. They were easily distinguished by the extent of their tattoos. The southern Lao adorned themselves sparingly, but the northern Lao looked as if their midriffs had been steeped in woad. Only the men went under the needle; the arabesques and floral patterns extended from the waist to the knee, and within this area no part was exempt. It gave them, when naked, a butch and booted appearance and explained why they were usually known as the 'Black-bellied Lao', their southern brethren thus being the 'White-bellied'.

Dividing human society into groups designated by their shared appearance was evidently the norm long before ethnologists and anthropologists took the field. Like birds, men, and especially women, were here distinguished by their plumage, so that spotting and recording new species could be as satisfying as ornithology. In the busy markets of Luang Prabang the expedition first began to appreciate the exotic variety of *sauvage* and *montagnard* tribes in Laos. Among the Hmong, for instance, there were Red Hmong, White Hmong, Blue Hmong and Striped Hmong. The expedition began to distinguish some of these, but they barely scraped the surface. The Kaw, or Akha, are divided into seven sub-species; the Yao, or Mien, uniquely and hence distinctively, into none. Other ethnic groups are named for the terrain and altitude that they favour, a practice now deemed more politically correct. Thus Lao Loum, or 'Lowland Lao', are the Lao-speaking 'White Bellies' and 'Black Bellies'; Lao Theung, or 'Upland Lao', are all those peoples, mostly not Lao-speaking and so not strictly speaking Lao, who live a bit higher up; and Lao Soung, or 'Mountain Lao', are all those who, not Lao-speaking at all and mostly recent migrants from Yunnan, live in the mountains.

It was in the nature of things that an expedition committed to the river had limited contact with the mountain peoples. But in the Bolovens region of southern Laos they had encountered the country's greatest concentration of ethnic minorities, and around Luang Prabang it seems that Louis de Carné, of all people, con-tinued this line of enquiry. Normally far from complimentary about native peoples, de Carné writes warmly of 'these children of the woods' and castigates the 'Bellies' for disparaging their lifestyle. Although shy at first, the hill peoples never failed him on his rambles, supplying food and shelter whenever required. He admired their cleverly woven huts and enjoyed 'positive feasts' within them. On one occasion an old man, 'amazed rather than alarmed by my beard', had taken as much delight in showing him round his fields of rice and maize 'as any civilised proprietor would'. 'And I cannot recall without gratitude the memory of my collation [there] which consisted of sticky rice, smoked iguana legs and pepper.'

Lagrée and Garnier concentrated on Luang Prabang's political status. Since the decline of the Lan Xang kingdom in the late seventeenth century, the state (whose dependent *muangs* covered most of upper Laos) had maintained a degree of autonomy not by defying the demands of its more formidable neighbours but by accommodating them. The Burmese could currently be ignored; they were too preoccupied with the British. But to Bangkok the king of Luang Prabang sent an annual tribute, to Hué a triennial tribute, and to Beijing two elephants every six years. Although the elephants were currently in arrears because of recent political upheavals in Yunnan, all these arrangements presumed the tributary's recognition of the suzerain's superior authority and protection. On the other hand, so many such relationships effectively cancelled one another out. The Thais, for instance, were wary of asserting their rights in Luang Prabang if it meant provoking the Vietnamese, and the Vietnamese likewise if it meant provoking China.

As noted, the French were already confident of inheriting Vietnam's rights in Laos. Lagrée favoured waiting until this happened. The French authorities should bide their time in the manner of the British, building good relations and holding out the promise of justice and order so that when they finally made their move, the bulk of the people would welcome them.

But Garnier read the situation quite differently. Caution, he argued, was misplaced. Luang Prabang was analogous to Cambodia before the French protectorate. Both had been in danger of being overrun by the Vietnamese and then by the Thais. In the case of Luang Prabang only the superior, if remote, authority of China deterred Thai aggression. But since the Taiping rebellion, and even more so since that in Yunnan, the influence of Beijing, 'the regulator in this whole region', had significantly declined.

Unless some other great power took over China's brief, Luang Prabang would be swallowed up by Bangkok.

Unlike any of his colleagues, Garnier had first-hand experience of China, having fought there in 1858. He respected the industry of the Chinese and admired their civilisation. He also thought them amazingly accommodating for, he insists, a China unable to exercise its traditional authority in northern Laos 'today bequeaths this role to the European powers'. Higher up the Mekong, where the Burmese king allegedly exercised sovereign rights over the Lao (or Shan) states, 'England finds herself called to succeed'. Why else had the British sent an expedition, albeit thirty years ago, from Burma through the Shan states to the Mekong? Undoubtedly, the British were coming, warned Garnier; only France could, and must, prevent them.

It is in Luang Prabang that the progress of English influence has to stop, if we [the French] *want to keep an equal balance and occupy in the* [south-east Asian] *peninsula the rank which our political and commercial interests invite us to take. France cannot abdicate the moral and civilising role that falls to her in the gradual emancipation of these fascinating peoples of inland Indo-China.*

The king of Luang Prabang must therefore be encouraged to look to France for his protection 'from now on'. Only by doing so could his independence be guaranteed and his power enhanced. Moreover he had nothing to lose. His country was too remote for 'direct subjection' by France. He would simply be exchanging 'some bothersome tutelages' for a protectorate that was 'effective but not onerous'.

Blinded by his ardour, Garnier failed to explain how French protection would be effective despite Luang Prabang's location when, because of it, subjection was unthinkable. This was the problem with which Dr Neis and Auguste Pavie would have to wrestle. Perhaps Lagrée, too, raised it. The discussion was evidently heated, and Lagrée remained totally unconvinced. '[*Le Commandant*]'s experience led him to find my views just a little bit premature,' says Garnier.

Meanwhile the sort of confidence-building preferred by Lagrée was bearing fruit. The king sent over a wooden clock that wouldn't work. Joubert replaced its rotten parts and got it running. The townspeople warmed to their visitors and invited them to participate in their festivities. A strange ritual – de Carné called it an orgy – at which a row of young men addressed cryptic compliments to the town's beauties, then singly retired into the darkness with the one of their choice, attracted special attention. So did a twenty-year-old princess who frequented the Commission's quarters 'with a boldness and familiarity that never displeased us'. She even brought along some of her girlfriends and 'recommended them'. The girls were 'so confident and so intimate that we were sometimes embarrassed by them'. Luckily, continues Garnier, they too supposed beards to be an indication of geriatric impotence, a reassurance that gains nothing from his repetition of it.

There was no hint of any urgency until, less than three weeks after their arrival, Lagrée abruptly issued orders to sort out the baggage. Each man was now to be allowed only one load. The rest was to be divided into three piles. One was for instruments and materials – mostly notebooks and botanical and geological specimens – that were to be sent back to Bangkok and Saigon; another was for tradable items that were to be left in Luang Prabang in case they had to return that way; and the third was for everything else, which was to be immediately distributed among the dignitaries and ladyfolk of Luang Prabang.

A week later, on 25 May, the expedition was back on the river, lightly laden and full of purpose, though still somewhat dazed. Instead of four months in Luang Prabang, they had been there barely four weeks; and instead of waiting out the rains, they were now to run before them, hell-bent for China.

This decision, so catastrophic in its consequences, seems to have been taken partly because of the expedition's dwindling reserves of cash and partly in the light of new information concerning the political situation in Yunnan. There a rebellion of Chinese Muslims in the west of the province, through which reportedly flowed the Mekong, had been ongoing for some years. Lagrée hoped to take advantage of a rumoured lull in hostilities, although the border districts were reported more unstable than ever. In any case, the rebels would not respect passports issued by Beijing and so the chances of progress in that direction were again diminished. It was, of course, possible that the authorities in Luang Prabang were exaggerating the dangers, perhaps even being encouraged to do so by the Chinese. But a rebuff at the border or robbery by the rebels, followed by a return through Laos, were looking increasingly likely. Hence the need to regard Luang Prabang as a base camp, and to stash some of their precious reserves there while they made a less encumbered dash for the Chinese border.

The cash crisis would be solved if they reached government-held regions of Yunnan, principally in the east of the province around Kunming. Thereabouts remote Catholic missions had been warned to expect them and would supply their immediate needs until their Beijing letters enabled them to raise more substantial sums. But if they could no longer count on reaching government-held Yunnan, they were potentially in trouble. To get there up the river they would have to pass through what might be Burmese territory, where their Thai passports would be useless and where they would therefore have to bribe the authorities for carriage and then pay the actual boatmen or porters whatever they demanded.

Their cash reserves were insufficient for such exactions on top of the expense of four months' gracious living in Luang Prabang. Again, the only solution was to cut short their stay and make a dash for China. If they failed, they could fall back on Luang Prabang and, using the reserve left there as petty cash and their Thai passports for transport, return on the cheap via Bangkok.

This seems to have been the gist of their reasoning. It has to be pieced together from various observations and is nowhere logically presented as a single explanation. Garnier, however, writes more convincingly of a simultaneous and no less fateful decision – that concerning their choice of route.

A few kilometres above Luang Prabang, the Mekong is joined from the north by the Nam Ou (pronounced 'Oo' but sometimes spelled 'Hou' or 'U'). A considerable tributary whose clear dark waters blend reluctantly with the yellow flood of the main river, the Ou is shorter than the Mekong and of less volume. Yet more traffic and trade reached Luang Prabang down the valley of the Ou than down that of the Mekong, and it even had some claim to be considered the parent river. In determining such matters, hydrologists may take account of the direction of a river's flow as well as its length and volume. The clear-sighted Ou, coming from just east of north and running on just west of south, makes no change of direction at the confluence. The bigger river, on the other hand, nearing the end of another of its great loops, performs an about-turn. On a map, therefore, the Ou appears to receive the Mekong rather than the Mekong the Ou. Its direction is the truer of the two and so purists sometimes award it precedence.

The loop in question, the second of the Mekong's feints towards Burma, lasts for the 180 kilometres to Chiang Khong in the Golden Triangle. After that the river again veers to the north and China. Lagrée and Garnier knew all this from the Dutch surveyor Duyshart. But in Luang Prabang they learned that by way of the Ou and its tributaries there was a much shorter route to China. It avoided the Mekong's long east–west detour. It also eliminated the need to pass through the Shan states, against whose general lawlessness Duyshart had warned them and from whose Burmese overlord the Commission had failed to obtain any accreditation.

Lagrée saw this route up the Ou as their salvation. Most of it lay through territories that formed part of the Luang Prabang kingdom. The king was happy to furnish them with letters to his subordinates; and if they failed to get into China, they could simply return the same way. It was safer, shorter and, as the recognised trade route from Yunnan, of considerable commercial interest.

But Garnier, typically, would have none of it. The Mekong mattered too much to him. It was his destiny, their prize, France's due. This time *le Commandant*'s 'experience' – a term, one suspects, laced with innuendo about his superior's age and caution – must not be allowed to triumph. There were both political and scientific objections, but he mentions only the latter. 'I vigorously pleaded that . . . our geographical work would appear less interesting and less complete if it did not comprise a complete map of the river's course, which at the time we still hoped to track up to its Tibetan origin.'

Lagrée remained unconvinced; Garnier continued adamant. Further enquiries were made, and on 18 May the decision to move out from Luang Prabang was taken. It was then, says Garnier, that Lagrée adopted the Mekong route 'despite his personal preference for the route via the Nam Ou'. In a footnote Garnier's brother, who would edit his account of the expedition, claims this as proof of Lagrée's high regard for his deputy and of his readiness to defer to his judgement. Had the decision possessed any merit, Garnier's triumph would indeed have been notable. In fact it would prove disastrous. Disappointingly little would be added to existing knowledge of the river; delays and exactions in the Shan states would reduce the expedition to abject penury; and months of needless exposure to a second monsoon would do nothing for the expedition's state of health.

More plausibly there may have been some kind of showdown between the two men. It went unrecorded in Garnier's narrative, but Lagrée's papers, had they survived, might have told a different story. That they would in fact be destroyed on Garnier's orders only fuels suspicion.

Young de Carné and the others seem not to have been party to the dispute, though they were well aware of a crisis. De Carné only hints at Lagrée's misgivings and tells of *le Commandant*'s endless questioning of Luang Prabang's traders 'in which he showed both the patience of a savant pursuing a difficult problem and the wisdom of an examining magistrate'. No longer interested in matters of historical detail or commercial potential, Lagrée's enquiries now bore exclusively on the route ahead and their chances of survival. But wary as ever of 'enthusiasm', *le Commandant* was, says de Carné, 'readier to communicate to us his fears and doubts rather than his hopes'. 'He retained, besides, from his military habits the liking of command, and formed his resolutions as a result of solitary thought; so that . . . his companions sometimes had reason to regret his silence at critical moments.'

That this was indeed a critical moment is obvious; but Lagrée evidently kept his own counsel; and Garnier's opinion, though noted, was probably not decisive. Distrusting all the information obtainable, Lagrée in the end determined 'to advance nearer to the scene of events'. Far from gambling on the Mekong route, his intention seems to have been simply to test the waters. The expedition's fate, in other words, would be determined by the river.

Leaving by pirogue on 25 May, a day's paddling brought them to the confluence with the Ou. The mood of the Mekong had already changed. From the well-behaved river that smiles its way past Luang Prabang it had reverted to a fractious deluge needlessly contending with the scoured reefs of its black bedrock. Gone was the lower river's 'infinite perspective in which the blue of water and sky merged . . . and in which only the distant rows of palm trees and of huts half-hidden in their shade interrupted the horizon'. Here, wrote Garnier, 'the river was not three hundred metres wide and its winding course was bordered by rocky walls over which towered the bizarre serrations of the mountains behind them'.

To survey the Ou's confluence, the explorers climbed to 'the Cave of a Thousand Buddhas', a cliff-face atrium patronised by every passing boatman as well as by the myriad Buddha images that protect him. Although there had so far been only showers, Garnier reckoned the river had already risen by more than a metre. That was nothing. A marker beside the cave indicated a usual flood height of eleven metres above the dry-season level, and an occasional one of seventeen and a half metres. Through these gorges the river in spate became a different creature. Its metamorphosis was about to begin; and they could only guess at the rainfall needed to effect it.

By contrast to the thrashing Mekong, the Ou glided serenely to its rendezvous. Another sheer limestone cliff comprised its right bank; beyond it the valley opened out invitingly into rice fields and fishing grounds. At dusk Garnier paddled up its stream to take soundings. The current was 'almost zero', the water as clear and silent as the Mekong's was murky and turbulent. A couple of eagles circled overhead and, as the light faded, after a hard day's surveying, Garnier lay back and dozed.

Lulled by the limpid Ou, his dreams ought to have been of its unexplored potential. While affording access to the Yunnan border via one of its tributaries, the Ou affords access to the Tonkin border by another. Down this way would come the Ho on their murderous path to Luang Prabang in 1887, and up it Auguste Pavie would eventually open a route through to Hanoi. By the same trail and others parallel to it, French forces would in the early 1890s march to complete the conquest of Tonkin, pacify the Ho, and impose the desired protectorate on Luang Prabang. Then, as ever, the Ou, not the Mekong, was the key to upper Laos.

The Mekong's second great feint to the west has, though, found recent favour as an alternative tourist trail to or from Luang Prabang. To avoid retracing RN13's tortuous curves through the mountains, excursionists from Thailand and further afield can opt for the tour operator's 'Mekong loop' – one way by road and the other by boat, in fact 'a trip of a lifetime through the Mekong Gorges'. This means a two-day passage in the wake of the expedition between Luang Prabang and Ban Houei Xai, the exit/entry point into Laos across the river from the Thai town of Chiang Khong.

During the dry season, clinker and clapboard country-boats compete for this trade with an unnecessarily pert launch, a masted sloop with restaurant and bar, and a swarm of frail yellow speed-boats powered by what sound like aero engines. The Mekong caters for all purses. In terms of tourists this is undoubtedly its busiest sector and, excluding the Delta, its only readily sail-able sector. Beyond Luang Prabang the few roads are unsurfaced and none of them follows the river's westward loop. For the locals, too, boats are a lifeline. Villages unseen in the folds of the hills depend on them to stock the dawn markets that flourish along the riverbank but are gone by noon, like the cascading morning glory that forms their backdrop.

The expedition took a creditable ten days for this spectacular 180-kilometre stretch. The boatmen proved capable and the rapids less formidable than those below Luang Prabang. It rained only occasionally. A single short portage was involved, and one night a pirogue was swept away by the current. Fortunately the man sleeping in it awoke just in time to ward off certain extinction in a *tourbillon formidable* ('big whirlpool').

Extravagant reports of nearby volcanoes persuaded Joubert, a keen vulcanologist, to undertake a hike into the hills south of the river. De Carné, who had found in the sturdy doctor a good friend, accompanied him, perhaps to continue his hill-tribe researches. They discovered no lava-spewing cones, only smoky fissures and hot springs. But in the course of this excursion they found themselves crossing the watershed between the Mekong and the Menam, Thailand's main artery. The waterway that served Bangkok had its source less than fifty kilometres from the banks of the Mekong.

Evidently old maps and persistent rumours that made the Menam a breakaway stream of the Mekong were not far wrong. Conceivably, they may one day even be right. By cutting a short canal the Menam could be made a branch of the Mekong and the geographical hiatus corrected. The idea would appeal especially to irredentist Frenchmen who believed that Thailand must be included in their Indo-Chinese empire. And it has since been revived as the solution to irrigating Thailand's drier northern zones. Bangkok governments that champion the scheme are rightly assured of popularity, votes and lucrative tendering procedures. But once again, the fish-and-flood-dependent populations of Cambodia and the Delta shudder to think of it.

Joubert and de Carné continued overland to rejoin both the river and their comrades at Chiang Khong. They therefore knew nothing of the further options for a more direct route to China that had presented themselves to the expedition in the interim. Garnier mentions these, but without enthusiasm. At Pak-beng, where the two-day Mekong tours now make their overnight halt, the expedition had disdained the shortcut by which a trail led to Udomxai and on to China. Likewise they had looked the other way at Pak-tha, where the Nam Tha (*nam* is 'river', *pak* its 'mouth') is navigable all the way to Luang Nam Tha, the town nearest to the present-day Chinese frontier-post. To be fair, there was at the time no reason to give up on the Mekong. The gorges were impressive and the rapids manageable. So far so good.

Approaching Chiang Khong the river opened out again, its surface smooth and wide, its current slow and deep, and its valley suddenly a capacious plain. Not since Vientiane had the horizon seemed so vast or the river so full and peaceful: 'Nowhere else had there been such a beautiful appearance of navigability,' sighed Garnier, adding a wry 'but unfortunately it would be a very brief truce with the river's wilder nature.' In truth its wilder nature is here not unrepresented; it is just underwater. Ambitious building and landscaping operations along the bank today positively proclaim the importance of this stretch of the river as perhaps the last deep-water retreat of its most elusive denizen.

Combining impenetrable reaches with unfathomable depths, the Mekong enjoys its fair share of myths and mysteries. At Nong Khai (near Vientiane) in October 2002 a crowd of many thousands assembled to witness the 'great balls of fire' emitted by the river's digestive system. Egg-sized but sometimes 'as big as beach balls', the orbs of light burped into the air singly, though not all from the same spot, only at night, and only around the time of the October new moon. They were red, orange or occasionally pink, and they left neither smoke nor smell. 'Scientists struggle for an answer', reported *The Times*, to what it called 'one of the great natural mysteries of the world'.

The Lao and Thai know the answer. The fireballs are generated by the Mekong *naga*, a snake-like monster that personifies the river to its Buddhist peoples just as the nine-headed dragon does to the Sinicised Vietnamese of the Delta. *Nagas* are amphibious but spend most of their time in the river, reposing in underwater caves at a great depth. They surface where the river is broadest and deepest; and they may get mistaken for floating trees, although their undulating humps, like those of their Loch Ness cousin, are a giveaway. Several have been photographed, including one of about eight metres long being manhandled by a dozen jolly US servicemen. The picture features on postcards; and since there were of course no US troops serving in Laos, it must have been taken in Vietnam.

Frequenting the same open reaches of the river, but very definitely a fish, the *pa beuk* or *pla buk* has also attained near-mythical status. Although the name (in Lao and Thai) means simply 'big fish', it is reserved exclusively for *pangasianodon gigas*, otherwise the Giant Mekong Catfish, a creature unique to the Mekong and probably the largest freshwater fish in the world. Other species of catfish, some of considerable proportions, also live in the river, but they all belong to the genus *pangasius*. Only the *pa beuk* has an '-*anodon*' added on. The Latin suffix appears to acknowledge the fish's Jurassic proportions by placing it in the same league as the iguanodon and the mastodon. (Sadly it does no such thing. The '-*don*' means simply 'with teeth', and the '-*nodon*' 'with no teeth'.)

In the nineteenth century *pa beuk* were comparatively plentiful. The expedition had witnessed the netting of one just below Luang Prabang. It was a metre and half long, 'as fat as a fatted pig', and required 'five or six men' to heave it onto the bank. Lagrée bought it for a tical, 'a little more than three francs'. According to de Carné, 'its flesh was the colour and consistency of beef'. Regretting that none of them was an ichthyologist, Garnier conjectured that it might be of the same species as the boat-size 'freshwater kings' in the Tonle Sap river in Cambodia. He also wondered whether, salmon-like, it migrated to spawning grounds in Tibet. 'The only thing that I can confirm is that the meat . . . was delicious.' All of which amounts to a positive identification, the *pa beuk*'s distribution, meaty flesh and supposed spawning habits being as distinctive as its size. Its other attributes are entirely negative –

no teeth, no barbels (the catfish's telltale 'whiskers'), and no markings save perhaps for a little white spot on the head.

Auguste Pavie would add further details. In Cambodia they called it 'the royal fish', and it often grew to two metres long. Large numbers ascended the Mekong during the rainy season, and they were thought to spawn not in Tibet but at Ta-ly, or Dali, in Yunnan, whose great lake Pavie knew to be the source of one of the river's main feeders from its prominence in the final chapters of the Mekong Exploration Commission's report.

A Lieutenant Lefèvre, one of those who under Pavie's direction would complete the French acquisition of Laos in the 1890s, reckoned Pavie had underestimated the fish. He came across a lagoon near Paklai that the migrating *pa beuk* had adopted as a rest stop. They stopped there 'to swim about in peace', he says, although the fishermen who came from afar to cash in on the bonanza had other ideas. Some of the fish taken were 'enormous', in fact a scarcely credible 'six metres in length'; their eggs alone weighed several kilograms; and they were, again, 'delicious'.

The delicacy rating increased as the numbers declined in the twentieth century. By the 1970s the annual average catch was down to 'between twenty and thirty' and the price per kilo was going through the roof. Fish were rarely seen any more in the vicinity of Luang Prabang but could still be taken in Cambodia, on that boring stretch of river north of Savannakhet, and in the great basin between Chiang Khong and Ban Houei Xai. The capture of one was now news. When in May 1974 a local fisherman of Ban Houei Xai found his driftnet bulging, word was immediately phoned through to the Vientiane residence of the British ambassador to the LPDR (there was in those days such a person, although there is no longer). A diplomatic dinner party was promptly interrupted ('No one was surprised. They all knew about the *pa beuk*') and transport was organised courtesy of the USAID mission ('ten times more flights than Lao Aviation').

Early next morning Her Britannic Majesty's ambassador was flying north.

Although the fish had been tethered in the river for the night, it had been slaughtered before the ambassador arrived. It measured just over two metres, 'so was a middle-sized specimen'. Luckily the ambassador was only interested in the head. 'It registered 49½ kilos,' and despite 'quite a high price' he bought it. Finding a helicopter returning to Vientiane, he 'had it in the Embassy freezer by the middle of the afternoon'.

The head was intended for the natural history department of the British Museum; and the ambassador was called Alan Davidson. Laos turned out to be Davidson's last posting. Already, he says, 'my enthusiasm was fish'. Thanks to the *pa beuk* it became his profession. He resigned from the Foreign Office, started writing about fish and more generally food, and was hailed as the finest English author in this field. To him we owe many facts about the *pa beuk* and almost as many questions. The largest authenticated specimen measured three metres and tipped the scales at over 250 kilos (a quarter of a ton, about the same as a juvenile elephant); the testes of a male may be forty-three centimetres long, while the ovaries of a female weigh sixteen kilos; and netting the fish depends on the careful observation of week-long propitiation rites plus, while actually manning the net, hurling a non-stop stream of abuse at one's fellow anglers. 'They had to call each other "bald-headed fool" and other even more uncomplimentary names; and they exchanged sexual insults in the most liberal manner,' recalls Davidson.

Answers to the many questions raised by Davidson – what do they eat? why don't they have teeth? why are there no small ones? could they get up the Khon Falls? – should by now be available from the 'World's First Giant Catfish Reproduction Centre'. This is the name prominently displayed on a large signboard above the building operations on the river's bank at Chiang Khong. But the sign does not refer to the smart new terraces and pavilions under construction. It is a relic from earlier earthworks in the riverbed, now breeched and overgrown but once evidently the large holding pools needed for a reproduction facility. The new buildings are intended for a Giant Catfish Museum and Aquarium. In less time than it takes a signpost to fall down, the *pa beuk* has been demoted from a food source in the promising care of the department of fisheries to a freak show at the demeaning disposal of the tourism and heritage department.

This is not to say that the fish is extinct, just so rare as to be more valuable as a tourist novelty than as a table delicacy. As of 2003, there had been no reported sightings in the area for two years; and of the last batch of fry released into the river, 95 per cent either died, were caught, or were 'washed away'. An occasional *pa beuk* is still caught in the Tonle Sap river in Cambodia. The fish is not so prized there, and this could be its salvation. On the other hand, well-intentioned efforts to understand its requirements by closer monitoring may be counter-productive. Two were caught in 2002. The first expired before its tracking device could be installed. The second, measuring 2.56 metres and weighing 165 kilos, was successfully implanted and released, but was washed up dead the next day.

In the 1890s, while inspecting the sapphire workings in the gravel banks across the river from the *pa beuk* station, Warington Smyth, His Siamese Majesty's prospector of mines and minerals, noted that within a day's march of Chiang Khong there was a Chiang Hon, a Chiang Kon, a Chiang Kan, and a Chiang Klan. According to Garnier, in this region the term 'Chiang' – or 'Xieng' as he spells it – replaces that of 'Muang' 'as used in the south to designate the capital of a province'. Unfortunately it is not quite as simple as that. 'Chiang' has military as well as administrative connotations; it implies the existence of a fort or garrison. On maps of Burma, which country here begins to loom large, a 'Chiang' becomes a 'Keng' (as in Kengtung), while in Chinese it is a 'Jing' (as in Jinghong). And throughout the region the *muang* in fact remains ubiquitous, being a *muong* in Burmese and a *meng* in Chinese.

As all this implies, the Mekong Exploration Commission was entering a zone of hideous demographic and political complexity. In the slipstream of distant rivalries, frontiers had a way of drifting about like fishing nets, here snagging an unwanted bit of bank, there feebly bellying from a promising lie. Even today the area is popularly best known – on the grounds of simplicity as much as notoriety – as the cartographically undefined 'Golden Triangle'. To the Commission it was clear only that Chiang Khong was the last river-town in Thai territory and so the last place at which the Bangkok passports would be of use. It was also the point from which Duyshart had begun his voyage downstream. Upstream no 'white man' had ever been before. From here on the river was a completely unknown quantity until it slid past Jinghong in Yunnan, some five hundred kilometres away. Report knew of scarcely any villages on the river, let alone towns. Traffic was non-existent, and the rapids were said to be such as to make progress by boat impossible. Garnier's infuriating habit of disparaging their labours as not perilous enough to count as 'real exploration' would here cease.

The journey [he writes] *now began to assume that unforesee-able and potentially dangerous character that it had so far lacked. The ease of movement provided by our Siamese pass-ports was at an end. We were about to be left to our own devices and dependent on our own diplomatic efforts . . . From here on there was nothing that could deprive us of the merit that comes from discovery or of the pleasure that comes from the unexpected.*

It took ten days to lay in the necessary supplies, convince the Thai authorities to allow them to proceed, and find boats and boatmen willing to venture the last few kilometres to the limits of Thai jurisdiction. The showers became heavier; in between, the sun was if anything stronger. Thorel's dysentery returned, and Garnier had a brief recurrence of fever. Meanwhile they fretted over their likely reception by peoples supposedly under Burmese sovereignty. Considering the weeks wasted while they sent back for the Chinese passports, their casual neglect of any such authorisation from the Burmese court at Ava (near Mandalay) appears surprising. Application had in fact been made via a French bishop in Burma, but it coincided with a palace revolution in Ava and elicited no answer. The more obvious approach of a request via the British in Rangoon had not even been attempted.

Lagrée seemed to think that it was enough that 'the court of Ava had been informed of our journey'. He wrote accordingly to the 'king of Xien Tong' (i.e. Kengtung, the largest Lao or Shan state to the north) advising of their approach and asking for transport. The messenger also carried a few small gifts for the king by way of a sweetener – a carpet, a fan, a bit of 'Algerian cloth', pipes, soap and handkerchiefs – but there was nothing for Kengtung's official Burmese Resident, although Lagrée now knew that such a dignitary was attached to each of the Shan states.

Amid these anxious preparations, the first anniversary of their departure from Saigon went unremarked. On 14 June they again took to the river. Six boats were needed, but they were barely half the size of the long pirogues of lower Laos. Instead of paddles, rudimentary oars augmented the inevitable pikes as, for the first two days, they were rowed in stately procession round the river's last idle meanderings. 'One might suppose the river was delighted to dally in this plain', ventured Garnier, 'and let its waters rest after their frenetic course amid the mountains and rocks.'

The hills kept their distance and the plain was covered with a more airy and orderly forest than they were accustomed to. In winter, a season whose existence is here for the first time acknowledged, large crimson blooms give a bullfinch blush to the silver tracery of the bombax trees whose leafless limbs look reefed and ready for northern gales. Teak grows plentifully and was at the time a subject of contention between British lumber concessionaries and the Thais. Fast-maturing and of exceptional quality, it was not, noted Garnier, a large tree except in respect of its leaves, which flapped like elephants' ears in the rush of wind that accompanied every shower.

Despite its timber, the whole region seemed under-inhabited. Disputed between the Burmese and the Thais, it had repeatedly served as a battlefield and was still 'a sort of neutral terrain'. Head-high grass smothered Chiang Saen, the ancient capital that had been abandoned in the eighteenth century in favour of Chiang Mai. The French party stopped there for lunch. The ruins were even more unrecognisably urban than those of Vientiane. Their only resident was a rhino. By rocking a mango tree until the fruit fell, it was enjoying a gargantuan dessert. No less surprised than the intruders, it took one look at them and made for the trees. 'We listened for a while as the sound of its quick heavy tread faded into the forest and none of us thought of pursuing so timid and inoffensive a pachyderm.' Their last encounter in Thailand passed off peacefully.

Next day the river's course swung resolutely to the north. The mountains closed in again; the country was 'utterly deserted'. When navigating became as tricky as anything they had experienced, the pikes had to be brought into play. The showers were now downpours, darkening the waters. Nature seemed to be conspiring with their own anxieties to depress the spirit. Cloud crept

Encounter with a rhinoceros in the ruins of Chiang Saen.

lower on the hills and mist streamed from the forest to meet it. Rock and leaf glistened with malicious intent. As the rain fell, the river rose. The monsoon was closing on them, crowding their field of vision, restricting their freedom of movement, drenching their remaining possessions.

On 18 June they reached a spot with no name that was as far as their boatmen would go. Indeed it was as far as any boatmen would go – or any boat. 'We had arrived at the foot of the Tang-ho rapids,' says Garnier, 'which offered an insurmountable obstacle to navigation at this season of the year.' They would see the river again, but they would never again travel on it. Unknowingly, they had rowed their last bend, paddled round their last whirlpool, and piked up their last rapid. They promptly camped on the west, the Burmese, bank. The boats were retained while Lagrée sent ahead for whatever the nearest village could supply by way of porterage. The east bank was still Laos, or at least 'Siamese Laos', and it remained so (and still does) 'for a very large distance upstream'.

On that side the Thai passports ought therefore have continued to work their magic. Why then opt for the Burmese side? Why embrace a route where, as Garnier puts it, 'from this moment on, the fate of our journey depended on unknown circumstances'?

None of the Commission's published accounts offers an explanation. The ground looks steeper and the forest thicker on the east bank. Progress along it might well have been slow and difficult. Or perhaps there was no hope of finding guides and porters there. But these reasons are not given, and suspicion is aroused. The Commission seems to have been as inexorably drawn to Burmese territory as the giant hawk-moths to their candles over dinner. They realised the risk but, reckoning they could extinguish it, felt bound to try. As ever in Garnier's case, the explorer's craving for adventure – and that obsession with the river itself to which he would here confess – coincided neatly with his patriotic determination to demonstrate that the Mekong was a no-man's land beholden to no one, Burmese and British not excluded.

Next day, as they waited for carriage, Garnier left early with compass and cold chicken for that Elysian ramble up the river. He was as lucky with the weather as with the wildlife. It rained only once, and a fine day during the monsoon having a magic unequalled, he made the most of it. The stag that came towards him and the elephant that bathed beside him were allegories. They were not rank inventions – there were animals everywhere – but conveniently instructive episodes. Sun, solitude and the beasts of the forest were combining to pledge acceptance on the threshold of rejection. All creation 'confirmed to me that man was absolutely unknown in these regions', he says. This was not, of course, literally the case. They were bivouacking with other travellers in a hut that de Carné describes as a 'haystack on trestles'; and the requested carriage was already on its way. Garnier's point was that nature here knew no fear of 'the white man'. In Eurocentric terms it was *terra incognita*; and that, in the nineteenth century, meant fair game.

EIGHT

❧

Heart of Darkness

'It had become a place of darkness. But there was in it one river
especially, a mighty river, that you could see on the map, resem-
bling an immense snake uncoiled, with its head in the sea, its
body at rest curving afar over a vast country, and its tail lost in
the depths of the land. And as I looked at the map . . . it fascinated
me as a snake would a bird – a silly little bird.'

JOSEPH CONRAD,
Heart of Darkness, 1902

AFTER THE MEKONG EXPLORATION COMMISSION,
there would be a ten-year lull in that 'Lesser Game' between
the British and French for supremacy in south-east Asia. Humili-
ated in the 1870 Franco–Prussian war, Paris temporarily lost its
appetite for colonial enterprises; so did Saigon when its first venture into Tonkin, inspired by the findings of the Mekong Exploration Commission, ended in disaster in 1873. Not until the 1880s
would the game resume in earnest. As noted, a new Tonkin offensive would lead to Annam becoming a protectorate in 1883; and
in 1885, as the British moved to annex Upper Burma, the French
would rekindle their interest in Laos with the despatch of Auguste
Pavie to Luang Prabang,

In the same year, 1885, two rather similar-looking books on
the area were published in London. They each ran to about 380
pages, and they were identically leather-bound with their titles

embossed on the spine in gold. Both authors were well informed about the Mekong Exploration Commission thanks to the 1872 English translation of de Carné's narrative (Garnier's version had not yet been translated, and the official report never would be); and both authors were decidedly alarmist about French expansion.

One of the writers was Archibald Ross Colquhoun, whose *Amongst the Shans* was the book that made such free and un-acknowledged use of Delaporte's drawings. Colquhoun had been attached to a mission sent to resolve those disputes over the British extraction of teak in northern Thailand. He reached Chiang Mai but cast his enquiries very much wider and returned with his head spinning over the commercial potential of the whole region. Specifically he championed a trade route between British Burma and Yunnan which echoed that proposed by Garnier between French Vietnam and Yunnan. Colquhoun's route would run from Rangoon to Chiang Mai, on to the rhino-infested ruins of Chiang Saen on the Mekong, and thence up to the Chinese border through the Shan states of Kengtung and Jinghong. He even had a name for his route. Chinese merchants apparently knew it as 'the Golden Road'. What Colquhoun was proposing was that it be upgraded to a 'Golden Railway'.

No doubt all these glittering epithets contributed to the much later coining of the phrase 'Golden Triangle'. From Tibet to Cambodia every silt-laden river was supposed to be rich in gold dust; hence the gilding on all those wats and stupas. The whole of mainland south-east Asia had once been known in the West as 'the Golden Chersonese', a term originating in Ptolemy's *Geography* and popularised by Isabella Bishop (*née* Bird) as the title of a travel book (which, coincidentally, was also published in 1885).

But the gold, and later opium, scarcely required a railway. Over a thousand kilometres of track would need to be laid, most of it through pestilential rainforest or round unstable mountainsides.

Thailand's teak was already depleted, and the potential of the Chinese trade was too uncertain to justify an initial outlay estimated by Colquhoun at £5 million. Even in an age of 'railway mania' and of government guarantees for railway investors, this was a track too far.

Colquhoun, though, had other arguments. His Golden Railway was not just about profits. By opening up hitherto inaccessible areas, he claimed that slavery would be eradicated – 'with the sound of the railway-whistle feudal oppression will disappear' – jobs would be created – 'fresh hands in the Manchester mills and growing activity on the Liverpool wharves' – and best of all, French expansion would be checked. The question, according to Colquhoun, was simply whether the region 'shall be opened up to our [i.e. British] commerce or whether we shall allow it to be annexed by the French, and permit our only feasible trade route to China to be blocked by French aggression'.

The twin to Colquhoun's book put it even more forcibly. *France and Tongking* was written by James George Scott, a journalist who had witnessed the French operations in Tonkin in the early 1880s. After the British annexation of Upper Burma, he would gain wider renown as the hyperactive 'Scott of the Shan States', frontier administrator and fearless explorer among the 'filthy Kaw' and the 'wild Wa'. A bluff and entertaining writer, Scott was convinced that the French would not stop until they had absorbed all the Shan states (in which he included the Lao states) as well as Thailand. French officers admitted as much, and he didn't blame them. On the whole he thought French rule a good thing. But historically the French had been 'troublesome enough neighbours at home, and if we had them on our Burmese frontier they would be simply unendurable'. In fact 'war would be ... practically inevitable'. Britain herself had, of course, no designs on Thailand. Her only requisite was that it should not become French; and for this Colquhoun's railway 'would supply all that is wanted'. Linked to Rangoon by 'the iron way' and heavily indebted to British capital, Thailand would cease to be 'the safe quarry she now is for sinister French designs'. And the same would go for the Shan states.

Colquhoun and Scott were thus in complete agreement. Their books marshalled the arguments and would set the scene for British policy over the following twenty years. But the odd thing about them was that, though agreeing on so much, they were wildly at variance in respect of the existing political status of the most critical part of the region. Both books had fold-out maps, and both maps predictably awarded all of what is today southern Laos to 'Siam' (Thailand). But north of there, the vast east–west swathe of terri-tory bordering China from Tonkin through northern Laos and across the Mekong to Kengtung was designated on Scott's map simply as 'BURMA', most of it *Unexplored*', while on Colquhoun's map it became 'INDEPENDENT SHAN COUNTRY'.

'Shan' and 'Lao' were interchangeable terms, the British prefer-ring 'Shan' and the French 'Lao'. But how the same 'country' could be an unexplored (not to mention unadministered) part of Burma on one map and an emphatically independent Shan/Lao entity on the other was a mystery. Was it any more independent than what Colquhoun designated as Thailand's 'Shan states' (i.e. Chiang Mai, Chiang Khong, etc.)? Was it any more Burmese? And west of the Mekong, would the 'Golden Railway' be winding its way through a bit of Burma, or a sovereign Shan/Lao state, or a jigsaw of small Shan/Lao *muangs*? Where indeed did Burma stop? And what came next?

Eighteen years earlier, the situation had been even less clear when Lagrée and Garnier wrestled with the same questions as they waited for transport in the place-with-no-name below the Tang-ho rapids. Naturally they hoped to demonstrate that Burmese sovereignty over the Shan 'country' beside the Mekong was a fiction. That was why they had not troubled themselves too much over passports from the Burmese court in Ava, and that was why Lagrée had sent neither a letter nor handkerchiefs, let alone 'Algerian cloth', to the Burmese Resident at the court of the Kengtung chief. If they could pass through this area without acknowledging the authority of Ava and its representatives, it would prove that such authority did not exist. The expedition could then claim precedence in the area over any Anglo–Burmese rivals. The French would thus get their 'revenge on the upper river' as foreseen by Lagrée, and instead of 'England finding herself called to succeed' imperial China as 'regulator in the region', France could forestall her. Stripped of all political obstructions right up to the Chinese border, the maidenly Mekong would then await the embrace of French rule and French technology like a bashful bride languishing for her worldly-wise *seigneur*.

Geography lent some support to this contention. West of the Mekong, between it and the Bay of Bengal, two other major rivers hurtled down from Tibet. The Irrawaddy rolled past Mandalay and so was obviously Burmese. But the Salween, which squeezed its way between the Irrawaddy and the Mekong, sliced right through the Shan 'country'. Burmese influence was well established on the Irrawaddy side of the Salween in what the British would call the 'Cis-Salween Shan States', but less so on the Mekong side of the Salween in the 'Trans-Salween Shan States'. There both the Thais and the Chinese had occasionally made good their own claims to suzerainty. Logically then, the Salween, or its watershed, commended itself to the French as a realistic Burmese border that would leave the Mekong basin intact, unspoken for, and so wide open to Gallic advances.

As the Commission would soon discover, the Mekong basin between Thailand and Yunnan was principally occupied by two Shan states. The most southerly of these was Kengtung (otherwise 'Chiang-', 'Tsiang-', 'Kiang-', 'Xieng-', 'Sien-', etc. 'tung', 'tun', 'tong', etc.). The actual town of Kengtung was to the north-west near the Salween watershed, but its dependent *muangs* extended as far as the Mekong, although not across it. In Kengtung Burmese influence would prove to be well entrenched, and this would very nearly frustrate the progress of the Mekong Exploration Commission.

Further north and east, the second Shan state was Jinghong (otherwise either 'Alévy', the place from where their interpreter came, or any of the usual permutations of 'Chiang-', 'Tsiang-', etc. and 'hung', 'hon', etc.). Jinghong bordered with Kengtung and sprawled across both banks of the Mekong. Burmese influence was there currently matched by that of China, a situation which would ultimately prove the salvation of explorers equipped with Chinese passports. But if, as seemed quite possible with Yunnan in turmoil, China's position in Jinghong should deteriorate and Ava's influence prevail, French hopes of controlling the whole river would be fatally prejudiced. Worse still, if the Burmese kingdom was annexed by Britain (as it would be in 1886), Albion would here acquire Ava's rights on both banks of the river. France would then find the Mekong, her thrashing young bride-to-be, bestraddled by her deadliest rival. And the war that Scott feared to contemplate might indeed be 'practically inevitable'.

For the Commission waiting below the Tang-ho rapids, the political uncertainties were aggravated by their shortage of funds and by the rapidly worsening weather. Garnier's idyllic ramble upriver from the rapids would prove to be the last nearly-dry day. On the next it rained non-stop. They were relieved by the sight of twelve saddled bullocks that had been sent from the nearest village as they had requested. Although twelve was not enough, the expedition moved out anyway, leaving Garnier to guard the remainder of the baggage until further transport could be arranged.

The rain continued. It was like living under a waterfall. The first monsoon downpours seemed not to fall but to be propelled with a deliberate velocity. Drops the size of cherries hammered through the canopy to explode like bomblets on the baked earth. Their splashback did the drenching, sending a fine spray into anything pretending shelter. Paths became streams and streams torrents. The main expedition waded up to their waists, with the bullocks alternately walking or swimming; it was hard to tell which. Hillsides turned to mudslides. On the steep gradients 'we could only advance by catching hold of the bare roots of trees, creepers and hanging branches', says de Carné.

This hand-over-hand progression served as a home-delivery service to the leeches that jockeyed for position on every twig and blade. Delaporte may have been reminded of the Falls of Khon. He again attracted more than his fair share, and his legs were soon spurting blood as freely as a watering can. His sketch of the expedition here shows them marching down a river. 'As for the oxen, they fell at every step, rolling over and over on top of one another.' The packs had to be removed and the loads broken up for the men to carry.

Back at the place-with-no-name, Garnier spent his solitary days on the banks of the river not indulging his obsessive '*mono-manie*' for it but trying to escape from it. In forty-eight hours the waters rose three metres. It was like watching the encroachment of a tide that never turned. Luckily he was encamped in a hut on stilts. By the third day, when a gang of porters arrived to rescue him, the water was halfway up the stilts and he was marooned. In the end it was more relief than wrench to get away from his beloved river.

At the nearest village they were delayed ten days while word of their fate was awaited from Kengtung. Every halt was now 'a delay'. Thorel was so weak with dysentery that he could barely stand; their leech wounds developed into suppurating ulcers that

The highlight of the expedition's long stay at Bassac (Champassak) in southern Laos was the October water festival. Delaporte was never busier, drawing the pirogue races by day and the fireworks by night.

The Mekong dictates the terms of its navigability. Below the Khon Falls in Cambodia and Vietnam new river-craft have been imported (*above*). Above the Falls all launches (*below*) and freighters (*above right*) must be locally constructed, portable speedboats (*below right*) being the only exception.

Overleaf 'Our whole odyssey could be said to be taking place in one unending forest. We entered it in Cambodia and we were not going to be out of it until we set foot in China . . .' Much primary forest remains, although heavily depleted and everywhere endangered, nowhere more so than along tributaries like the Nam Ngum.

With the river in spate, the expedition could progress only by punting (or 'piking') through the flooded forest. A running-board of bamboos lashed to the sides of the pirogues provided a walkway for the pike-men.

The old city of Luang Prabang, capital of upper Laos and now a World Heritage Site, has changed little since Delaporte drew his panorama from across the river in 1867.

Luang Prabang's Wat Mai, the 'New Wat' when Delaporte drew it (*above*), became the Royal Wat when the neighbouring palace was built. Promoted by the French as a symbol of Laos's sovereignty, the monarchy was liquidated by the Communist Pathet Lao. The palace is now a museum and the wat again 'Wat Mai' (*below*).

Delaporte entitled this anthropological illustration 'Laotians of the Burmese territories', so acknowledging Burma's suzerainty while insisting that the people pertained to Laos. Chronic confusion over the status of the Shan states brought Britain and France to the brink of war as they eyeballed one another across the upper Mekong.

A forbidden city and a bloodthirsty sultan being desirable ingredients in exploration literature, Garnier gambled on a final bid to regain the river by way of the walled city of Dali (Ta-ly). His party was effectively arrested the moment it entered its north gate.

In Chinese Yunnan the Mekong Exploration Commission lost touch with the Mekong. In an attempt to regain it, Garnier led a fraught and abortive foray via the gorges of the uppermost Yangtse towards Tibet.

left Delaporte unable to walk; and according to de Carné, all of them were suffering from malarial fever. Under normal circumstances a halt might have seemed a good idea. But, obsessed with the cash flow, Lagrée was determined to keep going. Carriage rates were so high that they were having to cut back on food purchases. Longingly they eyed the herds of fat cattle in the village pastures. There was a time when they would have bought bullocks for the pot without thinking. Now, according to their leader, they could scarcely afford to hire them as pack animals.

Conventional coinage was here unacceptable as currency. Their remaining fifty kilos of ticals, or about ten thousand francs, had to be melted down into silver ingots, and any payments then made by paring off bits with a hammer and chisel and weighing them. The Commission duly purchased its own scales and got the village blacksmith to do the smelting. But with both Burmese and Chinese weights in use, and with every set of scales seemingly discriminating against them, neither this transaction nor subsequent disbursements worked in their favour. 'By being as economical as possible,' announced Lagrée, 'we may hold out for five or six months. But then we will be staring ruin in the face.' Both he and Garnier railed against their miserly government in Saigon. With an extra twenty thousand francs they could have bought or bribed their way to success. As it was, they were on the lookout for someone not to bribe but from whom to borrow. It was deeply humiliating. And all the while, though wet, sick and increasingly hungry, they had somehow to maintain the appearance of great white lords.

The news from Kengtung, when it eventually arrived, was favourable. They might proceed back to the river and continue up it. Boats were mentioned, but they were not a serious option. The Tang-ho rapids continue, off and on, for over a hundred kilometres, making this one of the most spectacular but least navigable stretches of the whole river. Too low when they first arrived at the rapids, they now found the water too high, a dilemma that would account for the stranding of the *Lagrandière*, that pocket-steamer which made the nineteenth century's only attempt on the Tang-ho cataracts.

They regained the river at a place called Paleo (otherwise Muong Pa-liao). Unable either to walk on his ulcerated feet or to sit a saddle on his ulcerated backside, Delaporte had been carried prone for the two days it took to get there. A litter had been easily constructed, but the local porters refused to touch it. A man so incapacitated, they reasoned, must be infectious. It therefore fell to the Commission's remaining Vietnamese and Filipino ancillaries, those unsung and themselves fever-ridden heroes of the expedition, to shoulder the burden. Employing the same logic, wayside villagers redirected the strangers well away from their houses. Lagrée expostulated and threatened to report them to Kengtung. 'Write to whom you want,' came the reply. Nothing could be done about it; the expedition was at the mercy of a lawless and money-grabbing people. For the first time since Cambodia, the spirited Garnier had occasion to brandish his pistol.

'Covered with mud, shivering and worn out with fatigue and hunger', they straggled into Paleo after a thirty-kilometre scramble. When paying off the porters next morning, they found that this Calvary had cost them 150 francs. 'At that rate, we would not get far,' says Garnier, 'so we decided on a new reduction of the baggage.' It was a measure of their reduced circumstances that rather than give the stuff away they now bartered it.

A coat went for two chickens, a pair of trousers fetched a duck, a flannel vest a cucumber. We also decided to carry our own arms, to abandon the small mattresses which had shielded us from contact with the bare earth, and to manage from now on with only our blankets as both bedding and shelter. Thus we reduced our luggage to thirty just-about portable bundles, of which the medicines, instruments, ammunition and money formed the bulk.

De Carné confirms these prices and adds others. By way of gifts for the Catholic missionaries whom they hoped to encounter in China they had brought along a selection of small medallions depicting various saints. These had doubtless been blessed and might be attached to watch-chains, waistcoats or rosaries as pious keepsakes. They were not intended as currency. On the other hand, they were more in demand than flannel vests. After a silent prayer that 'God forgive us such simony', all were briskly traded. 'St Anthony of Padua went for a pumpkin, St Pancras for a basket of potatoes and St Gertrude for three cucumbers.' St Christopher, if they had one, was presumably spared.

Economising meant eating more like the locals. The river here proved to be crawling with alligators – Garnier calls them 'caymans' – and July was their laying season. Alligator eggs were therefore cheap and plentiful, as well as nutritious. Yet when served up for dinner they met with a diffidence and disgust 'that was almost general'. The one exception was Garnier.

I ventured to overcome the prejudice that always attaches to strange food and boldly ruptured the soft membrane of one of these shell-less eggs. The contents, of a yellowish colour, spread itself over my plate. I tasted it, disguising my digestive misgivings behind a deadpan expression; and then in the hope that someone would follow my example, I hastened to declare the egg of the alligator to be an edible delicacy. In truth, the floury, sweetish taste of the thick liquid was not entirely disgusting. When, however, not one person followed my example, I myself renounced this gastronomic experiment.

On 8 July they resumed their march. They would have left on the seventh but a cloudburst had made the Paleo river, a tributary of the Mekong, unfordable. Delaporte was still a passenger; through rice paddies that now had the consistency of rice puddings, four men bore his litter aloft as if to the pyre. By darkness they had regained the shelter of the forest and spent the night on its floor, fully dressed, between a bed of damp leaves and a thatch of sodden branches. The rain poured through regardless. Their papers, gunpowder and instruments were kept dry by wrapping them in skins, but the fire went out, the leeches and mosquitoes, 'inseparable companions at this time of year', fed freely, and the spot they had chosen turned out to be infested with some kind of 'winged tick' that burrowed into the scalp and caused an excruciating itch. Next day the forest, once again a tropical profusion of ferns and fronds, would have been magnificent had pain, exhaustion and anxiety disposed them to appreciate it.

Interpreter Alévy had been sent on ahead with one of the Vietnamese. These two managed to surprise a tiger in the act of killing an enormous stag and then to scare it away by discharging their rifles. A haunch of venison sufficient for several days was quickly skinned, butchered and salted. That was the only triumph that awaited the expedition at Siem Lap (Xieng Lap). When Lagrée asked for onward transport, the chief blankly refused. They would again have to wait till further instructions arrived from Kengtung. The only hospitality on offer was, as usual, that of the local monastery. They installed themselves in the corner of the prayer-hall and instantly transformed it into a hospital strewn with invalids. 'The expedition's state of health was deplorable . . . fever and foot lacerations meant that half our people took to their beds . . .'

Morale was no better. They did a bit more bartering, but shrank to think what old friends would make of their behaving like 'hawker-charlatans'. Not that it mattered. Friends would never recognise them, and officialdom had surely forgotten them. The familiar world beyond the mountains and the forests did not bear thinking about. It was too painful, too tempting of Providence. Only the river, splashing its way through the gloom in a cloud of spray, retained its promise. They clung to it as to a thread through a maze. Down its thunderous course lay all that was familiar and French; up it lay their only chance of regaining that world.

The endless delays, the invariably truculent and obstructive attitude of the local chiefs, and the exorbitant charges made for the barest of necessities pointed to just one conclusion. To unaccountable petty potentates on an unadministered frontier, their plight was of no account. They were now themselves fair game. Through its local subordinates, Kengtung was testing them, toying with them. Trapped, fleeced, and then bled dry, they would eventually either succumb to the climate or be discreetly butchered.

Neither Lagrée's well-bred pessimism nor Garnier's easy wrath would allow of any other explanation. Thorel and Delaporte were probably too incapacitated to care, while Joubert, normally a pillar of strength, here succumbed to a fever 'that had both typhoid and bilious characteristics'. Young de Carné, too, was visibly declining under repeated attacks of malaria and dysentery; yet it was he who ventured the only alternative explanation. It was, he says, the worst of seasons for travel; no one normally ventured from their village at such a time, and no one wanted to be responsible for leading an ailing band of strangers to their demise. The exorbitant carriage rates and the reluctance of officials to assist their progress reflected these considerations. They had chosen the wrong season; and their being in denial of Burmese authority only made things worse.

A new communication from Kengtung included an invitation to visit the capital. At least that was how Lagrée, when politely declining it, chose to interpret the message. Written in the Shan language, then translated by Alévy into Cambodian and by Lagrée into French, its subtle phrasing could reasonably have lost some-thing along the way. In fact it was almost certainly a command. Lagrée admitted as much, and de Carné reckoned that, whatever the form of words, an invitation from a 'sawbwa' (king) had the force of an order. But Kengtung was 150 kilometres away, nearly all of them in the wrong direction. Their funds were insufficient for such a detour and their state of health too precarious.

According to their host in Siem Lap, the only alternative was to stay put for the three moons until the rains stopped. Besides being unthinkable, this suggestion smacked of a detention order. Lagrée decided to put matters to the test and struck a deal with a rival chief for immediate transport up the riverbank. Joubert and Delaporte were to follow on behind when they felt able to. The rest left, unmolested, on 23 July. In the five weeks since they had started travelling by land they had covered just eighty kilometres.

They followed the river, climbing high into the forest by day and descending to the bank at night. 'It always rained,' says de Carné; but it was good to be back by the Mekong. They had become so accustomed to it that, away from it, they felt bereft, disorientated, exposed. Still on the rise, it swept past 'with its fearful current emitting a dull roar'. It was now on average about five hundred metres wide, had 'the colour of red copper' and conformed to the frothy consistency of a thick and well stirred soup. Into it whole hillsides slithered and were instantly absorbed, leaving only a dribble of vegetation at the water's edge and, down-stream, perhaps a suddenly surfacing tree trunk to be tossed amid the spray of the next cataract.

Sleeping by the river was preferable to the forest because there were fewer leeches there. On the other hand the sleepers risked being washed away by a sudden surge of water. Lagrée, with his groin painfully inflamed by a leech-induced abscess, despaired of slumber and volunteered to keep watch. Garnier, though suffering from a no less excruciating rheumatism of the knee, says he would have slept except that his companion kept waking him. 'Watch out, Garnier. River seems to be rising,' croaked *le Commandant* every time his deputy's eyes closed. Garnier suspected that he just wanted company.

In the next village they were once more detained. Joubert and Delaporte rejoined them but, having finally negotiated their departure, they again split up. As well as resting the sick, this relay system enabled them to use the same porters twice. Leapfrog fashion, they continued roughly north-east. The route diverged from the river up one of its tributaries, then crossed to another. Through the chaos of switchback hills and hidden valleys in what modern maps show as a stubby finger of remotest Burma, they blundered unsure of anything except the compass.

This was travel fraught enough for the most demanding of explorers. Between bouts of irritation and despair, Garnier claims to have at last been in his element. In conversation with some migrants from Jinghong he heard tell of places in Yunnan and Tonkin 'that had once seemed impossibly remote but were now impinging from all sides'. The exotic topography seemed to be making some claim on him and, not for the first time, seducing his sense of purpose, even urging him to desert. He cursed the constraints of official travel and longed, he says, to break away, go native, and immerse himself in these tantalising lands and their still-unknown peoples. Patriotism, science and celebrity might seemingly be cast aside as casually as shoes.

Not implausibly, he was teetering on the edge of that civilisational abyss that would so fascinate both Conrad and Coppola. It could have been Kurtz himself who wrote of 'my willingness to renounce both my companions and my instruments' and follow the whim of the moment, 'roaming on foot the various parts of northern Indo-China'. These were extravagant sentiments from someone who, but for his companions, would have been left for dead in Cambodia. But travelling alone and indefinitely was,

The flooded trail near Siem Lap in the Shan states.

Garnier insisted, the only way to get to know the country and to master it. It was probably also the only way to get back to the river. Increasingly he would pester Lagrée for a chance to indulge his *monomanie* and strike out on his own.

On 7 August they arrived in Muong Yong (Mong Yawng).

They were still managing no more than sixteen kilometres a week, but they did at last seem to be getting somewhere. Muong Yong dominated a wide valley covered with prosperous villages and extensive rice fields. There was a wooden bridge, the first they could remember for months, and the temples had turned-up roofs, surely a sign of their proximity to China. It was altogether 'a pleasant surprise'.

The same could not be said of their reception there. Lagrée and Delaporte (whose ulcerations had healed) had gone off to look at a nearby stupa and taken Alévy with them. It was left to the more confrontational Garnier to install the expedition in the village *sala* and perform the introductions. Without the interpreter, this would be taxing for a tired traveller. He therefore begged to be excused when asked to present himself before the local authorities. A second overture met with the same reply, only this time Garnier turned his back on the visiting dignitaries and had them evicted. This was conducted, he says, 'with less gentleness than I had requested', and 'they had to descend the steps rather abruptly'. Threats and hard words followed, some of them profane, although how either party divined the other's meaning is not explained.

From a bad start, matters soon turned worse. As elsewhere, although the Shan chief was obliging enough, his Burman minder seemed bent on obstruction. He insisted that reference must again be made to Kengtung, which meant another two-week delay; and why, he asked, had the expedition refused to go there in the first place? The honour of an invitation was not to be lightly declined; in view of their effrontery, he anticipated that any further advance would be prohibited. In all probability Kengtung's next orders would be for them to return the way they had come.

This came as a bombshell. 'We had to think hard; everyone was overcome with despair,' says Garnier. To be turned back within a fortnight's march of China was almost unthinkable. They might conceivably forestall such an order by visiting Kengtung in person.

On the other hand, Kengtung might refer the matter right back to Ava. It could then take months. Moreover the expense and effort of just reaching Kengtung were as far beyond their means as ever. Yet they had to try. Lagrée saw it as their only chance. In his finest hour, he proposed that he, accompanied by just Thorel and the indispensable Alévy, should set off immediately. The main party was to stay put in Muong Yong, recuperate, and await developments.

Evidently Lagrée's groin had subsided and Thorel's dysentery gone into remission. They left for Kengtung on 14 August. The others settled down in what de Carné calls their 'prison'. Garnier makes it sound more like a madhouse. All of them had malaria, and rarely were one or two of them not raving with delirium. In one such fit, Garnier himself went berserk. He attacked Pedro, the loyal and inoffensive Filipino who did the cooking. Pedro had been shadowing him on Dr Joubert's orders lest he do himself an injury, a responsibility which the Filipino continued to discharge but now from behind a tree.

On the whole Garnier thought that being delirious was less distressing than witnessing the delirium of others. Waiting, on the other hand, was the other way round. It was much better to be the ones waited for than the ones having to wait. Every day it rained. Every day 'the cynical and obnoxious Burman gave us more offence'. And every day dragged past with no word from Kengtung. Fevered imaginations all too easily feared the worst. Perhaps the matter had been referred to Ava. Perhaps Lagrée and Thorel had never reached Kengtung. How long should the rest of them wait? How long could they hold out?

In cooler moments they turned to study. Garnier undertook the research for a short history of Muong Yong, while de Carné 'endeavoured to discover the principal elements of which the population of Burman Laos [i.e. the Shan states] is composed, and to make as exact an account as possible of their respective conditions'.

The results were modest; but it helped to pass the time. As the days turned to weeks, China was receding and the Mekong becoming a distant memory.

Ironically, Garnier's mapping of the river had been frustrated from the moment that he declared his '*monomanie*' for it. North of Tang-ho, the expedition's long detours into the surrounding hills ended any chance of a continuous survey, while the weather often frustrated the few observations attempted. His map of this long reach on what is now the Burma–Laos border misses out entirely its one distinctive feature – a sharp kink in the river's course commanded by the Lao village of Xieng Kok – and bears so little relation to a modern map that it is difficult to track the expedition's route. Not that modern maps are altogether reliable. The combination of erratic orthography, ineffectual administrations and chaotic geography makes the apex of the Golden Triangle as baffling a cartographic challenge as anywhere in Asia.

The terrain alone would have put paid to Colquhoun's 'Golden Railway'. It was never built, and if one excludes Cambodia's rarely operational line from Phnom Penh to Battambang, the only 'iron way' anywhere near the Mekong remains that seven kilometres of track across the islands at the Falls of Khon. Nowhere in its entire length is the main river spanned by a railway bridge. And as for Burma and Thailand, the only line that would eventually unite them was the short-lived one built under Japanese direction that included a bridge over the so-called River Kwai.

The gold of south-east Asia proved uncommercial, while the trade of inland China would be more effectively tapped via other rivers, especially the Yangtse. Once the British and French had sorted out their differences over the upper Mekong, the region would revert to a mouldering inconsequence, and during the first half of the twentieth century it was perceived as neither golden nor triangular. The novelist Somerset Maugham whimsically savoured its delights in 1928–29 as he sauntered on a pony from the Salween to the Mekong by way of Kengtung. Of an evening Maugham played patience, read Proust, drank pink gin, fended off the mosquitoes and puffed on nothing more exotic than pipe tobacco. In the hundred pages of his travelogue, *The Gentleman in the Parlour*, that are devoted to this section of his itinerary, opium does not get a mention.

Not till twenty years later, and so after the Second World War, did opium come into its own in the region. Garnier and de Carné had noticed it only as an occasional item of trade and as a minor social vice to which the prevarication of unhelpful officials might often be ascribed. They reported no poppy fields in either Laos or the Shan states; the first they met with were well inside China. Twenty years later J.G. Scott did find opium in his 'Shan Hills', but insisted that addiction was rare among those who grew it. Applied more often than smoked, it was regarded as a medicine. Recreational use was restricted mainly to the Chinese community and to the more louche French officials. Personally Scott found it neither debilitating nor addictive. He saw no stigma in the occasional pipe, and in fact recommended it as an excellent restorative after a long day's hike.

In the nineteenth century it was on the China coast that the opium trade was flourishing. There, in defiance of Chinese prohibitions and at the expense of Chinese smokers, scruple-free European entrepreneurs enjoyed rich pickings and built commercial empires. The opium all came from India or the Middle East. Compared to such bulk shipments, the product of the poppy patches hidden in the hills of Yunnan, Tonkin and Burma/Laos was reckoned inferior and commercially irrelevant.

Matters changed only slowly when the British and others reined back their involvement in the coastal trade at the end of the nineteenth century. Production in Yunnan increased, but more significant was the encouragement afforded by the French in Indo-China. There, by the 1930s, taxation through an official monopoly of opium sales accounted for up to half of all colonial receipts. When the Second World War cut off supplies from outside Indo-China, the French turned to local growers in Tonkin and Laos. The Hmong and other upland peoples needed little persuading to switch from subsistence farming to a cash crop for which taxes might be commuted and for which demand seemed inexhaustible. Production in the hills above the Mekong soared.

Thus in the second half of the twentieth century, opium from the Golden Triangle completely reversed the flow of the earlier trade on the China coast. Increasingly it was now scruple-free Asians who enjoyed rich pickings at the expense of Western consumers and in defiance of Western prohibitions. The decisive factor in this reversal followed the triumph of Mao's Communists in the late 1940s. Opponents, notably the nationalist and anti-Communist Kuomintang (KMT), were driven back to the Chinese border in Yunnan and beyond it into, especially, the Shan states. To fund further resistance and arms purchases, the KMT exiles turned to whatever means lay to hand, and on the borders of Yunnan this meant opium. Thailand and the US provided the KMT with arms; ostensibly for operations against the Communists within China, the guns also came in handy for enforcing opium production.

Thanks to the KMT's activities in the Shan states, Burma's annual production of opium shot up from forty tons in 1942 to four hundred tons in 1962. The Shan states were now the largest producer region in the world and, following a similar escalation in Laos and northern Thailand, the Golden Triangle accounted for 70 per cent of the internationally traded crop. Cause and effect are hard to disentangle in this sudden bonanza, but clearly it owed little to indigenous initiative. Poppies in south-east Asia only thrive at altitude and on alkaline soils. They are grown as a cash-crop sideline by mountain cultivators who are invariably members of one of those Lao Soung or Lao Theung minorities – principally the Hmong, Akha (Kaw), Yao, Lahu, plus in Burma the Wa and Kachin. Lowland Shan/Lao/Thai were not traditionally involved in the production or distribution. According to both Garnier and Scott, in the nineteenth century the hill peoples, many of whom were themselves comparatively recent migrants from China, always sold their opium to Chinese intermediaries and indeed intermarried with them.

The exiled Chinese of the KMT inherited this relationship and exploited it. But their task was made easier by other factors – endemic insurgency as the hill minorities resisted central administration from national governments in Rangoon, Vientiane and Bangkok; the instability and venality of these same governments; and the involvement first of French crime syndicates and then of the CIA. In the 1960s the CIA's support of its Hmong 'secret army' in Laos saw its supply and reconnaissance operations doubling as an opium-collection service.

At about the same time a market for this crop in the much more lucrative form of 'morphine base', and then heroin, was discovered among the hundreds of thousands of US troops who came to serve in Vietnam. Heroin 'laboratories', operated by chemists supplied by the KMT, sprang up along the upper Mekong. They processed opium from both Laos and insurgent Burma, and they were run in collusion with senior members of the Lao and Thai governments and with the cognisance of the CIA. When the CIA's Hmong 'secret army' was driven back and dispersed in central Laos, Lao production was switched to the north-west of the country, thereby consolidating the Golden Triangle's reputation. More significantly, when American troops were withdrawn from Vietnam, the heroin trail simply followed them back to the United States.

In the 1970s the Golden Triangle enjoyed its golden decade as the West's principal supplier of its most prized narcotic. Subsequently other drugs and other producers overhauled it. Eradication programmes and crackdowns, especially in Thailand, also helped to staunch the flow. But in the 1990s business revived with the mass production of metamphetamines – chemical substitutes of innocuous appearance and inviting name, like 'speed' and 'ecstasy'. These readily disguised and easily popped 'designer' drugs are now the principal product of the deep green hills that crowd the upper Mekong above the Tang-ho rapids between Thailand and China.

With insurgency still rife, and with a few exotic terror-merchants now joining the drug-dealers and the gun-runners in here evading international scrutiny, this section of the river has today limited appeal to travellers of innocent purpose. To follow the tortured trail of the Mekong Exploration Commission from Thailand's Chiang Khong to China's Jinghong by way of the Shan states would be as perverse now as it was in the 1860s.

Chiang Khong, with its kilometre-long market and its Giant Mekong Catfish 'station', seems peaceful and aspires to commercial respectability. Across the river, Ban Houei Xai, its Lao equivalent, cultivates a dustier indolence, with its reputation as the hub of a whole cluster of major heroin facilities uncelebrated. But round the river's bend at Chiang Saen, the aspect changes. For three hundred kilometres the Mekong thrashes and weaves between seemingly uninhabited hillsides that yield few significant tributaries. To the unsuspicious eye its monotony suggests no secrets; thick and brown, the river swirls and foams beneath ragged hills whose slopes plunge to the water's edge in an eternity of shaggy vegetation. Those bankside terraces of market produce, the carefully staked fish-traps and the netsman's dugout canoe, are not to be seen. All is either river or leaf, and with nothing worthy of scrutiny, the mind wanders at leisure, rejoicing at the pristine emptiness. If nature is innocent, here is indeed a smiling Eden just as Garnier proposed.

But behind the leafy smile lurk wisps of smoke and the frown of dark dealings. Tucked into the foliage opposite the place-with-no-name in which Garnier was marooned lies Ban Khwan. There in June 1967 a widely reported 'Second Opium War' flared up (the First being the nineteenth-century Anglo–Chinese hostilities that included the British seizure of Hong Kong). At Ban Khwan KMT units ambushed a Sino-Shan warlord whose mule train of sixteen tons of raw opium threatened the KMT's near-monopoly. While so engaged, both sides came under fire from troops and planes of the Royal Lao government operating on behalf of a no less monopoly-minded Laotian general. The fighting, so appropriately triangular, lasted several days. In the end the KMT men made their point, the Lao general got the sixteen tons, and the Sino-Shan warlord got away; as the notorious Khun Sa, he would build a veritable opium empire in the 1970s. Fatalities in this 'war' ran to over a hundred.

Fifty kilometres upstream, Muong Pa-liao, the place where the Commission traded flannel vests for cucumbers and declined to eat the egg of the alligator, achieved notoriety as the KMT's headquarters in the 1950s. Arms came in by air in exchange for intelligence that went out by radio to the KMT's US backers. Opium came and went by mule, porter or boat in exchange for gold and consumer goods – fridges, torches, record players. Ten thousand KMT men were supposedly commanded from Muong Pa-liao. But in 1961 they were outnumbered and outgunned by Chinese Communist troops who had apparently crossed the border at Rangoon's invitation. Joined by Burmese government troops, this invading force stormed the place. When the KMT were expelled over the river into Laos, five tons of US-supplied armaments were discovered.

This was the KMT's last stand in the Shan states. Most of

them were then expatriated to their other sanctuary, the still-Nationalist island of Formosa, otherwise Taiwan. Yet enough stayed on in Laos and Thailand to enforce their opium interests, continue their intelligence-gathering and, come the heroin bonanza, bankroll the Triads and the other organised crime syndicates that distributed the drug.

As naturalised citizens of either the Lao PDR or the kingdom of Thailand, the KMT are still around. Others lasted less long. On the other side of the Mekong from Muong Pa-liao and well out of sight behind the first range of hills, there reigned and raved in the late 1960s the latter-day Kurtz who supposedly inspired the reworking of Conrad's all-too-short *Heart of Darkness* into Coppola's all-too-long *Apocalypse Now*. During America's 'Secret War' in Laos the Nam Yu, a tributary of the Nam Tha (itself a tributary of the Mekong), here hosted the CIA's command centre in the north-west of the country. By 1965 most of northern Laos was under the control of the Communist Pathet Lao, supported by the Ho Chi Minh government in Hanoi. The Nam Yu base therefore stood on the ideological faultline, a vital and well-hidden listening post as well as a handy hideout from which to launch guerrilla operations behind Communist lines.

To raise and train such guerrillas there came as post commander in 1965 one Tony Poe, a veteran of the Pacific and Korean wars and a man with an already impressive record of service as a paramilitary operative in the Free World's catalogue of lost Asian causes. Intermediary in an aborted rising against Sukarno in Indonesia, instructor to the Khamba horsemen of Tibet in their struggle against Beijing, and latterly an inspirational adviser with the Hmong 'secret army' in central Laos, Poe was noted for a fund of unverifiable anecdote and a willingness to share it with his impressionable recruits. He had married a Hmong widow who, though not the princess of later report, lent credibility to his identity of interest with the hill peoples of Laos.

Arriving in Nam Yu in the floppy combat hat of an ex-Marine and the slimline dark glasses of the CIA, Poe looked the part. He towered over the local hillmen and, as if anticipating Brando as Kurtz, retained a physical appeal that was somehow undiminished by thinning hair, greater girth and incoherent address. Like Conrad, Tony Poe was of Polish parentage, his real name being Anthony Poshepny. Like Kurtz, he took his work seriously. His methods, though unconventional, were his own and he thought them unexceptionable. War had brutalised him and liquor was poisoning him, but as he slipped from the CIA's control and lurched unsteadily towards that moral void at the 'heart of darkness', he too was probably idolised by his men.

Yet if right for the part, Poe had not read the book. He wrestled no demon darker than drink, acknowledged no authority beyond his own experience, and seemed unaware of the abyss that beckoned. Where Kurtz loved music, quoted verse and liked to paint, Poe mouthed obscenities, fondled a quart of alcohol, and romped with a bevy of call-girls. Whether he personally adorned Nam Yu with severed heads stuck on upright posts or was actively engaged in the opium trade is debatable. Skulls on posts were a speciality of 'the wild Wa', a headhunting hill people much written about by J.G. Scott. Wa opium may well have found its way through Nam Yu, and perhaps a few Wa recruits. But for the most part the Wa lived – and hunted their heads – on the other side of the Mekong beyond Kengtung.

Poe's army comprised mainly local Yao, Lahu and Akha (Kaw). Their womenfolk, flitting amongst the pollarded trunks of their upland cultivation in black outfits aglitter with silver balls and cowry shells, certainly grew opium; and the men themselves traded it. Sticky brown bundles of the stuff probably did find their way under the seats of returning helicopters. But while to Conrad's Kurtz the ivory trade was his sole rationale, to Poe opium was an incidental. He didn't touch the stuff, discouraged its use and indulged its trade only to humour recruits and allies.

It seems to have been certain press reports in 1970 which brought the irregularities at Nam Yu and the eccentricities of its commander to the attention of the American public (and so, presumably, of Coppola). Poe's men had surprised and, for six days, actually held the important Pathet Lao town of Luang Nam Tha. Unfortunately CIA headquarters in Thailand was as surprised as the Pathet Lao by this incursion, and no less incensed. The action invited Communist retaliation in an area of great sensitivity. It had not been authorised. And it was all too typical of a man whose gung-ho tactics had once led to fisticuffs with the Hmong commander-in-chief. Clearly Poe's insubordination was now verging on the mutinous.

Poe just thought the attack good for morale. It coincided with a local festival which his men duly celebrated with their Luang Nam Tha cousins while he himself sampled the town's fleshpots. Casualties were negligible and Poe's men were gone before the counter-attack. But the operation had necessitated a small airlift and would later entail some explaining to the Vientiane government. Poe was indeed becoming a liability. The scandalised press reports may have been intended to discredit him.

On the other hand, he never denied them. In fact he embellished them. A plastic sack was said to hang from the steps up to his bungalow as a receptacle for unattached ears. For every pair of ears accompanied by a Pathet Lao cap badge there was a bounty of five thousand Lao *kip*. It was a popular scheme, and Nam Yu's weekly report, accompanied by its grisly bag of evidence, made quite an impact back at CIA headquarters. But according to Poe, the scheme was abruptly terminated when he came upon an earless youth whose father admitted to having had a pressing need for cash. Poe regretted this sabotaging of his incentive scheme, marvelled at the savage single-mindedness of the patriarch concerned, and expressed not a hint of remorse, indeed appeared cheerfully oblivious of any personal responsibility whatsoever.

Kurtz's famous last words ('The horror . . . the horror') would have meant nothing to Poe. Yet in his own way he too had crossed the line, slipped the leash. He had to go. There was no need for an upriver odyssey to remove him. He was relieved of his command by air after being extracted from his booze-stuffed bungalow without so much as a scuffle. Far from dying in an agonising welter of recrimination like Kurtz, he lived on in carefree and dissolute abandon, first in northern Thailand, then in the United States, until 2003.

By then a new and still more puzzling presence was reported on the banks of the upper Mekong in this no-man's land at the apex of the Golden Triangle. The place at which Garnier and his companions, as they waited for news of Lagrée's desperate mission to Kengtung, had fought off delirium and boredom was called Muong Yong. An anxious month there had seemed like an eternity before, amid contradictory reports, word was finally received from Lagrée. He had secured the necessary authority to proceed to Jinghong, the last of the Shan states. They were therefore free to move out. They were to meet up with him on the Nam Loy at a place called Muong You.

It was only a two-day march. But to have escaped from their Muong Yong detention and to be again heading north put all of them, says Garnier, 'in cheerful mood'. They climbed back into the hills – which reminded them of the Cévennes – and on 10 September debouched into the valley of the Nam Loy (Loi, Leui). This river was said to join the Mekong about fifty kilometres to

Making camp in the hills after leaving Muong Yong.

the east. It was bigger than most of the tributaries they had lately encountered, indeed 'larger than the Seine and just as winding' according to de Carné. It was also just as navigable. Down the Loy, after their rendezvous with Lagrée and Thorel, they once again sailed. Albeit for only a few hours, the reunited expedition was back in boats. Thanks to Delaporte's timely rediscovery of his fiddle, Garnier had *La Belle Hélène* lodged in his brain. (How the instrument had survived both the drastic baggage reductions and an *al fresco* monsoon is not explained.) A fierce sun hammered down on the river. China again loomed large. Even the rains seemed to be coming to an end.

To the navigability of the Loy were added other unexpected discoveries. Returning from Kengtung, Lagrée had passed through a village of cutlers and gunsmiths. Working at half a dozen forges, about a hundred 'Doe' (Dai, i.e. Thai or Shan) smiths turned out three thousand breech-loaders a year, boring their own barrels and turning their own screws. Meanwhile Garnier had reported similar skills in woodworking. Muong You had its own sawmill, the first they had seen. The architecture of the local palace no less than various civic novelties, like benches and bridges, testified to a high standard of joinery. Here were hints of an industrial capacity quite out of keeping with either the wilderness aspect of the Shan hills or their dismal reputation for chronic lawlessness. With such skills to hand even cargo-carrying boats might one day be built to sail down the navigable Loy.

De Carné regretted that further enquiries were impossible. 'It was ever our misfortune', he says, 'to be detained amongst hostile peoples in places devoid of interest while obliged to rush through anywhere that useful information of any sort might be acquired.' They had to press ahead lest their safe-conduct from Kengtung be countermanded by orders from the Burmese government in Ava. More on the industrial achievements of the 'Doe' was not therefore forthcoming.

But if latitude be allowed in respect of all conjecture to do with the Triangle, it may not be fanciful to suppose that these skills and traditions continued into the twentieth century. They could then provide a clue to the late-twentieth-century identification of this same district along the river Loy as the seat of a deeply mysterious entity known as '9:11'.

Possibly rendered as 'Nine-one-one', the 'Nine-eleven' in the Shan states is not a terrorist outrage but a territorial enclave. It predates the Twin Towers and may be so named after another 11 September, perhaps the day of the enclave's foundation sometime in the late 1990s. Alternatively the number is either that once assigned to the area as a military district or that assigned to the unit that once held this military district. The point about '9:11' is that it is a place, arguably a state, outside the jurisdiction of its better-known neighbours, like Burma and China; and that in 2002, from its port on the Mekong at Sop Loy ('Mouth of the Loy'), a busy trade was for the very first time being conducted down the Mekong river to Thailand.

According to an informant at the multinational Mekong River

Commission in Phnom Penh, in 2002 a thousand buffalo a week were being shipped downriver from '9:11'. They were being disembarked at Chiang Khong and were thence finding their way as ribs and steaks onto Bangkok menus. It was all thanks to the Chinese, whose floating drilling rigs, under an agreement with the Lao government, have been boring and blasting at the Tang-ho rapids for seven years. Sizeable ships will soon be able to sail all the way from Yunnan to Thailand when the river is high enough. The Golden Triangle is at last being wrenched into the twenty-first century as an 'Economic Growth Quadrangle', with the buffalo boats from '9:11' pioneering this new trade corridor.

It all sounded admirable; and although a suspicious mind might leap to the conclusion that inside those buffalo there could be something more valuable than ribs, this proved not to be the case. Water buffalo doubling as drugs mules was evidently too obvious a ploy. There is, though, a suspect dimension to the trade. According to Bertil and Hseng Noung Lintner, unchallenged authorities on the mind-boggling complexities of dissent and drugs in the Golden Triangle, '9:11' is the brain-child and exclusive preserve of an outfit known as the United Wa State Army (UWSA).

When, after that 1967 'Second Opium War', the Chinese Nationalist KMT moved out of the Shan states, the Burmese Communist Party moved in. Like the Kuomintang, the CPB (Communist Party of Burma) had lit on the Shan states and the neighbouring Wa states as a place of sanctuary from which to challenge ideological opponents. But in this new scenario the opponent was the military regime of General Ne Win in Rangoon (which had seized power in 1962), while Mao's China was the CPB's paymaster and arms supplier.

Supported in the rear by the Chinese, the CPB soon controlled substantial pockets of territory along the China border from the Mekong to the Wa states. Through the 1970s and eighties the CPB, divided into various numbered military commands, represented Rangoon's most formidable opponent. Alongside it the Shan, Wa and Kachin peoples continued their resistance to Rangoon's encroachment on mainly ethnic grounds, and the opium/ heroin traders, whether KMT, Lao, Thai, Wa or Shan, continued their resistance on economic grounds. The Golden Triangle, popularly seen as a three-sided figure comprised of Burma, Thailand and Laos, would have been better represented as a three-sided free-for-all in which ideology, ethnic insurgency and various forms of counter-insurgency scrummaged untidily for a territorial advantage that was more about opium than governance.

The situation changed dramatically in the late 1980s. In 1988 the military regime in Rangoon was rocked by the success, and then vilified for the repression, of the Burmese democracy movement led by Aung San Suu Kyi. And in 1989, like Communist parties elsewhere in the world, the CPB fell apart. Its several units went their separate ways and adopted new names that stressed only their 'democratic' or ethnic credentials. The largest of these in terms of battle-hardened troops was based in the Wa states, an important opium-growing area, and as the UWSA began expanding its activities.

Faced with the possibility of democratic activists who had escaped the 1988 crackdown making common cause with such formidable and now ideology-free insurgents, Rangoon moved swiftly to neutralise the latter. The ex-CPB groups were offered a limited autonomy plus what the Lintners call 'unofficial permission' to engage in narcotics production. In return they must suspend military operations against the Rangoon forces and forswear all alliances with other dissident groups. Most of the ex-CPB groups, including the UWSA, accepted these arrangements. The amnesties were dressed up with pious talk about developing the hill states and weaning them off opium production that went down well with agencies like the United Nations International Drug Control Programme. But the number of opium laboratories in fact increased, say the Lintners. 'The heroin trade took off with a speed that caught almost every observer of the south-east Asia drug scene by surprise'; and it is now, says Bertil Lintner, 'clear that the druglords in the north-east [of Burma] are enjoying protection from the highest level of Burma's military establishment'.

Sop Loy and '9:11' represent a new venture by the UWSA to secure an outlet to Thailand via the now occasionally navigable Mekong. Around 1999 troops under the brother of the UWSA's founder-commander moved down the Nam Loy to manage operations. His sizeable vessels may well be built there by the descendants of those smiths and joiners who so impressed Garnier and Lagrée. As for the buffaloes, they could be a sideline but are more probably a money-laundering exercise. 'We're talking heroin and metamphetamines,' stresses Lintner. But while the 'Wild Wa' in their 1970s guise as Maoist revolutionaries were said to still hunt heads and set them up on poles, in their new guise as shippers and import-export entrepreneurs the UWSA leaders hobnob with governments and set up corporations.

NINE

❖

Into the Light

'The conquest of the world . . . is not a pretty thing when you look into it too much. What redeems it is the idea only. An idea at the back of it; not a sentimental pretence but an idea; and an unselfish belief in the idea – something you can set up, and bow down before, and offer a sacrifice to . . .'

JOSEPH CONRAD,
Heart of Darkness, 1902

THE NINETEENTH-CENTURY EXPLORER was popularly supposed to scan the map for empty spaces and then set himself the task of crossing them. Coast to coast or river to river, in Africa, Australia or Arabia, he typically traversed an unknown 'interior' between two known 'exteriors', one a convenient departure point and the other an eagerly sought destination. It was less straightforward for the Mekong Exploration Commission. Without a map and with only the vaguest notion of where the river was taking them, the members of the Commission lacked the satisfaction that comes of counting down their progress towards a predetermined conclusion. It was more like travelling blindfold. They groped at whatever presented itself as evidence of progression, unsure of where they were heading and hopelessly ignorant of when the blindfold might finally be removed.

China was so big and distinctive they could scarcely miss it. It served as a goal of sorts, and in the Shan states they sensed they were getting near it. But they had little idea of where, once they arrived there, their enquiries would take them, or of how much further they would have to travel. No foreign expedition had ever entered China from south-east Asia. Yunnan, the province which occupied this remotest corner of the Celestial Empire, was practically unknown, as well as being in political turmoil. And the Mekong, if past experience was anything to go by, could not be counted on to conduct them directly or expeditiously anywhere.

Whenever possible Garnier had continued to take observations for latitude. Starting ten degrees north of the equator, the expedition was now about twenty-two degrees north, which was roughly equivalent to having travelled the length of Central America from the Panama Canal to the US–Mexico border. How far west they had come was less certain, longitude being much more difficult to establish, although by logging the approximate distances covered each day and the bearings followed, Garnier's route map provided some idea of progress.

Much more satisfying, because indicative of what lay ahead, were observable changes in temperature, vegetation and fauna. Rising in the tundra of Tibet and debouching in the sweltering Delta, the Mekong traverses a global spectrum of climatic zones from the glacial to the equatorial. Yet halfway up it, the temperature was still in the thirties centigrade and the humidity high enough to keep long beards dripping and leeches lunging. After over two thousand kilometres of tropical rainforest, the expedition felt entitled to expect change, and hence their delight in the slightly barer, Cévennes-like hills of northern Kengtung. In a local market they recognised, alongside the reddish tubers of the sweet potato, a handful of their rounder, waxier namesakes. They were the first genuine spuds they had met with and a sure sign of more temperate lands ahead.

Another revelation came courtesy of *le Commandant* Lagrée's successful excursion to Kengtung. When he, Thorel and Alévy rejoined the others at Muong You in what is now the opiate enclave of '9:11', they arrived on horseback. Kengtung's *sawbwa* ('king') had presented Lagrée with a pony; and he had since bought two more. Despite the cash crisis, he reckoned ponies a sound investment in that they would reduce the number of porters required and would be available to carry the sick.

The last time any member of the expedition had enjoyed the luxury of a ride had been on elephants in lower Laos. In the Shan states, though tigers still abounded, elephants were becoming scarce and rhinos non-existent. An equine presence promised a smarter pace across less exotic terrain. Tethered to a cotton tree beside some monastic *sala*, the ponies emitted familiar snorts and a sweet stable odour that reminded the Frenchmen of dew-drenched swards, firmer going, cooler climes, higher ground.

'Royal', as Lagrée had named his mount, and his two companions would lend to the expedition a heightened sense of purpose. They might also confer a touch of respectability, something in short supply among men who, but for the tricolour that they affixed to every hut, boat and beast they patronised, increasingly resembled a gang of demented desperadoes, gaunt-faced, fevereyed, covered in scabs wherever their clotted hair and shredded rags permitted inspection, and without a boot or shoe between them. In supposing that their ill treatment in the Shan states might have something to do with their unprepossessing appearance, Garnier was probably right. He was certainly right to worry about how China's notoriously fastidious officials, all of them mandarins minutely schooled in the niceties of Confucian etiquette, would react. In imperial China all foreigners were regarded as 'barbarians', but they did not normally indulge this conceit by actually looking barbaric.

Armed with the Kengtung safe-conduct, from Muong You the expedition had drifted pleasantly down the Nam Loy (the baggage and ponies followed by land), and then climbed again over the switchback hills west of the Mekong. They crossed another watershed between two of its tributaries and learned that this was the boundary between Kengtung and Jinghong. Muong Long, the next halt, was therefore the first place in the last Shan state. As they strode into the town over the Nam Nga, they found a paved road and then a humpback bridge. The bridge was not of timber but of well-wrought stonework with the wedge-shaped *voussoirs* of a true arch, an architectural device unknown even at Angkor. Gargoyles grimaced from the keystones, and on the pedestals at the bridge's approaches stone lions had apparently once sat.

A curious crowd of always trousered Shans pressed around them. In the mêlée they noticed two women peddlers in long dresses. The feverish de Carné stared in disbelief. 'Their tiny feet were enclosed in microscopic shoes,' he says. Could it be? Or were his bloodshot eyes deceiving him? Then the truth dawned on him and the tears welled up.

> *They were Chinese women, real Chinese women. There was no longer any doubt about it; how could these ladies with mutilated feet and that bridge of cut stone be other than indicators of a different civilisation? Had we not then emerged from Laos? Venus Astarte rising from the Nam Nga, or the Parthenon suddenly materialising from behind the bamboos, could not have more charmed the eye or excited the heart . . . Fifteen months of exhaustion, privation and suffering were forgotten in an instant. China at last! It was the goal of our journey, the starting point for our return.*

Garnier, assuming the air of an old China hand, confirmed the observation and shared the relief, but he derided the idea of two pigeon-toed harridans being any sort of compensation for the hell they had been through. 'Such acquaintances were usually obtained with less effort,' he sniffed, 'especially if one was a sailor.' For all the excitement, the expedition was quickly reminded that it was still in the Shan states and still at the mercy of their capricious chiefs and the obstructive Burman Residents. The safe-conducts from Kengtung here expired. And in case they had imagined otherwise, the local authorities were again brandishing orders, this time from Jinghong, directing that the foreigners be turned back and 'forced to take the road by which they have come'.

Garnier suspected more Burmese intrigue. Lagrée, who was inclined to think better of both Shans and Burmans after his gracious reception in Kengtung, suspected Chinese intrigue. Both were wrong. The Jinghong rebuff would be revealed as a classic case of mistranslation. Well-meant letters designed merely to warn the expedition about giving a wide berth to the civil war in Yunnan had been sent by both the governor of that province and the head of its Catholic mission. But the one being in Chinese and the other in French, they had been misinterpreted in Jinghong and their caution taken for the more usual interdiction.

Luckily Alévy rose to the occasion. Jinghong, after all, was his birthplace. From there, as a monk, he had wandered all over south-east Asia and, returning now as the interpreter for a prestigious European commission, he would suffer unthinkable loss of face if his superiors were rebuffed in his own home town. Sent on ahead, he confronted the authorities with a wild mixture of intimidation and threat, pledged his life for the honourable conduct of the great French mandarins, and secured permission for them to advance to Jinghong town, there to plead their cause in person.

They arrived on 1 October. The trail, through rounded hills and closely cultivated valleys, had carried enough bullock traffic to qualify as a trade route. Pine trees made their scented debut on the heights, and the local cultivators were almost entirely Akha hill-people. Garnier called them either 'Kho', presumably a rendering of 'Kaw' (the Burmese version of 'Akha'), or sometimes 'Miao', a more derogatory term that derived from the Chinese written character for a cat. Evidently the Chinese thought the Akha scrambled up their hills like cats, and so assigned to them the onomatopoeic ideogram used for cat in Chinese writing. Sounded as a typically moggy 'mi-aou', the word had taken on a life of its own in Lao and Shan parlance and was applied to all the northern hill-peoples, not excluding the Hmong. To CIA agents like Tony Poe, America's main surrogate force during the 'Secret War' in Laos was not an army of Hmong but of 'Mi-aous' or 'Meos'.

The Akha girls made a big impression on the expedition. Bare-kneed between their boot-length leggings and their very short skirts, with bespangled boleros and a helmet-like headgear festooned with jackdaw trinkets, they reminded de Carné of Calabrian peasants. According to J.G. Scott, who knew them better, the jackets never met in the middle and the skirts fell off at the slightest exertion; even when fully hitched, they left a gap that exposed a part of the Akha anatomy which was 'not the part that a European, at least, is accustomed to see'. Like the apple trees and the occasional aubergine field, these girls immediately brought to Garnier's mind '*la patrie*'. 'To people long accustomed to the peculiar features of tropical nature,' he says, 'the change was utterly delightful and entirely new.'

Jinghong, then 'more a market town than a population centre', sprawled across a wide and well watered plain hemmed in by hillsides that were in places denuded of vegetation. The scene was so unexpected to men accustomed to nothing but greenery that, when describing it, Garnier almost forgot to mention the Mekong. In fact it flowed – 'I beg pardon for not having spoken of it yet,' he interposes – hard by the town, was three to four hundred metres wide, and sped peacefully along between high sandy banks. Not since Siem Lap, eight weeks ago, had they so much as glimpsed the river. It deserved a more ecstatic greeting, and as if to make amends, Garnier skipped the expedition's formal audience with the king of Jinghong for another solitary ramble upstream.

[But] *I did not find those grandiose and solitary landscapes which had delighted me during* [the Tang-ho excursion]. *On the contrary I met with almost insurmountable obstacles to travel. The banks were lined with bamboo thickets and spiky shrubs in which one's clothes, if not one's skin, would be shredded. Elsewhere rocky cliffs barred the way and made a boat indispensable for getting any further . . . I contented myself with noting that, after its expansion in the Jinghong plain, the Mekong resumes that wild and tormented aspect – its bed confined and rock-encumbered, its waters deep and fast – that had characterised it ever since Vien Chan* [Vientiane].

At the time he feared that this might in fact be his last sighting of the river; and when he came to write his narrative, of course, he knew it was. But he made no attempt to disguise the ill-tempered nature of the encounter. For weeks thereafter he continued to remind Lagrée that the expedition would be judged on its river-work and to pester *le Commandant* about making another push for its Tibetan source. But in retrospect the Mekong had let him down. It had let the expedition down, let France down. A rapturous parting would have been inappropriate.

The remotest of the Shan states, Jinghong today confronts the visitor with as many surprises as it did the Commission. Once known as the Sipsong-panna – which is usually translated as the 'Twelve [Sip-song] Thousand Rice Fields [Pan-na]' – it is now notable for its 'twelve thousand rubber plantations'. Above the neatly terraced vegetable plots and rice paddies, hills that once rejoiced in a shaggy chaos of forest sit politely groomed and combed in regimented plantings of the latex-oozing *hevea*. Deciduous, in winter this block monoculture turns brown and downs leaves with a very untropical synchronism. To an otherwise indifferent and still lush landscape, the rubber trees impart the strict dormitory discipline of four distinct seasons. Any surviving natural forest (and the odd wild elephant) is increasingly confined to designated 'sanctuaries'. Here lavishly labelled, amenitised and policed, the big green trees are undergoing the same transition from defining species to museum specimens as the Giant Mekong Catfish.

The river too, although intimidating enough on Garnier's upstream ramble, is now less 'wild and tormented'. One might have thought that, having shunned aggressive exploitation all the way up from the Delta, the main river (if not its tributaries) would have had a good chance of sustaining a wilderness aspect until released to range across the Tibetan plateau. But not so. Those rocky cliffs that frustrated Garnier, and beyond them the dusky defiles and wild gorges through which the Mekong plunges down from Tibet, have proved irresistible. Here China's insatiable passion for resource management runs unchecked. Four, possibly six, hydro-electric dams are envisaged; two have already been built. If the Giant Mekong Catfish ever did migrate up to spawning grounds in Lake Dali, it can no longer – which may indeed explain its decline.

Downstream of Jinghong the hard-hatted workers of China's economic miracle labour to clear the river; upstream they labour to dam it. Whichever the direction, whatever the object, the river is being harnessed for mainly Chinese priorities, and there is little the other riparian states can do about it. Fortunately only about a quarter of the river's discharge in the Delta comes from China, the other three-quarters being the product of its Lao, Burmese, Thai and Cambodian tributaries. Beijing might also argue that China's water and nutrient-rich silt have too long been lavished free of charge on Cambodian and Vietnamese fields. An upstream state is as entitled to benefit from the river's munificence as those downstream, especially when the state in question happens to be the regional superpower. The Mekong river authority in its Phnom Penh headquarters just has to grin and bear it.

At Jinghong itself, for the first and only time, the river submits to the indignity of manicured embankments sporting a pedestrian corniche and some heavy urban development. Apartment blocks and office complexes exchange flickered neon greetings across its chastened flow. Instead of a humpback bridge, the traffic rumbles relentlessly over a six-lane highway suspended from a futuristic pylon which rears, fairy-lit, from the bedrock in midriver. On the east bank, industry stands ready to flourish among the truck repair shops. On the west bank, taxis prowl streets bright with shopping malls and showrooms, boutiques and burger bars. A cable car promises views from the nearest hilltop; the botanical gardens are world famous. Over two thousand kilometres from its mouth and nearly as many from its furthest source, Jinghong is today the Mekong's only real city.

Except that the Mekong here is no longer the Mekong, and Jinghong – never these days 'Xieng Hong' or 'Kenghung' – is no longer a Shan state. To the Mekong Exploration Commission in 1867 the place had felt much like a bit of China. Sure enough, within a generation it was a bit of China. The river at Jinghong was thereby awarded its Chinese name of 'Lancang Jiang', the Sipsong-panna became the Sinicised 'Xishuangbanna', and the indigenous Shan people became the 'Dai' (i.e. 'Thai') people, the largest of many proudly protected ethnic minorities in the Xishuangbanna Autonomous Dai Prefecture. Seemingly peoples too are a manageable resource fit to be shoved in a showcase, like big fish and natural forest.

All these changes originated in events back in the 1890s. Informed by the discoveries of the Mekong Exploration Commission, the transition would owe much to Auguste Pavie, the one-time French consul at Luang Prabang; to James George Scott, he of the Shan hills; and to a typically convoluted Anglo–French tiff over the Mekong basin that constituted the highlight of that obscure 'Lesser Game' for supremacy in south-east Asia.

To recap, the Mekong Exploration Commission took the field in the 1860s. In the 1870s not much happened in the region apart from a first French intervention in Tonkin that would prove to be the nemesis of Francis Garnier. In the 1880s the tempo quickened as the British snapped up Upper Burma while the French, assuming sovereignty over Vietnam, made good their claim to Tonkin. And in the 1890s the alarm bells sounded internationally as the British, in what they took to be the Shan states, and the French, in what they insisted were the Lao states, came face to face on the upper Mekong. The confrontation would decide the political fate of the region and endow it with the twisted skein of nation states that exists to this day. And of these states, the most important and contentious, around which the whole affair would revolve, was the kingdom of Siam (Thailand).

The trouble started in early 1893 when a conjunction of complacency in London, colonialist ascendancy in Paris, and French resolve in the East produced a series of incidents along the lower Mekong in Laos. The pace was set by the new French minister (i.e. ambassador) in Bangkok, who was none other than Pavie, the 'timid' erstwhile erector of Cambodian telegraph poles. Ever since his 1885 assistance to Luang Prabang's royal fugitives amid the Mekong rapids, Pavie had been probing the Siamese position in Laos while ostensibly masterminding the country's exploration and scooping geographical awards. Echoing Lagrée and Garnier, Pavie contended that Thai sovereignty over Lao territories on the east bank of the river lacked either legitimacy or substance; and again like the Commission, he desperately sought a legal basis for this contention in the rights supposedly once exercised by the now French-protected Annamite (Vietnamese) emperor of Hué.

But after seven years Pavie had failed to add to the Commission's findings, and admitted as much. Annam, and so France, had few claims on Lao territory that would withstand scrutiny and none that Thailand could not match. Some other justification was needed for ousting the Thais and enabling France to gain access to the Mekong under the guise of 'protecting' the east-bank Lao states. With this end in view Pavie catalogued a succession of minor grievances and incidents, on the basis of which a French claim to the entire east bank was first officially advanced in early 1893.

Funds and then troops for a forward move were voted through in Paris when the British government showed no interest in upholding the Thai position. The Liberal Lord Rosebery, Foreign Secretary in Gladstone's last government, preferred a clear-cut frontier accepted by all parties to one that was uncertain and contentious. If this meant encouraging Bangkok to make concessions, so be it. There was no harm in indulging the French on the Mekong provided Thailand's sovereignty, and so the desired 'buffer' between the French and British spheres of influence, was thereby secured within internationally recognised borders. Rosebery was seemingly unaware at the time that in the far north there was in fact no Thai territory between the Mekong and what were now Britain's Shan states.

French operations began in the extreme south with 'a police action' in April 1893 to seize Stung Treng, the Khon Falls and Khong Island. It was in the wake of this advance that those two pocket steamships were heroically manhandled across Khon to fly the flag above the Falls. No resistance was offered initially, and another offensive was launched further north where the river begins its westward loop to Vientiane. Again Thai officials and garrisons quietly withdrew. But in Bangkok there was consternation. Court and government could not decide on their response. If they fought back, the French would use it as a pretext to demand territories as yet unaffected, like Luang Prabang. On the other hand, if they tried to negotiate, the French would take it as weakness and exploit their advantage to raise the stakes anyway.

Trusting to British support if matters got worse, Bangkok decided to fight. In his reports from the Thai capital Pavie may have exaggerated, but arms were certainly purchased and a mobilisation of Thai forces got underway. In May this counter-offensive regained some of the Khon Falls region, capturing a French officer in the process. And in June, in the most serious incident to date, a Thai garrison withdrawing from Khammouan in eastern Laos ambushed a French police unit and killed its *Inspecteur*.

A disinterested observer might have concluded that honours were now more or less even. But this was the heyday of a bigoted if paternalistic imperialism that deemed any suggestion of parity between a European power and an Asian autocracy absurd. It was tantamount to equating francs with ticals, or men with monkeys. 'A weak Asiatic kingdom may not argue a question of right and wrong with a first-class European power on a basis of equality,' wrote Warington Smyth, then in the middle of his *Five Years in Siam*. This was 'undoubtedly hard', he continued, but it was 'a fact in practical politics that should not be ignored'. The deployment, in pestilential regions halfway round the world, of highly trained, expensively armed and European-officered units was not to be compared with the despatch of a mob of conscripted natives armed with muzzle-loaders. Nor could the acquisition of a few thousand square kilometres of tropical forest, with river frontage, begin to compensate for the loss of an *Inspecteur Civil*.

The howls of French protest over such incidents were accompanied by rapidly escalating demands for more territory, albeit disguised as compensation for losses already suffered and expenses incurred. These claims now embraced the 'kingdom' of Luang

Prabang (so most of northern Laos) and sundry islands in the Gulf of Thailand; even the inclusion of those 'lost' Cambodian provinces around Angkor (Siem Reap and Battambang) was mooted. Pavie went still further. In the spirit of Francis Garnier, he saw the situation as ready-made for the ultimate resolution of south-east Asia's untidy configuration with the extinction of its last independent kingdom. No less than the establishment of a French protectorate over Thailand itself, he claimed, would 'round off' France's position in south-east Asia and elevate French Indo-China to an equivalent of British India.

Unwittingly the British very nearly precipitated just that. Becoming alarmed by the French demands, Rosebery supposed that a show of force might lead to their being moderated. In time-honoured fashion, therefore, he despatched to Bangkok two gunboats. One duly arrived in late June, but its presence only made matters worse. For the Thais, rejoicing at what they took to be a positive indication of British support, were less inclined to negotiate; and likewise the French who, with their suspicions of Anglo–Thai collaboration confirmed, were understandably incensed. In fact, far from moderating their demands, the French matched the British move by ordering two of their own gunboats to Bangkok. Simultaneously a detachment of the Foreign Legion sailed from Algiers and a senior plenipotentiary was sent from France.

The French gunboats reached the mouth of the Menam, or Chao Phraya, in July. They were there informed that the river had been mined and that any attempt to sail up to Bangkok would be contested. This was contrary to an existing agreement on free passage, and so further grounds for French protest. Given the welcome just accorded to the British, it was also insupportable. Despite last-minute pleas and some not unusual confusion over delayed telegrams, the French gunboats entered the Menam at Paknam ('River's Mouth') on the evening of 13 July. They were duly challenged, then fired on from Thai vessels. They responded in kind. Warington Smyth, who followed the whole affair with the rapt attention he otherwise lavished on those diurnal tides, says that the action began at 6.45 p.m. and lasted less than half an hour, 'the flood tide being very strong, and a rain squall increasing the darkness of the short twilight'. The shooting, though reckless, claimed three lives on the French ships and fifteen on the Thai side. A small French merchant vessel was incapacitated. The two French gunboats proceeded up to Bangkok.

A ceasefire and then a succession of French ultimatums followed. When the Thais effectively rejected the first ultimatum, Pavie prepared for action. A blockade of the Menam was announced while he himself was to be evacuated to a French man-of-war. The blockade would affect mainly the British, whose shipping accounted for nearly 90 per cent of the country's external trade. In fact Rosebery interpreted the French '*blocus*' as a ban on British commerce 'in order to obtain a coterminous [French] frontier with India [i.e. Burma] which will impose great perils and burdens upon us'.

Rosebery was thinking especially of the Shan states. The significance of the French obtaining Luang Prabang – and so the whole east bank of the upper Mekong as far as Jinghong – had now dawned on him. Here, with no intervening Thai territory, the world's two greatest empires would be eyeball to eyeball, separated only by the variable width of a 'wild and tormented' river. An Anglo–French frontier on the upper Mekong could prove more vulnerable than that in the straits of Dover. British, as opposed to native, troops would be required to man it; roads would have to be cut and barracks built; the expense would be crippling.

In this treehouse of empire, therefore, a mini-buffer of neutral forest between the two colonial superpowers was imperative; and with the idea of creating one, Rosebery engaged in some distinctly creative geography. In March 1893 a treaty was signed with Beijing whereby Jinghong, never the most convincing or the most convenient of the Shan states, was transferred to China; the only condition was that no part of it could be alienated to anyone else, like the French. That effectively bunged up the northern end of the mini-buffer. *Le tampon*, as it was called in French, would be half Chinese.

South of Jinghong down to Thai territory, in that angle of the river where opium wars would one day flare and Tony Poe would amass his ears, the *tampon* could only be continued by interposing a supposed Shan entity. In case this should be contested, in 1894 British troops actually occupied the area; and as French troops massed nearby, there was a genuine little war-scare. By raising the Union Jack in Muong Sing, a rat-infested outpost to the north of Luang Nam Tha that was the only town, the British had for the first time laid claim to territory east of the Mekong. Pavie and his patrons in France saw their worst fears being realised: the British were making their grab for the upper reaches of the maidenly Mekong; deceased members of the Mekong Exploration Commission would be turning in their graves.

But the occupation of Muong Sing was supposed to be only temporary. Graciously and at a price, the British intended to hand the town over to Bangkok, so completing the *tampon* with a wodge of Siamese territory. The French therefore bided their time. Compared to the 1885 'Penjdeh Affair' – when a similar border crisis had threatened an imperial armageddon between the British and the Russians over the Afghan frontier – or the 1898 'Fashoda Affair' – when the British and French would nearly come to blows on the upper Nile – the 'Muong Sing Affair' of 1894–95 scarcely registered on the Richter scale of global upheavals.

It remained only to reconcile the French to the *tampon*. With the idea of sacrificing as much Thai territory elsewhere as was needed to win French approval, the British had engaged in the search for a settlement to the Franco–Thai crisis prompted by the 'Paknam Affair' and the Menam blockade. It was not as difficult as some feared. All along, while colonial interests in France demanded ever greater chunks of Thai territory, the Quai d'Orsay (in charge of external affairs) had been reassuring the British that Thailand's sovereignty and independence would be respected. In Europe and Africa, France needed British goodwill; the repercussions of her appropriating Thailand would be militarily dangerous and diplomatically horrendous. The Quai d'Orsay had therefore ensured that no demand for a protectorate over Thailand was tabled, and that even the 'lost' provinces in Cambodia were not officially claimed.

Instead, under a Franco–Thai agreement of August 1893, Bangkok had been obliged to make a series of lesser concessions. All Thai rights on the east bank of the Mekong were renounced, and by agreeing not to deploy troops within a twenty-five-kilometre zone down its west bank, Bangkok effectively handed over the river itself. Cambodia's 'lost provinces' were to be subject to the same immunity from Thai troops. And by way of a surety that these and other conditions would be met, Bangkok had been obliged to acquiesce in the French occupation of Chantaburi, a Thai port strategically situated between Bangkok and the 'lost' Cambodian provinces.

In effect, France had obtained exclusive rights over the whole of what is now the Lao PDR, plus a say of great potential in the 'lost' Cambodian provinces and in that strip of Thai territory twenty-five kilometres wide but about 1500 long, and indefinite possession of an important Thai town and port (Chantaburi). But this was only the beginning; for though the Quai d'Orsay intended the agreement as a final settlement, gung-ho colonialists like Pavie interpreted it as a charter for further encroachment. As Rosebery would put it, Thailand was being 'eaten like an artichoke – leaf by leaf'. With about half of the country – admittedly not the most fleshy bits – now detached, its more succulent heartland in the Menam basin was exposed. Thailand's independence was still far from assured, and safeguarding what remained of the kingdom within its diminished borders now became a British obsession.

Alongside this life-and-death struggle for the survival of a major Asian state, the future of the upriver *tampon* seemed less important. The French had duly agreed to a delimitation of the mini-buffer on site, and this was where the redoubtable James George Scott came in. While for seven years Pavie had been chalking out the ground for French rule in Laos, Scott had been doing much the same for British rule in the Shan states. The two men had then crossed swords in Bangkok, where Scott briefly served as the British Chargé d'Affaires, and they were now, in 1895, to head their respective border commissions in the joint demarcation of the mini-buffer south of Jinghong.

Scott thoroughly approved of the British occupation of Muong Sing. He was confident that the area pertained to one of the Shan states and eagerly championed Colquhoun's 'Golden Railway' as the best possible ploy for making the British position on the upper Mekong unassailable. A fanatical games-player, he had been responsible for introducing the Burmese, the Shans and even the 'wild Wa' to soccer; while other travellers distributed seed potatoes, Scott doled out footballs. Famously he had once led out a scratch team with an ex-rugby player in goal. England – it was 'England v. Burma' – were 3–0 down before it dawned on him that the goalie, while launching himself acrobatically at anything that flew over the bar, merely turned to retrieve anything that passed under it.

Much the same misunderstanding now torpedoed Scott's efforts in Muong Sing. Despite fielding an impressive team, including the formidable Mrs Scott, he found his Commission fatally handicapped when Pavie produced incontrovertible evidence that Muong Sing in fact already belonged to Thailand. It could not be regarded as anything to do with the Shan states because its chief had acknowledged Thai suzerainty as recently as

1892. Pavie had the papers to prove it, and since all Thai territory on the east bank was now under French protection, Scott and his commissioners were trespassing. The British occupation was illegal and the Union Jack must be hauled down immediately.

Scott, of course, refused; he could do no such thing without orders from above. And Pavie, of course, declined to proceed with the demarcation. The *état de tampon* was dead. But the British still held Muong Sing and, though duty-bound to surrender it, determined to exact a price commensurate with the acute embarrassment that retreat would entail. This took the form of an 1896 Anglo–French agreement under the terms of which both sides solemnly agreed never to move troops into Thailand's Menam basin 'without the consent of the other, in any event, or under any circumstances'. In effect, for the price of another leaf, the heart of the artichoke was thus removed from the plate.

French colonial interests thought they had got a bargain. The British nose had been bloodied in Muong Sing; and further south, between the west bank of the Mekong and the now reserved Menam basin, many square kilometres of Thai territory might yet be detached 'leaf by leaf'. But the British also thought they had a bargain. Press reports of a 'Siamese surrender' by Lord Salisbury's new government might delight the French, but were hopelessly misinformed. For as Warington Smyth put it, 'the Menam valley, for practical purposes, *is* Siam'. It contained 80 per cent of the country's population and accounted for about 90 per cent of its revenues. In return for what was now reckoned the worthless Muong Sing, London had secured a guaranteed future for one of its better markets and had erected an insuperable impediment to any French protectorate over Thailand.

The matter did not end there. The Thais still demanded the return of Chantaburi while the French detected enough infringements of the 1893 agreement to hang on to it. In fact Pavie's successors proved just as adept at exploiting the situation as Pavie himself. Mutual recrimination led to a further Franco–Thai convention in 1904 and to a further Franco–Thai treaty in 1907, both of which benefited from the 1904 Anglo–French global trade-off known as the *Entente Cordiale*.

In the first of these transactions, the French swapped Chantaburi for Kratt, a place of less significance, and exchanged that twenty-five-kilometre exclusion zone down the west bank of the Mekong for two permanent west bank acquisitions. One was the triangular wedge between Ubon and the Cambodian border that brought Bassac and its laid-back sirens under French rule; Lagrée and his colleagues would thoroughly have approved of that. The other was the long strip of Luang Prabang territory that, starting opposite the town, extended down to Paklai, the place to which in 1885 the town's royal fugitives had been whirled through the rapids. Pavie's befriending of them had not been in vain.

Another clause in the 1904 convention continued the gradual alienation – or liberation – from Thai control of those still 'lost' Cambodian provinces. This reclamation process was completed by the 1907 treaty. For the return of Kratt and other minor concessions, Bangkok finally signed over to Phnom Penh, and so to France, the provinces of Siem Reap, Battambang and Sisophon, comprising the whole of the western end of the Great Lake's basin including, of course, 'the Khmer Versailles' of Angkor. If Lagrée, who knew and loved the place better than any of his companions, had made a deathbed wish, it would have been for just that. As it was, the satisfaction of a job well done fell to Louis Delaporte, who by 1907 was acknowledged as the foremost '*explorateur d'Angkor*'.

This completed the territorial carve-up of the region. *Le tampon* had been flushed down the Mekong; the heart of the Thai artichoke had survived intact; and from its detached leaves, the French had begun experimenting with the short-lived and never very rewarding concoction known as *l'Union Indo-Chinoise*. Time was not on their side. The man who would call himself Ho Chi Minh was already ten years old in 1907. The Tonkinese irregulars who were still opposing the imposition of French rule would seamlessly mutate into the nationalist and then Communist cadres who overthrew it.

Yet despite subsequent wars both hot and cold, secret and sensational, and despite interminable insurgencies, unwanted interventions, and revolutions too numerous to relate, the frontiers so contentiously drawn up at the turn of the nineteenth century have survived into the twenty-first century. If their meanderings take little account of geography it is because they still, with extra-ordinary fidelity, correspond to the wish-list of prestigious sites, strategic positions and congenial fiefs compiled by Lagrée and his companions in the course of their upriver journey to China.

As the Mekong Exploration Commission finally fought its way free of south-east Asia's malarial forests and impenetrable allegiances, there was an understandable sense of mission accomplished. The Mekong itself was not a natural highway, yet against all odds the expedition had traced its course, discovered lands of both political and commercial potential, and pioneered a route that led into the deepest and least-known recesses of the Chinese empire. Geographers would be grateful even if colonial prospectors were unconvinced.

Poised at Jinghong on the threshold of China, Lagrée and Garnier anticipated no further surprises. An assessment of Yunnan's political condition, a careful cataloguing of its produce and requirements, and perhaps some further sightings of the Mekong as it issued from Tibet looked to be the most they might achieve. Then they would head for the Yangtse, whose navigability from neighbouring Sichuan down to Shanghai and the China coast was well attested. With the Mekong discredited as a highway into western China, the Yangtse's pre-eminence looked assured. Had the expedition's findings in Laos and Burma comprised its only discoveries, the dream of a French empire in the East would probably have been abandoned. France would have sadly turned her back on Indo-China – just as Lagrée and his men now did. But, unsuspected at the time, their most decisive addition to that wish-list of future acquisitions had yet to come.

To the Commission, Jinghong's 1893 transfer to China would have seemed quite logical. Those crimped feet and humped bridges noted by de Carné clearly advertised the proximity of the Celestial Empire, and the expedition's official contacts confirmed its influence. Here Burma's representative was an irrelevance. 'He was not taken too seriously,' says Garnier. A galaxy of exotic hill tribes made the last of the Shan states scarcely Shan at all. When, before Jinghong's council, Lagrée drew from its envelope the expedition's Chinese letter of accreditation, 'there came a great silence'. A Chinese secretary certified that the document was genuine, and as it was read aloud, the entire gathering 'prostrated themselves in respect'. Despite appearances, the foreign vagabonds evidently were the great mandarins they pretended to be. Porters and guides would be at their disposal as soon as required.

They left Jinghong after barely a week, crossing the Mekong for the last time on a ferry comprised of a platform lashed between two boats. Next day they zigzagged steeply out of the valley up cliffs that rise to 1300 metres. It was the highest they had yet been, and from the top they got their last glimpse of the river. A gash of silver in the middle distance, it bellied to gulp down a wayward tributary before burrowing back into the hills. Garnier stood entranced, savouring thoughts of its still elusive headwaters.

A misty drizzle that had hung about the mountain cleared, and a warm sun bathed this distant landscape in light. To

*the east and north there were visible only endless waves of
sizeable mountains rearing higher and higher like the heavy
swell of a petrified ocean.*

The mountains to the north marked the frontier of Chinese Yunnan. Still climbing, the expedition snaked along ridges covered in
pine forest. At night they descended to villages where the houses
were no longer on stilts and there were fleas instead of mosquitoes.
Here they found furniture – real cabinets and cupboards, benches
and tables. Thanks to their Beijing passports, food was provided
free and they sat on chairs to eat it. 'To appreciate our delight at
what may seem rather puerile pleasures, you have to have sought
in vain, for months on end, for a comfortable position in which
to eat crouching,' says Garnier. Peas and beans grew in the fields,
and pears and plums in the hedgerows. The pigs were bigger, the
chickens meatier. It was hard not to get excited because, coming
from the tropical south, they were being constantly reminded of
France. Entering China was like a homecoming.

Their excitement may be gauged by that of the modern traveller heading in the opposite direction. Few cross into the Xishuangbanna Autonomous Dai Prefecture by the checkpoints from
Muong Sing and Luang Nam Tha in Laos, but hordes, foreign
as well as Chinese, bus or fly into Jinghong from all over China.
Hothouse vegetation, exotically attired minorities and allegedly
'wild' elephants command a premium in the People's Republic.
The balmy winters are especially attractive. Honeymooners come
in coachloads to pose beside banana plants and find romance
among the rubber trees. 'Tropical' supposes 'paradise'; and over
workers from the bleak cities of the north, the heavy air of
Xishuangbanna exercises a Californian fascination. No one likes
to be reminded that it was in fact paranoid imperialists who here
so obligingly invited China to thrust out a toe into the soft steamy
world of the south-east Asian rainforest.

The rest of Yunnan is a less yielding and less wooded land. Elevated, riven by deep valleys, it serves, like Afghanistan, as a rugged hook over which to tuck and gather an untidy end of the swagged Himalayas. The mountains, like the rivers, tumble from the Tibetan plateau to sweep in subsiding folds that run south-east across the province, corrugating what would otherwise be rolling upland. While cresting the ridge of one such fold, the expedition caught sight of Semao. Known as Muong La in Lao/Shan, de Carné gave it only its Chinese name. It was, after all, their first Chinese town.

At last, on the afternoon of 18 October 1867, five months after our departure from Luang Prabang and sixteen months after leaving Saigon, from the summit of a high mountain, a great plain lay stretched out before our eyes, and at its extremity, on a low hill, was a veritable town with white gables, red walls and tiled roofs. We were about to tread the soil which supports one of the oldest and least known peoples in the world; all our hearts beat with joy and our eyes were moist with tears; if I had to die on the journey, I would have wished to expire there, like Moses on Mount Nebo embracing with his last look the land of Canaan.

Though not destined to die just yet, de Carné probably was the weakest of the party. Whereas recurrent malaria – or dysentery in Thorel's case – affected the others in delirious bouts, the young man from the Quai d'Orsay seems to have suffered from a less erratic and unremitting fever. Joubert, his closest (and perhaps only) friend, looked after him and would continue to do so when the expedition was over. But the damage seems already to have been done. At twenty-three years old, Louis de Carné was a dying man. If he hailed their first Chinese town with tears, it was not because, like Garnier, he felt at home in China but because, as he had once himself put it, home lay through China.

'A strange country, full of mysteries and contrasts', Yunnan confronted the expedition with both devastation and abundance. Markets displaying produce of every conceivable description delighted Thorel; mines – for copper, zinc, silver, lead, iron, coal – laid a heavy claim on Joubert's time. Yet in this land of plenty, the population lived in acute distress. Semao, though a sizeable place and certainly the largest town they had seen since Saigon, lay half in ruins with whole suburbs reduced to a mass of blackened timbers and rubble. Troops of the self-styled 'Sultan of Dali (or Ta-ly)' had lately sacked it and were still in the vicinity. The war had been going on for five years, and now divided the province along a front that ebbed and flowed in a great north–south arc.

To the west of this arc, all was under Muslim control from the grey-walled city of Dali. The city flanked a great lake of the same name, out of which flowed a tributary of the Mekong. In fact the river itself, throughout its headlong dash down the margin of Yunnan, ran almost entirely through mountains currently under Dali's control. On the other hand, the east of the province, with its capital of Kunming (then known as Yunnan-fu), acknowledged Beijing's authority and was administered by mandarins appointed by the imperial court. Travellers with a letter of recommendation from this same court could here expect every assistance, whereas in Dali such accreditation would be useless and possibly dangerous.

The expedition was therefore faced with a choice. Either they could stick with the Mekong, hope to slip unchallenged across the warring front line, and then be prepared to chance their luck with the Dali Muslims – this was Garnier's preference, and he volunteered to go alone – or they could play safe, defer investigation of the Mekong, and head for Kunming. There, unless the news of Dali was more encouraging, they would be well situated to strike out for the Yangtse and a boat to Shanghai. This was the course chosen by *le Commandant*.

Mindful of their difficulties in the Shan states, Lagrée was determined not to repeat the mistake of venturing into a disturbed land uninvited. Additionally, according to de Carné, now that the Mekong had been revealed as unnavigable, Lagrée had 'renounced' its exploration and 'felt it would be useful' to investigate another river. This other waterway was the Red River (Song Hong, Yuan Jiang). It was known to flow to the sea through Tonkin (north Vietnam) where, says de Carné, 'our flag would be able to secure an easy entrance'; and its upper reaches were supposedly in Yunnan, probably to the east of Semao. But if the expedition headed north-west for the Mekong, it would almost certainly miss them.

Garnier thus found his preference for the Mekong rejected, and he made no secret of his disgust. In fact he insists he was not the only one to be disappointed, for 'we were all', he says, 'young and in love with adventure'. But not so Lagrée, nor the failing de Carné. The tensions that had been kept in check during more perilous times were becoming hard to disguise.

They surfaced again when the invaluable Alévy here took his departure. His fluency in Lao would be of little further use and he was anxious to return to his family in Phnom Penh. With a plausible story about the loss of his finger, he duly did so, arriving in French territory to deliver a progress report on the expedition just ahead of the expedition's own return. Without Alévy, and with no Chinese interpreter, they were now dependent on Tei, one of their Vietnamese auxiliaries. Though unable to converse with their hosts, Tei could read and write the Chinese characters (they were the same as those used in Vietnam). It meant that everything had to be written down, but Garnier reckoned it was worth the trouble. Lagrée disagreed. He doubted whether Tei's skills were up to the subtleties of political discourse, and he was reluctant to trust him in matters that might decide the expedition's fate. Again Garnier found his leader's caution incomprehensible, and said so.

In Yunnan, apart from the war, the only obvious danger lay

in the insatiable curiosity of the Yunnanese. After months in the solitude of the forest, crowds in themselves were a welcome novelty, but Semao's crowds were nothing like the gently buzzing Buddhist throng that had so charmed them at Luang Prabang. Here they were mobbed unmercifully from the moment they entered the place. The pagoda in which they were billeted was under permanent attack, its open hall so densely packed that even sticks failed to clear a path across it, and the door to its upper apartment so closely besieged that only drawn bayonets thrust through its panels prevented its being crushed. The roof, when not being stripped of tiles, was so laden with clamouring humanity that it threatened to collapse.

This was by no means exceptional. Except in Kunming, where the expedition would have its own walled compound, Yunnan's baying masses respected neither peace, privacy, nor personal dignity. The explorers no longer thought much of being the first 'white men' in this remote corner of China. It was impossible to eat, sleep, write or walk without being scrutinised and mauled like some new family pet. For the most innocent and intimate of excursions an armed guard was essential. When Delaporte, ignoring this precaution, was discovered quietly sketching, the press of bodies led to a knife fight, then a riot.

Missiles were a constant hazard, though presumably thrown less in anger than frustration. Garnier would suffer a nasty head wound when struck by a brick; it was like a biblical stoning, he says. The authorities were not indifferent, affording protection when they could and, in the case of the brick-thrower, effecting a quick arrest. Next day, on enquiring after the culprit, Garnier was advised not to bother himself as the man had already been executed.

Leaving Semao they vowed to halt, when possible, in wayside inns rather than risk more urban hospitality. With new shoes all round, and with the paths through the paddy fields here paved, they made good speed to Puer ('Pou-eul'), then as now a tea-growing centre where the road to Dali (and the Mekong) forks off from that to Kunming. Inevitably Garnier made another plea for permission to take the fork. He reckoned that, travelling light and alone, he could reach the river, follow it for a bit and then double back to rejoin the main party without occasioning any delay.

But Lagrée would have none of it. They must stick together. The country even here was being ravaged by bands of brigands who might be either desperate refugees or unruly soldiery. Who would care for Garnier if he went down with another fit of fever? How would they explain matters if he got killed? And what if they came across the possibly navigable Red River while their hydrographer was off flirting with the definitely unnavigable Mekong?

In growing discord they slogged on, scaling ever higher, barer ridges and slithering down to ever more intensively cultivated valleys. Thorel was appalled at the deforestation. Timber for rebuilding those villages destroyed in the fighting, even firewood, was virtually unobtainable. People cooked on smoky pyres of grass or cow dung. Flash floods washed away their fields while the streams needed for irrigation were drying up. There was a lesson here, thought Thorel, for the management of the Lao forests, should they become a French responsibility. Lagrée and Garnier were more concerned about where the water went. Unable to decide whether they had yet crossed the watershed from the Mekong to the Red River, they quarrelled about that too.

It was now November. In response to the altitude as much as the latitude (they were still technically just within the tropics), the thermometer was plummeting. One night it touched 4°. On men accustomed to and equipped for equatorial conditions, the wind registered a biting chill-factor and the cold rain felt wetter than the heaviest monsoon downpour. In Semao they had ordered new tailoring, but more for appearances than warmth. They envied the

Chinese who travelled sandwiched between 'mattresses' (presumably a form of quilting) under which they cradled 'a true warmer' (perhaps a clay fire-pot). The mandarins wore thermal underwear that was stitched from 'another product of the region', namely a fine cloth woven from the spun thread of a particular kind of spider.

Climbing to 1800 metres the expedition passed a decapitated head in a cage and then 'the first opium poppy fields that we had so far seen'. Neither of these novelties was the work of the Wa, whose distribution did not extend to western Yunnan. The decapitated head was intended as a warning to bandits and the opium was for local consumption.

Ahead, deep gorges rent the ground in the shape of a star. They began to descend into one of them which opened into a wide valley of 'wild, burnt colours' where stood 'a town whose crenellations were reflected in the waves of a splendid river'. Garnier was reminded of the Middle East. There were palm trees beside the river, and orange groves and fields of sugarcane. Warm breezes fluttered to meet them. Down there they would be back in the tropics proper.

The town and the river were both called Yuan Jiang. Rivers in China changed their name every few hundred kilometres, but for once Lagrée and Garnier were in agreement. This could well be what the Vietnamese called the Song Hong, the Red River, the great artery that linked Haiphong to Hanoi and upper Tonkin. Not as big as the Mekong at Jinghong, it was still a noble stream, wider than they had expected, of impressive volume, and definitely a bit reddish. Boats were visible on the banks, and though the current appeared strong, its potential was well worth investigating. Lagrée's gamble looked as if it might pay off. As de Carné put it, in abandoning the Mekong for the Red River, they had discarded a subject of 'purely geographical interest for a political one of the first order'.

TEN

❧

Death in Yunnan

'A journey up the Mekong is [today] impossible for both geographical and political reasons.'
MICHEL PEISSEL,
The Last Barbarians, 1997

AT YUAN JIANG the expedition found itself not just expected but welcomed. Though a place of no great significance, the town had been notified of their approach and, less affected by the war, decided to make the most of it. Mandarins in their finest robes waited at the gates while two hundred pigtailed soldiers and standard-bearers lined the route. In front ran a pack of boys not taunting the Frenchmen with obscenities but carrying placards with messages of greeting. The entire population seemed to have turned out to watch them pass. Gongs boomed, trumpets blared, and an artillery salute competed with the rattle of firecrackers.

Most gratifying of all to cold-pinched travellers from the uplands was the heat that radiated from the mud walls and stone paving. It was like descending into an oven. The fiery zephyrs left de Carné, still unaccustomed to Yunnan's harsh seasonal variations, feeling quite 'intoxicated'. The expedition was housed in a magnificent three-hundred-year-old pagoda secluded on the outskirts of the town. 'We found everything we could wish for in this oasis, even straw to sleep on.' Basic foodstuffs were much cheaper here, though they scarcely needed to buy any. In a mark of unusual respect, the city's mandarins paid the first visit, each being announced by a large red poster and an edible gift – 'a hog, a ram, capons . . . baskets of oranges and tea'. The slender trumpets that heralded their arrival brought to de Carné's mind those given to the angels on the Day of Judgement by Michelangelo. All in all, it felt a lot like paradise.

Never, during the course of their entire journey, had the expedition experienced a reception like that at Yuan Jiang. In fact, 'never before had we been taken so seriously', says Garnier. Nor would they receive the like again. It was as if the city fathers of this remote township not only appreciated the standing of an official French commission, but had somehow divined the crucial role that it would award to their very own river.

The governor, a kindly and expansive mandarin, might have been more knowledgeable but he could not have been more helpful. Lagrée, desperate to glean all he could about the river, patiently formulated his questions in French, then asked them in Vietnamese so that Tei could render them into Chinese characters for the governor to read. The responses came back the same way. It was hard work, and there were many misunderstandings. But uniquely this inquisition benefited from the use of maps. Lagrée had a chart of the Chinese empire that had been compiled by French Jesuits in the seventeenth century and on which, during the march from Puer, they had at last recognised a place name and been able to locate themselves. The governor also had a map. Though annoyingly vague about natural features – mountains were depicted as identical green sugarlumps and every watercourse, however insignificant, as a wiggle of uniform width – it was unexpectedly accurate as to distances.

After hours of interrogation and intense scrutiny of both maps, a consensus began to emerge. The river at Yuan Jiang was neither the Mekong nor the Yangtse. It, too, rose somewhere in the mountains of the far north-west, yet it flowed neither south like the Mekong nor east like the Yangtse, but somewhat in between. At no great distance below Yuan Jiang it ceased to be navigable. It became so again in the vicinity of mountains that marked the frontier with Tonkin. And thereafter it flowed to the sea through Tonkin.

Meanwhile Garnier had measured its width at between 150 and three hundred metres. His barometer made its height above sea level about five hundred metres, which was much the same as the Mekong at Jinghong. It proved nothing except that the expedition's hydrographer was still coming to terms with his '*nostalgie de Mékong*'.

By way of establishing a claim of precedence to what now seemed indeed to be the Red River, the expedition hired boats, hoisted the tricolour on a makeshift mast, and sailed a short way downstream. Encountering impossibly broken water, they landed and left Garnier to continue this reconnaissance as best he could. The expedition would wait for him at Jianshui.

In the end, it was Garnier who would have to wait for the expedition. Travelling mostly in boats, but with some difficult rock-clambering in between, he managed only a day and a half before having to give up. The governor of Yuan Jiang had been right: this section of the river was unnavigable. Whereas a penchant for forests endeared the Mekong to naturalists, the Red River was clearly designed for geologists. Instead of traversing the country, it mined it, boring into the ground to create its own roofless shaft of twisting canyon and sheer-walled gorge. Strata of schist, limestone and conglomerate slanted diagonally across the cliffs, which in places were 1800 metres high. Rocks crashed from above into the stream; tributaries shunted barriers of shingle across it. Low water allowed one to climb round the worst obstructions, but in spate there would be no footing for the pedestrian and no safe channel for the sailor.

Yet extensive enquiry once again confirmed that this was definitely the Red River of Tonkin, and that 150 kilometres down-stream it was indeed navigable. To a place called Mang-ko, which was not far from the Tonkin border, Vietnamese merchants used once to travel upriver from Hanoi to exchange salt and tropical produce for Yunnan's ores, especially copper and zinc for the Viet-namese coinage. The trade had declined during the Taiping rebellion and had not been revived; Beijing and Hué were still at daggers drawn. But according to de Carné, the French ascendancy in southern Vietnam 'compels us not to remain indifferent'. On the evidence of the mines they had seen, Yunnan could become 'the most important metallurgical supplier in the world'. It was vital, urged the young man from the Quai d'Orsay, that French diplomatic leverage at Hué and Beijing be deployed to get this route reopened.

[For] *the so-long-sought communication by which Western China's abundance of riches must one day flow into a French port is to be expected by way of the Sonkhoi* [the Red River], *not by the Mekong. This is an undisputed truth that must surely prompt the exploration of the Tonkin river.*

Garnier seconded this, but without much enthusiasm. He must have resented the undisguised delight over what de Carné called 'purely geographical questions' having been discarded and 'illu-sions' about the Mekong 'finally' discredited. At the time, the man to whom history would award the first French conquests in Tonkin showed absolutely no premonition of the role he would himself play in the revival of the Red River trade route.

On the contrary, Garnier still pined for the Mekong and was again fretting at the limitations of group travel. In his account of Yuan Jiang and its river, he deliberates at length on the local tribes and in discreet detail on a more intimate 'trip' that was organised by a Chinese customs official with a long black pipe. He implies that this diversion was for purely medicinal reasons and entirely fortuitous, just like the bathing belles in Laos. He happened to be suffering severely at the time – 'from a very dry cough that almost prevented me from speaking . . . my eyes starting out of my head . . . [and] an excruciating migraine'. The customs official took pity on him and made him lie down on a camp bed. The pipe, the flame, the needle and the poppy resin just happened to be ranged beside the bed. The *douanier* prepared the dose and Garnier took a few puffs, then a few more. His sore throat eased and the migraine vanished 'as if by magic'.

'Several' pipes followed. 'It was the first time in a while that I had smoked opium, and the experience convinced me that, correctly administered, the drug can become a useful remedy; only abuse makes it a deadly poison.' Seemingly its remedial qualities were as much psychological as physical. 'Mademoiselle Buonaparte' was beginning to feel her old self again.

Reunited at Jianshui, in which place Garnier was hit by the brick, the expedition began its final push for Kunming. It was 9 December, over six months since they had left Luang Prabang and a year and a half since they had set off from Saigon. Back on Yunnan's Tibet-like plateau, it seemed incredible that they were only now crossing the Tropic of Cancer. The cold was so intense that it snowed. This was a great novelty to their Vietnamese and Filipino followers. For fifteen minutes they chased snowflakes and laughed maniacally, then for the rest of the day they wept as their shoeless feet turned a purplish blue and their gloveless hands unaccountably ached. Their masters sympathised; icicles tinkled in long French beards, and compass and pencil slipped from Garnier's benumbed fingers.

The prospect of Kunming kept them going. Nowadays a city of four million with something of a slick Seattle about it, Yunnan's capital was even then a genuine metropolis. Its battlemented walls rose theatrically above a rolling plain dotted with vast lakes. The walls enclosed an area of at least ten square kilometres, within which the streets were lined with stylish shops, restaurants and business houses, each distinguished by its own gilt-lettered sign-board. Like rustics on the loose, the new arrivals gawped as palanquins bearing doll-like dowagers wrapped in ermine and exquisite silks pushed past them. 'We felt ourselves blushing over our appearance and our stained and scruffy clothes,' says Garnier. They reckoned the population, probably the most ethnically mixed in all China, at about fifty thousand. Before the war with the Muslims of Dali it had been more like two hundred thousand.

Apart from creature comforts, what the explorers wanted above all else was news. They needed to know how far it was to the Yangtse, whether it was worth chancing a final visit to the Mekong, and where they could raise a loan. More desperately they longed for word of the outside world, of war and peace among nations, of the fortunes of fellow countrymen and the doings of loved ones. The priority, then, was an interpreter, and the most likely candidate a missionary. Even if Chinese, he would surely speak Latin.

Their prayers were answered as soon as they arrived. It happened to be Christmas Eve and, heaven be praised, a Père Protteau was waiting for them. He was one of those long-serving missionaries who had so identified with his flock that he lived, and even looked, like a Chinese. But at the sound of his French, albeit somewhat rusty, they fell upon him, bombarding him with camaraderie and questions. The good Protteau did his best; but as is ever the way after a long absence, the tidings fell well short of the travellers' expectations. In fact 'he was unable to give us any more recent news from Europe than we already had'.

The best he could do was to refer them to Père Fenouil, the Vicar Apostolic for Yunnan. It was Fenouil who had written one of those letters warning of the war in Yunnan which the Jinghong authorities had mistaken for a prohibition. He was evidently a more worldly cleric than Protteau. Normally resident in the city, he had just had to vacate his house because its magazine, in which he manufactured gunpowder for the military, had blown up. Arson was suspected and Fenouil had decamped to a safe distance. He was sent for but would not arrive until after the New Year.

Christmas 1866 had passed unnoticed. It had been the day of that touching send-off by the good people of Bassac in lower Laos, a scene so sun-flushed and lush that it seemed a world apart and a lifetime ago. They made devotional amends in 1867, trooping off to mass on Christmas Day as part of Protteau's minuscule congregation. On Boxing Day Lagrée began the rounds of the civil and military authorities and at last, thanks to Protteau's translation, began to get a clearer picture of the war with the Muslims of Dali and of the extent to which this might dictate their future movements.

The first revelation was that Kunming itself was in imminent danger. It had been sacked once before, and now the rebels were again within fifty kilometres. A general exodus of the more prosperous traders was already underway. Lest the expedition be cut off or become besieged, it was imperative that it too move out as soon as possible. They stayed only long enough to conduct their business, and would be back on the road within a couple of weeks.

A loan was negotiated with General Ma, the military commander-in-chief. Their financial worries had eased in China thanks to the official status accorded them by the Beijing passports. Food, accommodation and carriage were free. But from guests so honoured a commensurate level of liberality and respectable demeanour was expected. With their stocks of European guns and knick-knacks almost exhausted, the travellers needed cash just to support their condition. The business community proved reluctant to help; times were too uncertain. But General Ma, a redoubtable warlord with a passion for firearms and a ragtag army to equip, offered as much cash as they wanted and the easiest of terms. He was indifferent to the duration of the loan, asking only that repayment be made in guns and ammunition of the very latest European manufacture. They could be shipped via his agent in Canton. At this stage it did not occur to the Commission that an arms shipment might be the perfect excuse to pioneer the reopening of the Red River trade route.

A topsy-turvy banquet with the General introduced them to Chinese dining. The dessert of pomegranate pips and pineapples came first and the bowls of bird's nest soup last. In between, dishes by the hundred ran the gamut of Yunnan's edible productions, from fish-guts to lichen salad and 'worms of every description'. It lasted three hours, yet the General himself ate nothing. He was fasting, he explained, this being Ramadan and he a Muslim. Much of Kunming's population was Muslim. Clearly the battle lines of this 'war of religion' were not quite analogous to those of Catholics and Huguenots or Christians and Moors with which the Commission was familiar.

The war had in fact originated as an industrial dispute involving the terms and conditions offered to miners, many of them Muslims, in western Yunnan. It had then acquired a decidedly religious dimension as a result of reciprocal massacres, but had since degenerated into a confused struggle typical of China's borderlands in which local warlords fiercely contested, and occasionally endorsed, Beijing's currently impaired authority. The General had originally taken his orders from the rebels of Dali. After capturing Kunming, he had defected to Beijing and been appointed its commander-in-chief; but whether he was now poised to repel or to welcome the new onslaught was uncertain. Father Fenouil was actively intriguing on Beijing's behalf to prevent another defection, and in this context the loan to Lagrée and the promise of guns was most timely.

In another anomaly, the Grand Mufti, the spiritual leader of Yunnan's Muslims, had also thrown in his lot with Beijing. He too was in Kunming and, on Fenouil's insistence, Lagrée and Garnier eventually secured an audience with him. So far, no one had encouraged them to renew their designs on the Mekong. It was said to be impossible to reach the river without entering territory under Dali's control, and any introduction obtained in Kunming would there be worthless. Dali's sultan would be especially suspicious of anyone travelling under Beijing's protection. He was said to execute all foreigners unless they were merchants; the only exception had been for some Europeans who were rumoured to be producing guns and gunpowder for him.

This last piece of news did not pass unchallenged by the vigilant Garnier. Any mention of Europeans in the Mekong basin was as a red rag to so bullish a patriot. 'Was this', he wondered, 'an English expedition which, starting from the frontiers of Burma, had entered China and then altered its purpose?' If the British were already in Dali, a further attempt to reach the uppermost Mekong suddenly became highly desirable, in fact a priority. The previous year's panic over the Dutch surveyor Duyshart seemed to be repeating itself, although, recalling that fiasco, Garnier claims that they viewed the new rumours with more caution.

The matter was clinched by the Grand Mufti. An octogenarian who had once made the pilgrimage to Mecca, this so-called 'Lao Papa' had little regard for infidel strangers but a passion for astronomy. Garnier, as a surveyor, duly indulged it. When he also reassembled the Mufti's telescope and actually got it to focus, the old man was delighted. Convinced that he was dealing with genuine men of science, he could see no objection to their pursuing their enquiries at Dali or beyond. He therefore volunteered, and duly penned, a warm letter of commendation to the rebel sultan.

'With one word from me,' he claimed, 'you can travel freely throughout the whole land.' Although de Carné thought him both 'deranged' and 'a braggart', they now had the authority to give Dali a try.

When the Commission left Kunming on 8 January, the Mekong was thus again their goal, with Dali as its gateway. Yet this final and fateful excursion is still the least explicable of the entire journey. Except for the mad Mufti, everyone from General Ma to Père Fenouil and the entire civil and military establishment of Yunnan advised most strongly against it. The season – midwinter – was as unpropitious as the political climate. Apart from the extreme cold that awaited them at heights of up to three thousand metres, they would have barely three months in which to reach the river and return to some navigable part of the Yangtse before the spring thaw made the roads impassable. The most they could hope for would be a geographically insignificant glimpse of the Mekong amid terrain of quite exceptional difficulty and no conceivable colonial value.

Additionally, after a twenty-month ordeal of tropical enervation and now arctic discomfort, none of them was in a remotely fit state to address the inclines of the eastern Himalayas. Life expectancy among Europeans in eighteenth-century India had proverbially been put at 'two monsoons'. The Commission had had its two monsoons, admittedly with the benefit of quinine but in far more fever-ridden conditions and invariably without the consolation of a solid roof. Garnier's malaria and Thorel's dysentery continued to recur. Delaporte would register alarming new fever symptoms, de Carné was visibly fading, and most worryingly of all, Lagrée himself seemed to be losing his grip. De Carné dates *le Commandant*'s decline to early December, perhaps in the course of their bleak march from Yuan Jiang. His perennial laryngitis was exacerbated by the cold, and to it were now added amoebic dysentery and an as yet undiagnosed liver condition. Leaving Kunming he was unable to walk and within a couple of days he could no longer ride. He was transferred to a litter.

How far Lagrée's condition affected his decision-making – or whether he was actually making any decisions – is far from clear. Garnier says that while in Kunming all of them endorsed the need for a final bid for the Mekong, and that they did so in the form of 'a moral pact'. The term implies consultation and suggests that some sort of consensus was reached. Lagrée is said to have sub-scribed to the pact; but he is not credited with having proposed it, and there is no mention of the uncommunicative agonising that so exasperated his colleagues at other critical moments. It looks very much as if *le Commandant* was no longer commanding and that, if he had any misgivings, they were brushed aside. When a week later the die was finally cast at Dongchuan, any such reser-vations would be discounted on the grounds of his physical and mental incapacity.

Dongchuan ('Tong-tchouen') lies about 150 kilometres due north of Kunming near the Yangtse. A similar distance further north, at a place called Yanjin (or 'La-wa-tan'), a tributary of the Yangtse reportedly became navigable. There the ordeal would be over, in so far as the voyage downriver by junk and steamer thence to Shanghai and the China coast should be an undemanding for-mality. Kunming, then, was almost the end of their overland travels. As de Carné had cheerfully noted on their arrival in the city, 'we had no longer any real difficulties to encounter, and our return by Shanghai was virtually assured'. Allowing a week to reach Dongchuan, another week to attain Yanjin, and a few days for delays on the way, they could be boat-borne on the Yangtse by the end of January, and tucked up in the French legation in Shang-hai by mid-February. Little more than a month separated them from the world they knew and the recognition they craved; Lagrée was that close to a hospital bed and a chance of survival.

But not if they persisted in making a last excursion to the

Mekong. Back at its confluence with the Nam Ou above Luang Prabang they had given the Mekong the benefit of the doubt, resolving to stick with the main river despite the onset of the monsoon and the uncertainties of the Shan states. The same thing was happening again. Three months had elapsed since their last glimpse of that gash of silver from above Jinghong, and still the river held the fate of the expedition in its thundering waters.

For Garnier in particular, that *monomanie de Mékong* would not go away. While aware that reaching the river's Tibetan head-waters was now probably out of the question, he interpreted the expedition's instructions as commanding them to make the attempt. Admiral de Lagrandière's orders did mention pushing their geographical reconnaissance 'as far as possible', and under the heading of 'Information Required' they were indeed to report their findings 'on the question of the sources of the river'. But Garnier chose to conflate these two directives, to assume that information on the sources of the river could only come from their own on-the-spot observations, and to ignore another paragraph that made 'the health of the men and the scale of difficulty' the determining factors in any decision on this score.

Geographical science demanded a last effort, said Garnier; so did national pride. Only another attempt to reach the headwaters would 'crown' their 'triumph'. For him – and, it would emerge, preferably for him alone – the river retained its promise. It was no longer the promise just of a trade route into the interior, of a highway to China or even of an empire for the taking, but of a passion to be gratified, an obsession exorcised, a reputation secured.

Though 'morally' pledged to return west to the Mekong, they left Kunming heading north on the road to Dongchuan. To circum-vent the fighting it had been thought advisable to make a long detour, arcing through the neighbouring province of Sichuan and the less populated regions of northern Yunnan before homing in on Dali and then the river itself. This had the added attraction of enabling them to inspect a section of the upper Yangtse that had not yet been surveyed by Europeans. It also gave them the option of detaching unneeded baggage at Dongchuan for early forwarding to Yanjin and Shanghai. Several of their loyal followers from Saigon were reckoned too weak and susceptible to the cold for a further excursion. They too would be detached and sent downriver in charge of the baggage.

The march to Dongchuan took just over a week. With Lagrée's condition rapidly deteriorating, he was transferred from a saddle to the stretcher and then to a bed. After a day's rest, they continued. As if in sympathy with his master, Lagrée's pony, the 'Royal' presented to him at Kengtung, then collapsed and died almost instantly. Poison was suspected but Joubert, acting as vet, pronounced it a case of chronic indigestion. That night all except Frenchmen dined on pony stew.

At Dongchuan Lagrée's condition became critical. 'Serious symptoms of an afflicted liver manifested themselves,' says Garnier. 'He had to stay in bed all the time.' Obviously *le Commandant* could not manage an excursion to the Mekong, yet he 'felt a great pain when he had to admit that the evil had won and that he was unable to endure further exertions'.

Solicitude, loyalty, even plain common sense now surely dictated that the Mekong excursion be abandoned. According to de Carné, Lagrée's only hope was to wait until he felt well enough to make the short journey to Yanjin and then be whisked down the Yangtse to proper medical care. He could be in Shanghai within the month. They all knew this, and so did Lagrée himself.

A letter from Fenouil, the meddlesome cleric, and pleas from the mandarins of Dongchuan again urged them not to risk an excursion into the sultan of Dali's territory. Lagrée himself had probably never been that keen on the idea. Had anyone else been the invalid, he would almost certainly have countermanded the trip. But such was his selfless devotion to the success of the expedition that, according to de Carné, 'he could not bring himself to force us to renounce it solely on the grounds of his own ill-health'.

Garnier puts it differently and, in the opinion of many, less believably. In his version, *le Commandant* followed the admission that he could go no further with an order.

> *He charged me* [Garnier] *with fulfilling the moral agreement made at Yunnan* [Kunming] *to complete our journey with an excursion to Ta-ly* [Dali]. *I had no illusion about the numerous difficulties that this task entailed . . . I could not inspire in my travelling companions, to the same extent as M. de Lagrée, that confidence which is the prerequisite of success in an enterprise such as this. I counted on their good will and co-operation, which in the outcome would not fail me. Nevertheless I asked my chief for instructions in writing which, by outlining a general line of conduct, would give still more weight to my authority. He begged me to write them myself and bring them to him for signature.*

Garnier's orders as drafted by himself allowed for Joubert to stay behind to care for Lagrée. Delaporte, de Carné and Thorel, plus five of their remaining followers, were to accompany Garnier up the Yangtse and then, with a view to reaching the upper Mekong, across the hills to either Dali or Lijiang (a city north of Dali but under the same rebel jurisdiction). He was not to approach either of these places without having requested authorisation; and once there, he was to strike out for the Mekong 'alone and in the most expeditious manner possible'. They were all to be back within three months for a rendezvous at Yanjin.

Evidently 'the moral pact' had changed. Now it was only Garnier who was to have the honour of 'crowning their success' with further observations of the Mekong. His companions were simply coming along to lend weight to the enterprise should the rebel authorities prove unco-operative. 'If there was no danger, [I was] to leave my companions and escort behind to save them unnecessary fatigue,' Garnier explains. De Carné, on the other hand, was still looking forward to 'revisiting the Mekong', probably near Lijiang 'where having barely issued from Tibet it flows at the foot of a mountain five thousand metres high'. No European had ever been in the area. The prospect was sufficiently mouthwatering to overshadow the direst warnings, banish exhaustion, and 'rekindle our almost extinct ardour', says de Carné.

> *Had it been given to us to read the future, to foresee the reverse that was awaiting us at Dali and the sorrow that would greet us back at Dongchuan, perhaps the decision would have been different. But we were abrim with youthful confidence, and we resolved to start.*

In a cameo sadly unrecorded in Delaporte's sketchpad, they gathered for final farewells round *le Commandant*'s bed. Dr Joubert was understandably anxious, but the trembling handshakes and the whispered farewells owed most of their poignancy to retrospect. 'We departed on 30 January [1868] deeply upset at the state in which we left M. de Lagrée but still with high hopes of his recovery,' says Garnier.

They would be gone for just over two months, and would cover in that time more ground than on any comparable stage in the whole expedition. The baggage had again been reduced to the barest essentials; additional ponies were purchased so that each man could ride for at least some of each day; and they stayed mostly in wayside inns that rarely invited more than one night's rest. The urgency was dictated partly by the distances and by the need to forestall any opposition, and partly by the change of leader. Garnier liked to lead from the front. A phenomenal walker despite his size, he shot off ahead claiming that he needed peace and quiet to count his strides, take bearings and make calculations. The others, whether Vietnamese, Filipino or French, trailed in his wake, all of them very definitely followers.

If Lagrée's style of command had erred on the side of the inscrutable, Garnier's veered sharply towards the adversarial. Guns, till now scarcely mentioned other than as gifts or sporting pieces, suddenly achieve prominence; they are ever to hand, need constant loading, get menacingly 'presented', and are often slept beside. Rightly or wrongly, hostility is always expected and insolence readily imputed. Even his colleagues are not spared. Their confidence, which he was so keen to win, cannot have been increased by his recording every mishap, and in marked contrast to the restraint exercised by Lagrée, invariably identifying the culprit. When a gold bar representing half their exchequer was lost in the course of a hurried exodus, the finger was pointed at Delaporte. Thorel, as was his wont, escaped either censure or notice, but de Carné's transgressions received close attention. He was held up to ridicule when an outcry resulted from his improvising a trough for the horses out of a coffin 'whose proprietor was already at rest in it'. And when in Dali the mob pressed them hard, it was de Carné who was accused of using fists and a rifle butt to unnecessarily provocative effect.

The first two weeks of the march were through a corner of Sichuan and presented no difficulties other than those of the terrain. They crossed the upper Yangtse by ferry ('not since the time of Marco Polo had a traveller seen the Blue River so far from its mouth'), climbed through deep snow to the highest point in the entire journey ('the barometer indicated more than 3000 metres'), and then crossed back over the Yangtse into Yunnan. In the absence of any interpreter (the Chinese-reading Tei had been one of those left behind on health grounds) Father Lu, a Chinese missionary, gave them a chance to show off their Latin. From him they learned that to approach Lijiang without securing authority from Dali would be suicidal. Before all else they must present themselves to the sultan in the capital.

Entering territory under Dali's control, they strode past the first outpost and barged past the second. The country had been devastated; villagers huddled within the barricaded ruins of their houses. They crossed a watershed, then another; one of them was that between the tributaries of the Yangtse and those of the Mekong. Delaporte shot a pheasant, then went down with fever. Decapitated heads on spikes lined the trail and a gibbet from which hung an entire corpse stood out horribly well against the snowy hills. '*Memento homo quia pulvis es*,' intoned a Father Fang in almost unidentifiable Latin. It was Ash Wednesday.

Yet another priest, this time French, awaited them in the hills north of Lake Dali. The wisdom of relying on beleaguered Catholic missionaries in a determinedly Islamic sultanate was questionable, but they had no other means of making themselves understood. Father Leguilcher, their new facilitator, was little more than a fugitive, hiding up among the hill tribes whenever danger threatened. The risk that he would take in conducting them into the lions' den of Dali was thought to exceed that of men armed with the Grand Mufti's letter. Yet he took little persuading, perhaps because he saw the expedition's protection as his best chance of extricating himself from a clearly futile ministry.

On 29 February – 1868 was a leap year – they descended to the great expanse of sky and water that is Lake Dali. Lying north–south and about forty kilometres long, it lapped at a ledge of intensive cultivation dotted with lakeside pagodas and low-lying villages. Hills, bare in winter, converged from all directions and, along the west bank, reared up into a wall of mountains fretted with caves and snowy pinnacles. Through the fields between this wall and the lake, like an invitation to an ambush, ran the road to Dali itself. A fortalice guarded the northern approaches, and there the travellers were stopped while orders were awaited from the city.

Delaporte took the opportunity to sketch one of the finest panoramas they had met with. Why would he do this, asked suspicious onlookers, if not with a view to conquest? Meanwhile Garnier was treated to cautionary tales about the last 'Europeans' to present themselves at the gates of the city. All twenty had been put to death. The sheer scale of this massacre convinced him that, though foreigners, the victims were probably not real Europeans but Malays or Burmans. When a favourable response came from Dali, de Carné 'felt relieved of a heavy load of anxiety'. On 2 March they advanced to the walled city that stood four-square like a grit-grey sandcastle between the wave-flecked lake and a mountain of streaky white marble.

Forbidden cities, a desirable ingredient in any nineteenth-century travelogue, had not yet featured in the Commission's itinerary. Nor had religious fanaticism. The Buddhism of south-east Asia had rarely outraged the expedition's sensibilities and never presented any kind of a threat. On the whole, whether philosophically minded Catholics like de Carné or near-atheists like Garnier, they had found much to admire in the monastic traditions of Laos, especially the hospitality of the wats, and had noted enough similarities in devotional practice to prompt lively discussion on the relationship between Buddhism and Christianity.

Islam, though, was a very different matter. Of a 'Mussulman' despot, like the sultan of Dali, anything was possible. A fanatic by definition, the Islamic potentate was supposed to rule by terror, persecuting infidels as a matter of course and inflicting horrific punishments for any infringement of his arbitrary demands. De Carné relays stories of flayings, executions and of people being buried alive. Garnier, primed on the narratives of other explorers, simply recognised the value of a spine-chilling sultan and a forbidden city. Though no Mecca, Dali would serve as the expedition's Bukhara, Timbuktu and Riyadh all rolled into one.

As they approached the city, 'unsettling rumours' again assailed them. Father Leguilcher's few Christian disciples deserted him at the last moment, and the porters seemed minded to do likewise. 'At 3.30 p.m. we arrived at the town's north gate.' Each of the city's walls had – and has again thanks to some ambitious 'conservation' – an elaborate central gateway, more fortress than portal, with many galleries and upturned roofs. From its deep shadow they emerged onto the paved street flanked with timbered buildings that cuts clean through the city to a similar gateway in the southern wall. This was their processional route, and it was immediately crammed with 'a huge crowd' intent on minute inspection of the newcomers. Halfway along, they were halted in front of a large crenellated building of a particularly 'dark and forbidding aspect'. The mob pressed closer, hauled them from their ponies and snatched off their hats. That was when de Carné lashed out. There ensued 'an indescribable turmoil' in which the Frenchmen's fears of being lynched were genuine enough. Only later did they concede that, the building being the sultan's palace, the removal of their hats was probably to gratify either his peeping curiosity or his vanity.

A fixing of bayonets quelled the turmoil and they resumed their march. They emerged from the southern gateway and were conducted to lodgings outside the walls. There a senior mandarin requested details of their identity and business. Garnier was delighted with the man's 'cordiality and finesse', especially when he confirmed an audience with the sultan for the next day. From Dali it was only four days' march to the Mekong. Dali's lake was itself the source of one of the Mekong's tributaries, the spiritual home of its *nagas* and possibly the spawning ground of the Giant Mekong Catfish. He was practically there.

Next morning Father Leguilcher was summoned to the palace first. He left in trepidation and came back quivering. For bringing strangers into the kingdom he had been upbraided, sentenced to death, and reprieved only on condition of immediately extracting them. There would be no audience, no further inspection of the city, no Mekong. They must leave in the morning and return by the way they had come.

> 'Go tell these foreigners,' the Sultan had said, 'that they may take all the lands watered by the Lancang [Mekong] from the sea to Yunnan but that here they will be obliged to stop. Had they conquered the whole of China, the invincible kingdom of Dali would still prove an insuperable barrier to their ambition. I have put many a stranger to death and these insolent fellows who yesterday shed the blood of one of my soldiers before my eyes may expect the same fate. I spare them only because they have been recommended by one venerated by all Mussulmans [i.e. the Grand Mufti].'

As his hopes clattered to the cold stone floor around him, Garnier desperately sought an explanation. Perhaps it had something to do with their sketching and mapmaking. Any power 'born of rebellion ... repressive ... exacting ... and that lived only by terror and crime must naturally be cruel and suspicious'. Either that or the sultan had mistaken them for Englishmen. This was a common error in Garnier's book, and in conversation with the mandarin he had laboured to counter it. He had stressed their French identity, dangled the prospect of a commercial alliance with France and perhaps made too much of the thrusting little colony at the mouth of the Mekong. He had also refused point blank to attend an audience to which he was expected to come unarmed and willing to kowtow. He thought that this was understood, and indeed it was. But so delicate a matter of protocol, over which Lagrée would have soothingly debated for days, Garnier presumed to have settled in seconds. To one so naturally confrontational, the silky skills of diplomacy were as unattainable as Tibet.

During an edgy night, with their lodgings now a gaol, a guard on the door, and their guns 'capped and loaded by myself with the greatest of care', Garnier and his men slept little and then left before first light. They were conducted round the city rather than through it, and reached the outer fortalice at the head of the lake that night. Whether the detachment of the sultan's troops that accompanied them was an escort or an execution squad was unclear. Accommodation within the fort was rejected on the grounds that it must mean imprisonment. A tense stand-off ensued. It was when, under cover of darkness, the expedition here tried to slip away from their guards that Delaporte discovered the loss of the gold bar. They retraced their footsteps, hunting for it in vain, and then camped beside the fort. They resumed their march unopposed on the morrow. Another fort and more 'intemperate demands' led to a further scuffle. Bayonets were now permanently fixed.

> *Each man received a revolver in addition to his rifle, and Father Leguilcher himself agreed to bear arms. I had all the streets and the inn guarded, and we passed the night awake. There were only ten of us but, with a revolver and rifle each, we had seventy bullets before we needed to reload. That was enough to hold a Muslim regiment at a distance.*

Aware of the obvious criticism, Garnier would vehemently reject the idea that he was being either alarmist or unnecessarily provocative. Far from regretting his rashness, he would marvel at his moderation. He wished, he said, that he had taken more risks, and later he would insist that, but for his concern for his companions' safety, he would have done. Courageous to the point of recklessness, he would be an odd choice, five years later, for a colonial initiative that was supposed to be pacific.

On the 'night of the seventy bullets', not one was needed. 'Nobody showed up,' says Garnier. They left next morning unmolested and with a joke from the fort's commandant by way of a parting salvo. Three long days later they were clear of Dali's menace; and three gruelling weeks after that they were again within striking distance of Dongchuan.

Instead of 'a crowning success', the trip could only be accounted a dismal failure. For nine weeks of hardship, all they had to show was a route map, some not very original information – on local tribes, cormorant-fishing in Lake Dali, and the kingdom's trade – most of it gleaned from Leguilcher, and the unpleasant recollection of a thirty-minute walk down the main thoroughfare of Dali itself. Far from reaching the Mekong, they had not even been able to inspect its tributary that issued from Lake Dali.

Yet two years later, when Garnier went to London to receive the accolades of the Royal Geographical Society, it would be this short and abortive side trip that figured most prominently in the citation for his gold medal. In his own estimation the main significance of the excursion lay in its having extended to the mountain fringes of Tibet the explorations conducted up the Yangtse by the British. France had again stolen a march on its rival, in other words. But in London he paid generous tribute to the Society's role in encouraging scientific exploration in inland Asia, and compared it favourably with French official indifference. This went down well with British geographers, and the Society responded by complimenting his endeavours in so far as they extended their own. Yunnan thus became the focus as well as the 'crowning achievement' of the whole journey. The Mekong was scarcely mentioned by the RGS's president, nor was the eighteen-month odyssey up it, nor were any of Garnier's colleagues with the exception of Lagrée.

But there was another reason for this curious emphasis. The RGS awarded two medals a year, and in 1870 the other, its Patron's Medal, was destined for George Hayward. Hayward's travels had mirrored those of Garnier at the other end of the Himalayas. He too had reached a 'forbidden city' on the borders of China that was then under 'tyrannical' Muslim rule, namely Kashgar in Xinjiang, and he had there been detained. Subsequently 'He fell among thieves' in the Hindu Kush as per the Henry Newbolt poem written in his memory. Hayward's was therefore a posthumous award. Garnier claims to have argued that his own award, the Victoria Medal, should in fact have been dedicated to Lagrée. But the RGS demurred. The medal must go to Garnier – and so be for the Yunnan excursion – since it would make for a dull ceremony, and might even be thought macabre, for both the year's medals to be posthumous awards.

Lagrée's death had occurred on 12 March 1868, just as Garnier and his companions were emerging from the sultan of Dali's clutches. Complete rest and Dr Joubert's devoted attentions had failed to revive *le Commandant*. For a couple of weeks he had sunk rapidly until, under conditions impossible to imagine, Joubert had felt obliged to operate. The affected part of the liver was drained; and briefly Lagrée rallied. But as an autopsy would confirm, the surgery had addressed only part of the problem. When the patient relapsed, a further operation was out of the question. He died bravely, in the arms of Moëlho (or Morello), the Breton sailor and sole survivor of the original European escort, with Joubert in attendance.

A sad little funeral had been held in Dongchuan. Lagrée's body was buried, minus the heart (for which Joubert had a casket made); but his papers were preserved, despite his wish that they be burned. Joubert understandably baulked at incinerating what presumably constituted an important record of the journey and especially of its more critical debates.

Garnier, arriving three weeks later, promptly reversed both these moves. He insisted that the body be exhumed and the paper-work destroyed. The logic in respect of the corpse is clear. The grave in such an out-of-the-way spot might be desecrated. So noble a leader deserved a more secure resting place. Additionally, Garnier foresaw an official funeral in Saigon being a useful means of impressing the colonial authorities with the extent of their sacrifice. In death, as arguably in life, Lagrée became a talisman and, trans-ferred to a more elaborate coffin, he was duly lugged across the hills, installed on deck down the Yangtse, and then shipped in his own cabin via Hong Kong to Saigon, so completing the expedition in the company of his men. This whole return journey would resemble a protracted funeral procession, in that guarding the coffin and punishing any disrespect to it became a major preoccupation.

Lagrée's papers, on the other hand, are never so much as mentioned. That they existed at all, let alone that Garnier over-ruled Joubert and had them burnt, is known only from sources other than the published accounts of the expedition. Garnier claimed to be respecting the wishes of the deceased. If the papers were of a private and intimate nature, burning them was the right thing to do. On the other hand, if they were indeed purely per-sonal, why did Lagrée not have them destroyed while he lay dying? Expressing a wish but delegating the decision was how he had dealt with the question of the last Mekong excursion. Perhaps he had again done the decent thing, issuing an instruction that would spare his companions any embarrassment yet leave them free to act as they thought best.

If this surmise is correct, it may be assumed that the papers included professional notes and drafts relative to the conduct of the expedition. These should surely have been retained, and that was presumably Joubert's argument. That Garnier unhesitatingly ordered their destruction strongly implies that they contained observations at variance with those of himself and his colleagues and perhaps unfavourable to them. As with most expeditions and despite, in this case, a variety of sources, the Mekong Exploration Commission thereby left a legacy of controversy and generous scope for conjecture.

'On 7 April we left Dongchuan to return at last,' writes Garnier. 'We were all at the end of our tether.' More than half of them were sick, with the Vietnamese and Filipinos especially affected. 'Sometimes I had them transported in chairs by porters to prevent the march being retarded.' In just under two weeks they reached Yanjin ('La-wa-tan'), 'where navigation on the river began'. 'Thus,' says de Carné, 'exactly one year after leaving our canoes and setting foot in Burma on the banks of the Mekong, we again found vessels in China on an affluent of the Blue River [Yangtse].' A short voyage brought them to the main river, where they hired junks. By 13 May they were in Chongqin (Chungking). Gliding on through the famous gorges, they went ashore at the French consulate in Wuhan (Hankow) on 6 June. It was two years to the day since they had boarded the *canonnières* in Saigon.

'Our mission was accomplished,' sighs de Carné. Further observations were superfluous and even the thirst for news had gone. On de Carné a heavy cloud of exhaustion settled and became indistinguishable from his perennial lugubrium. During the voyage by steamer from Hankow to Shanghai and on to Hong Kong and Saigon, he would shut himself in his cabin. Sea sickness added to his woes as their vessel entered the South China Sea. He thought more fondly of cramped pirogues and the rambling gait of the Laotian elephant.

In Hankow, where steam navigation started and many of the great powers had consulates, a chance meeting with a fellow countryman had unforeseen results. Jean Dupuis was a fortune-seeking adventurer long resident in China who dealt especially in armaments. Joubert apparently fell into conversation with him because they hailed from the same part of France. Although Dupuis may well have heard of the Red River of Tonkin, Joubert's report of its being navigable as far as Yunnan did not pass unnoticed; nor did his news of the war in that province and of General Ma's urgent need for arms. To a resourceful arms dealer, this was sufficient. Dupuis would head for Hanoi 'as a result of our journey' and 'on the basis of our information', says Joubert, and there set in motion the sequence of events that would finally engulf Francis Garnier.

It was also in Hankow that the commander of a British gunboat, 'not satisfied with verbal accounts of our adventure', demanded a photograph of the explorers. In fact he insisted that, for it, they should don the garb they had worn in the south-east Asian forest. It was bad enough having been an object of curiosity to the Chinese nation, grumbled de Carné; now they were 'threatened with the same fate amongst civilised people'. Happily for posterity they agreed; and as at Angkor of distant memory, the picture is eloquent.

This time their followers are included, though to judge by the subsequent engraving, somewhat out of focus. A genuine bond had been forged with these largely nameless heroes. Their attachment to Lagrée had been especially touching, and they guarded his coffin with proprietary zeal. When, on the grounds of their non-European race, they were denied first-class cabins on the Yangtse steamer, the explorers would be outraged.

The coffin does not appear in the picture. Guns, haggard stares and an air of desperate abandon tell their own story. Delaporte in a pork-pie hat looks like a deflated old man, de Carné in a Vietnamese straw cone like an Oriental mystic. Seniority has deferred to a slumped informality. Joubert in safari suit towers over a wild-eyed Garnier who, but for his naval jacket, would be indistinguishable from the elusive Thorel. The self-conscious machismo of the

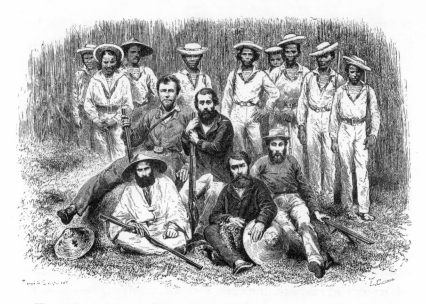

*The survivors of the expedition at Hankow, June 1868. Left to right: de Carné,
Joubert, Garnier, Thorel, Delaporte.*

Angkor portrait has been swept away, torn to shreds in the scrub
of the Shan hills or sucked to extinction in a Mekong whirlpool.

Back in Saigon, where the expedition had begun with a subdued send-off, it ended with a subdued funeral. Headed by the
governor, 'the entire colony accompanied the body of *le Commandant* Lagrée to the cemetery'. De Carné expressed the hope that
the French authorities would emulate the British in the matter of
honouring explorers by erecting a statue in his honour. They never
did. But many years later 'a sort of Angkor-style pagoda' with a
plaque was put up in Grenoble, Lagrée's home town. Like Lagrée
himself, it was subsequently dug up and relocated near the place of
his birth at Saint Vincent de Mercuze in the Savoy Alps. Obscurely
memorialised, the Mekong Exploration Commission would retain
its tenuous hold on public attention thanks less to memorials than
to subsequent acrimony, then disaster.

Epilogue

FROM SAIGON the surviving members of the expedition headed for France. De Carné was dying, Delaporte needed convalescence, the two doctors were no longer required, and Garnier had maps to draw and reports to write. Three new provinces in the Mekong Delta had just been added to the three already under French control, so there was little prospect of immediate action being taken on the expedition's upriver recommendations. As even de Carné conceded, the geographical achievements of the Mekong Exploration Commission had greatly exceeded its political and commercial discoveries. Geographical laurels were imminently expected; and it was over them that controversy would surface.

In all, the expedition had travelled overland (including by river and including side trips) a distance of about eleven thousand kilometres, which was considerably more than the length of Africa. They had conducted a survey across over six thousand kilometres, most of which had never before been mapped. They had resolved the mystery surrounding the course of one of the world's great rivers, recorded its tributaries, and surmounted the formidable obstacles posed by what de Carné called its 'extreme individuality'. They had also endured that full Heart of Darkness 'horror' – the disease and danger, heat and cold, hostility and hunger. But it was the sheer scale of the thing that was the hardest to take in. As Sir

Roderick Murchison, the President of the RGS, would put it, the expedition must have 'traversed a greater amount of absolutely new country than ... had been accomplished for years'. If the journey had produced no political results whatsoever and had remained just a geographical curiosity, it would still have been 'one of the most remarkable and successful expeditions of the nineteenth century', declared Murchison.

The trouble ostensibly arose over how the credit for it was to be apportioned. Garnier, as one of the original projectors, the principal surveyor, second-in-command and official memorialist, was the obvious candidate for the geographical plaudits. He readily accepted this role and duly scooped the awards at the Société Géographique de Paris in 1869, the RGS in 1870 and the International Geographical Congress in Antwerp in 1871. But in doing so, he was not as careful as he might have been to stress the debt due to Admiral de Lagrandière, who had despatched the expedition, or Doudart de Lagrée, who for all but the last few weeks had led it. Nor was he punctilious in acknowledging the support, and sometimes even the existence, of his other colleagues.

The objections came principally from Louis de Carné who, near death and not under the restraints of naval service, could speak freely on behalf of the others. He did so both privately to friends and publicly in letters to the press. Garnier was accused of drawing attention to himself by disparaging the role of others, especially Lagrée, and exaggerating the period of his command and its importance. According to the British consul in Hankow, he had already been describing himself as '*chef de la mission*' in 1868. In Europe, while championing the expedition and presenting its results in a popular serialisation, an official report and several scientific papers, Garnier continued to shoulder the responsibilities of '*chef*', battling with the official indifference as well as basking in the professional applause.

A sorry affair that would rumble on long after both de Carné's death in 1871 and his own in 1873, the controversy had perhaps less to do with conflicting personalities and more with differing perceptions of what exploration was all about. Garnier was fired by the particularly British idea of the explorer as a competitive pioneering individual, privately funded and supposedly operating beyond either official constraint or protection. His models were Africanists like James Bruce, Mungo Park and Hanning Speke. Hayward and Livingstone, with whom he was jointly honoured in London and Antwerp, fell into the same category; the one was an adventurer whose links with British Indian intelligence were flatly denied and the other a missionary part-sponsored by the RGS but not under government direction.

The Mekong Exploration Commission was very different. Conceived from the first as a governmental initiative, officially funded, diplomatically accredited, formally constituted with a hierarchy of command and responsibilities, and burdened with the resources and personnel necessary for all sorts of scientific, commercial, cultural and political activities, it was essentially a great national undertaking. Its directives had been drawn up by the government, and when things went wrong – the delayed Chinese passports, the cash crisis in the Shan states – the government was blamed.

The self-conscious formality of that group photo at Angkor, and the flag so proudly flown from every campsite and conveyance, proclaimed a structured patriotism that flatly contradicted notions of individual endeavour and personal celebrity as championed by the nineteenth-century RGS and cherished by Garnier. Often resentful of his colleagues and ever eager to strike out on his own, Garnier wanted it both ways. Like Kurtz he clung to the certainties and status of a familiar world while espousing the allure of a more wayward and outlandish existence. In practical terms, the contrast was even more obvious: but for his colleagues he might have been left for dead at Stung Treng, yet but for his colleagues he might have exorcised that *monomanie de Mékong* and sneaked onto the Tibetan plateau.

In 1869, while the controversy spluttered, and while Garnier wrestled with official indifference to the expedition's political and commercial findings, he unexpectedly discovered the need for what he calls 'a soul-mate'. He married Claire Knight, the daughter of a Scots father and a Provençale mother, in early 1870, just as France gravitated towards war with Prussia.

Joubert had already resigned from the navy but would rejoin as an auxiliary doctor. After the Franco–Prussian war he attended his dying friend de Carné before going into private practice. Thorel, too, resigned, and then married a rich widow. Until his death in 1911, the Thorels lived in Paris; at their house Delaporte would be introduced to the seventeen-year-old who would become his bride.

Delaporte and Garnier both served with distinction in the defence of Paris against the Prussian army. And after the war both again set their sights on the East. Garnier, though, had been highly critical of the terms of the French capitulation and, after completing the official report of the expedition, remained in some disgrace. He headed for China on unpaid leave in 1872. At about the same time Delaporte was rewarded with commissions to explore the navigable potential of the Red River and to continue at Angkor the work of study and conservation (which included the amassing of a collection that would form the nucleus of the Musée Guimet in Paris).

Free at last to indulge his own notion of exploration, Garnier proposed to resume the quest for Tibet and the uppermost reaches of the Mekong. The *monomanie* was still upon him, but he also needed to raise funds. He hoped either to be appointed French consul in Yunnan or to exploit the silk and tea trades at source. Claire and their first child came with him as far as Shanghai. He then obtained a passport in Beijing and set off alone, heading for the Yangtse and without an interpreter so that he might learn Chinese more quickly.

Despite the title – *De Paris à Tibet* – of his posthumously published account of these wanderings, he never saw Tibet or revisited Yunnan. He got no further than Chongqin; and it was on returning from there to Shanghai in 1873 that he found waiting for him an urgent summons from the governor in Saigon. His services, it transpired, were needed for a most delicate mission. Delaporte's Red River expedition had just been aborted because of the latter's ill health. Meanwhile a confused, if not explosive, situation in Tonkin was rapidly deteriorating. It required a man of the utmost decision who understood what was at stake. And Garnier, though not the first choice, was both readily available and rash enough to take it on. '*Carte blanche*' was how he would triumphantly describe his orders. Back in uniform, in command of his own mission, with the eyes of all Asia upon him, he felt his heart 'fit to burst'. A farewell salute from French vessels in Saigon's port 'moved me deeply'. His hour had come.

The cause of all the trouble was Jean Dupuis, the arms dealer whom they had met in Hankow in 1868. Acting on the information obtained from Dr Joubert, Dupuis had himself investigated the Red River's navigability, secured orders for armaments from General Ma in Kunming, obtained encouragement and some authorisation from Paris, and duly sailed up the Red River with a flotilla of vessels carrying soldiers and guns in 1872. A tidy profit resulted, and in 1873 Dupuis returned downriver with more troops provided by General Ma. But the Vietnamese authorities, though far from united, had opposed the first shipment and were adamant that there should be no more.

Dupuis, ensconced in Hanoi with perhaps two hundred men and ample munitions, refused to budge. In fact he began organising another shipment up to Yunnan, this time of salt. He flew the French flag and acted as if French commerce in Hanoi enjoyed the same rights and immunities as in Shanghai. The Vietnamese halted the salt shipment and tried to arrest him. With hostilities threatening, both parties then appealed to Saigon. The Vietnamese demanded Dupuis' removal – and that was indeed the official reason for despatching Garnier. But Dupuis demanded French backing for the opening of the Red River – and that seems to have been the real reason.

Garnier sailed up the Vietnamese coast from Saigon with two ships; one was lost on the way, but two others joined him. There were only a hundred troops, possibly because more would have meant appointing an officer of higher rank than a lieutenant. With the addition of Dupuis' mercenaries and the ships' crews, the total may have been four hundred well-armed infantrymen and a few artillery pieces.

Once in Hanoi, Garnier handled the Vietnamese mandarins as brusquely as he would like to have done their counterparts in Dali. When they refused to open the river to French vessels, he simply took it upon himself to declare it open. Far from deporting Dupuis, he concerted operations with him. Signs of armed resistance from the Vietnamese mandarins brought a French ultimatum for the withdrawal from Hanoi of all Vietnamese troops. And the mandarins' refusal to make Hanoi's citadel available as a safe billet for French troops brought a dawn attack and an overwhelming victory.

The rest of the city was then taken. Other forts in its vicinity were overrun one by one. Styling himself 'Le Grand Mandarin de France', three weeks after his arrival Garnier was pleased to inform the governor in Saigon that 'the province of Hanoi is now completely pacified. The entire administration is in our hands ... brigandage suppressed ... the people sympathetic...' Four hundred men had secured a land of 'two million souls'.

But Paris had not authorised such action, the emperor in Hué was livid, the governor in Saigon was getting cold feet, and within two weeks of that triumphalist report, the horribly mutilated body of Francis Garnier lay spattered and dead in the soft mud at the edge of a Tonkin paddy field. The 'pacification' had been an illusion. Resistance had gathered pace as Chinese 'Flags' – those marauding armies later known to Pavie as 'Ho' (Haw) – joined the Vietnamese. Although their combined attempt to expel the French from the Hanoi citadel was repulsed, it was in pursuit of the attackers that the hotheaded Garnier led out his ill-fated sortie.

Initially twelve men, this flying column strayed far from the citadel and split up to engage the enemy. Garnier had only two companions to cover him when he fell while crossing a ditch. One of these men was simultaneously hit by a bullet. 'Le Grand Mandarin', stuck in the ditch, 'fired six shots with his revolver and was massacred'.

His death, the rising tide of resistance, and the ambivalence of the French authorities could have only one result. Another plenipotentiary was sent from Saigon to Hanoi, and an embarrassed retraction followed. Garnier's bullying might have been expected of conquistadors like Cortés and Pizarro; it might have been tolerated in nabobs like Dupleix or Clive and forgiven of a national hero like Napoleon. But in the 1870s, in the diminutive person of a controversial naval lieutenant acting in the name of a nation already reeling from defeat in Europe, it was inconvenient and utterly reprehensible. Not until ten years later would the conquest of Tonkin be resumed in earnest, and not until two years after that would Auguste Pavie be despatched from Cambodia to Luang Prabang, there to reprise the dreams and substantially realise the hopes of the Mekong Exploration Commission for an *Indo-Chine Française*.

A SHORT BIBLIOGRAPHY

Bassenne, Marthe, *Au Laos et au Siam*, in *Le Tour du Monde*, vol. 18 (NS), Paris 1912; transl. *In Laos and Siam*, Bangkok 1995

Beauvais, René, *Louis Delaporte, Explorateur*, Paris 1929

Bizot, François, *The Gate*, London 2003

Booth, Martin, *Opium: A History*, London 1996

Clifford, Hugh, *Further India: The Story of Exploration from the Earliest Times in Burma, Malaya, Siam and Indo-China*, London 1904, repr. Bangkok 1990

Colquhoun, A.R., *Amongst the Shans*, London 1885

Conrad, Joseph, *Heart of Darkness*, London 1902

Davidson, Alan, *Fish and Fish Dishes of Laos*, Rutland 1975

Davidson, Alan, *A Kipper with My Tea*, London 1988

De Carné, Louis, *Voyage en Indo-Chine et dans l'Empire Chinois*, Paris 1872; transl. *Travels in Indo-China and the Chinese Empire*, London 1872, repr. Bangkok 1995

Delaporte, Louis, and Garnier, Francis, *A Pictorial Journey on the Old Mekong: Cambodia, Laos and Yunnan. The Mekong Exploration Commission Report – Volume 3*, repr. Bangkok 1998

Fairbank, John King, *The Great Chinese Revolution 1800–1985*, New York 1986

Gargan, Edward A., *The River's Tale: A Year on the Mekong*, New York 2002

Garnier, Francis et al., *Voyage d'exploration en Indo-Chine effectué pendant les années 1866, 1867 et 1868*, 3/4 vols, Paris 1873

Garnier, Francis, *Voyage d'exploration en Indo-Chine*, Paris 1885

Garnier, Francis, *Travels in Cambodia and Part of Laos: The Mekong Exploration Commission Report (1866–8) – Volume 1*, Bangkok 1996

Garnier, Francis, *Further Travels in Laos and Yunnan: The Mekong Exploration Commission Report (1866–8) – Volume 2*, Bangkok 1996

Gomane, Jean-Pierre, *L'Exploration de Mékong: La Mission Ernest Doudart de Lagrée–Francis Garnier*, Paris 1994

Groslier, Bernard-Philippe, and Boxer, C.R., *Angkor et le Cambodge au XVIe siècle après les sources Portuguaises et Espagnoles*, Paris 1958

Groslier, Georges, *A l'Ombre d'Angkor*, Paris 1916

Hall, D.G.E., *A History of South-East Asia*, 4th edn, London 1981

Harmand, Jules, *Laos and the Hill Tribes of Indo-China*, repr. Bangkok 1997

Jumsai, M., *A New History of Laos*, 2nd edn, Bangkok 1971

King, Victor T. (ed.), *Explorers of South-East Asia: Six Lives*, Kuala Lumpur 1995

Lacroze, Luc, *Les Grands pionniers du Mékong: Une cinquantaine d'années d'aventures, 1884–1935*, Paris 1996

Lefèvre, E., *Travels in Laos: The Fate of the Sip Song Panna and Muong Sing (1894–6)*, repr. Bangkok 1995

Lintner, Bertil, *Burma in Revolt: Opium and Insurgency Since 1948*, Chiang Mai 1994

McAleavy, Henry, *Black Flags in Vietnam*, London 1968

McCarthy, James, *Surveying in Siam*, London 1900

McCoy, Alfred W., *The Politics of Heroin in Southeast Asia*, New York 1972

Mannika, Eleanor, *Angkor Wat: Time, Space and Kingship*, Honolulu 1996

Mansfield, Stephen, *Lao Hill Tribes*, Selangor Darul Ehsan 2000

Maugham, W. Somerset, *The Gentleman in the Parlour: A Record of a Journey from Rangoon to Haiphong*, London 1930

Mitton, G.E., *Scott of the Shan Hills*, London 1936

Mouhot, Henri, *Travels in the Central Parts of Indo-China (Siam), Cambodia and Laos (1858–64)*, London 1864

Neis, Paul-Marie, *Travels in Upper Laos and Siam, with an Account of the Chinese Haw Invasion and Puan Resistance*, repr. Bangkok 1997

Nguyen Thi Dieu, *The Mekong River and the Struggle for Indo-China*, Westport 1999

Osborne, Milton, *River Road to China: The Search for the Source of the Mekong, 1866–73*, London 1975, Singapore 1996

Osborne, Milton, *The Mekong: Turbulent Past, Uncertain Future*, New York 2000

Pavie, Auguste, *Mission Pavie en Indo-Chine (1879–95): Géographie et voyages vol. 1: Exposé des travaux de la mission*, Paris 1901

Pavie, Auguste, *A la Conquête des Coeurs*, Paris 1947

Pavie, Auguste, *Au Pays des million éléphants et du parasol blanc (A la Conquête des Coeurs)*, repr. Rennes 1995

Scott, J.G., *France and Tongking*, London 1885

Scott, J.G., *Burma and Beyond*, London 1932

Stuart-Fox, Martin, *A History of Laos*, Cambridge 1997

Taboulet, Georges, *La Geste française en Indochine*, Paris 1956

Toye, Hugh, *Laos: Buffer State or Battleground*, London 1968

Tuck Patrick, *The French Wolf and the Siamese Lamb: The French Threat to Siamese Independence*, Bangkok 1995

Warington Smyth, H., *Five Years in Siam*, London 1998; repr. Bangkok 1999

Warner, Roger, *Shooting at the Moon: The Story of America's Clandestine War in Laos*, South Royalton 1996

INDEX

Lanten, 105
Lao (black-bellied, white-bellied, etc.),
 67–8, 98, 170, 195
Laos: history and politics, 8, 39, 92, 93–6,
 109–12, 125–6, 137, 143, 146–7, 154,
 158–65, 215–18, 233–43; borders, 7, 15,
 68, 69, 70–1, 80, 103, 158, 195, 209,
 233–43; Mekong in, 36, 54, 123–4 *et
 passim*; as Shangri-La, 99–100; opium
 in, 210–15, 222
Lefèvre, Lieut., 184
Leguilcher, Father, 268, 270, 271, 272,
 273
Leonowens, Anna, 110, 160
Leonowens, Louis, 160
'Lesser Game, The', 161, 192, 233
Lewis, Norman, 99–100, 168
Lijiang, 265, 266, 268
Lintner, Bertil and Hseng Noung, 221–3
Livingstone, David, xvii, 8, 106, 117, 281
Lon Nol, Gen., 38
Lu, Father, 268
Luang Nam Tha, 182, 217, 238, 245
Luang Prabang, 81, 83, 95, 113, 124, 147,
 149, 154, 157, 158, 160, 161, 162, 165,
 166–76, 177, 178, 180, 183, 184, 192, 232,
 233, 235, 237, 242, 249, 256, 263, 285

McCarthy, James, 160, 161, 164
Ma, Gen., 258–9, 261, 277, 283
Malaya, 26
Mandalay, 188, 196
Mang-ko, 255
Mao tse Tung, 211, 221
Massie (gun sloop), 81, 82
Maugham, W. Somerset, 210
Maximilian, Emperor of Mexico, 25, 58
Mekong Delta, xxi, 3, 10, 12, 14, 15, 17–22,
 26, 27, 28, 36, 38, 40, 52, 56, 82, 90,
 109, 126, 146, 166, 180, 225, 231, 279
Mekong Exploration Commission
 (MEC), *passim*: historiography and
 status, xviii, 8–9, 42, 193, 224; inception
 and objectives, 13–4, 16, 28–9, 41, 65,
 154, 263, 281; consequences, 58, 76, 78,
 95–6, 109–11, 158, 196, 232–4, 276,
 278–80, 285; supernumeraries, 66–8; *see
 also* Lagrée, Garnier, etc.
'Mekong Highway' (RN13), 124, 125, 147,
 180
Mekong River Commission, 36, 220–1

Menam River (Chao Phraya), 13, 20, 110,
 181, 236, 237, 238, 239, 241
Meru, Mount, 40, 167
Messageries Fluviales, 122, 123, 125
Mississippi River, 55, 58, 78
Moëlho, 118, 274
Mouhot, Henri, 154, 156, 168, 169
Muang Khong, 90
Mukdahan, 123, 134
Muong Long, 227
Muong Pa-liao, *see* Paleo
Muong Sing, 238, 240–1, 245
Muong Sing Affair (1894–95), 238–41
Muong Yong, 206–8, 218, 226
Muong You, 218, 219
Murchison, Sir Roderick, 52, 280
Musée Guimet (Paris), xviii, 282
My-tho, 17, 19, 21

Nagas, 182–3, 270
Nam Khan, 168
Nam Loy, 218–19, 223, 226
Nam Nga, 227
Nam Ngum, 146
Nam Ou, 176–7, 179–80, 263
Nam San, 146
Nam Tha, 181, 215
Nam Yu, 215, 216, 217
Napoleon Bonaparte, 25, 40
Napoleon III (Louis Napoleon), 25, 27,
 28, 108
Ne Win, Gen., 221
Neis, Dr Paul-Marie, 160, 174
Netherlands East India Company, 66
Nile River, 10, 152, 161
'9:11', 220–3, 226
Nixon, President Richard M., 49
Nong Khai, 144, 146, 152, 182
Norodom, King, 12, 51, 52, 69, 101, 133

opium, 193, 210–13, 214, 216–17, 221–3,
 226, 256

pa beuk, *see* Giant Mekong Catfish
Pak-beng, 181
Paklai, 157–9, 164, 184, 242
Paknam, 236, 238
Pakse, 103, 111, 125, 127
Pak-tha, 181
Paleo (Muong Pa-liao), 200, 202, 214
Papheng Falls, 74–5, 87